THE ESSENCE OF

PROFESSIONAL ISSUES IN COMPUTING

THE ESSENCE OF COMPUTING SERIES

Published titles

The Essence of Program Design
The Essence of Discrete Mathematics
The Essence of Logic
The Essence of Programming Using C++
The Essence of Databases
The Essence of Artificial Intelligence
The Essence of Human-Computer Interaction
The Essence of Systems Analysis and Design

Forthcoming titles

The Essence of Z
The Essence of Compilers

THE ESSENCE OF

PROFESSIONAL ISSUES IN COMPUTING

Robert Ayres
Royal Military College of Science
Cranfield University

Prentice
Hall

An imprint of **Pearson Education**

Harlow, England · London · New York · Reading, Massachusetts · San Francisco
Toronto · Don Mills, Ontario · Sydney · Tokyo · Singapore · Hong Kong · Seoul
Taipei · Cape Town · Madrid · Mexico City · Amsterdam · Munich · Paris · Milan

Pearson Education Limited
Edinburgh Gate
Harlow
Essex, CM20 2JE
England

and Associated Companies throughout the world

Visit us on the World Wide Web at:
http://www.pearsoneduc.com

First published 1999 by
Prentice Hall Europe

Typeset in 10/12pt Times
by Photoprint, Torquay

Printed an bound in Great Britain by Biddles Ltd,
www.biddles.co.uk

Library of Congress Cataloging-in-Publication Data

Available from the publisher

British Library Cataloguing in Publication Data

A catalogue record for this book is available from
the British Library

ISBN 0-13-908740-0

10 9 8 7 6 5 4 3

06 05 04 03 02

Contents

Foreword

As the consulting editor for the Essence of Computing Series it is my role to encourage the production of well-focused, high-quality textbooks at prices which students can afford. Since most computing courses are modular in structure, we aim to produce books which will cover the essential material for a typical module.

I want to maintain a consistent style for the series so that whenever you pick up an Essence book you know what to expect. For example, each book contains important features such as end-of-chapter summaries and exercises and a glossary of terms, if appropriate. Of course, the quality of the series depends crucially on the skills of its authors and all the books are written by lecturers who have honed their material in the classroom. Each book in the series takes a pragmatic approach and emphasises practical examples and case studies.

Our aim is that each book will become essential reading material for students attending core modules in computing. However, we expect students to want to go beyond the Essence books and so all books contain guidance on further reading and related work.

Coverage of professional issues is an essential component of accredited degree programmes in computing and both the BCS and IEE are seeking to raise the standards of professionalism in computing. This book provides an excellent starting point for raising awareness of the major issues in this area. There are three major components, covering social, legal and ethical issues, and I found them all stimulating. There are many small case studies to illustrate points and thought-provoking questions at the ends of chapters. I think this book will prove very useful to many computing lecturers trying to instil a sense of professionalism in their students; it will certainly be on my reading list for next year!

RAY WELLAND
Department of Computing Science
University of Glasgow
(e-mail: ray@dcs.gla.ac.uk)

Preface

Social change in response to technology is not new to this century; the Industrial Revolution brought about the end of a way of life which had altered little for hundreds of years. These changes were arguably just as rapid and possibly more profound than anything that has occurred in the present century.

One of the most dramatic examples of the early effects of industrialization was the impact of the railways. In 1830 there were virtually no railway lines in Britain and the only means of transport were horse or coach, and canal for goods. In the following twenty years some 6000 miles of railway were laid; most of this during the two 'railway manias' of 1835–7 and 1845–7. The rush to build railways resulted in many ill-conceived schemes being financed and terrible loss of life occurred on some of the construction projects. As a consequence of this hectic period of development, most of the current railway network was in place by 1850, a little under fifty years after the first working locomotive had been demonstrated.

The impact of rail travel was tremendous: it dramatically cut journey times, it brought about unprecedented mobility, and it led to the modernization of rural areas which had seen few changes in hundreds of years. Moreover, in changing the rural economy and lifestyle, the railways affected everyone, whether they travelled on them or not. Railways even prompted a general change from solar time to Greenwich Mean Time, since a difference of a few minutes between the local time and the GMT railway timetable could be the cause of a missed train. Such was the impact that in the nineteenth century the word 'railway' was synonymous with 'modern' and 'advanced' in the same way that 'computer' or 'electronic' are today.

Railway construction was also a factor in the transformation of engineering itself into a modern profession. Engineers had to build bridges, viaducts, and tunnels on a far greater scale than ever before; they were forced to confront new technological problems and adopt more rigorous approaches to design and analysis. These challenges led engineers to form professional societies to facilitate the exchange of knowledge and pooling of experience. The increasing complexity of engineering practice along with the outcry after various disasters, including one where a bridge over the Tay collapsed killing more than 70 people, forced these professional engineering bodies to define and enforce standards of training and practice. Consequently, by the end of the nineteenth century the training of engineers had been completely transformed. Whereas most engineers at the beginning of the century had learned as apprentices, by the end many came into the profession equipped with a formal university-level education in the relevant science and mathematics.

It is now a little over 50 years since the first electronic computers were used for tasks such as code-breaking and calculating shell trajectories. There are many parallels between the development of railway construction in the nineteenth century and the current status of software engineering: for instance, the lack of standard railway gauges caused problems then just as software incompatibilities do today, most early railway engineers had little formal training just as many software developers have learned by experience, and the many ill-conceived and abortive railway projects of the nineteenth century are mirrored by the failed, and in some cases fatal, software developments of current times. Nevertheless, just as railways became a major industry in the nineteenth century, so computing has in the twentieth and computers are now used to control everything from car-ignition systems and automated teller machines to air-traffic control and electronic funds transfer.

Similarly, the tremendous impact of information technology and the technical difficulties of software development and maintenance have created pressures for software production to become increasingly professionalized. One aspect of such professionalization is the growing awareness of the need for software developers to consider the broader implications of their work and to be aware of how the law has responded to, and now affects, their activities. This is one of the reasons why the British Computer Society, the leading professional body of computer professionals and software engineers, insists that university computing courses contain a 'Professional Issues' component, that is, one or more courses which cover topics such as the social implications of computing, legal issues, professional bodies for computer scientists, ethical issues and so on.

This book is aimed at computer science and software engineering students who are likely to pursue careers in or related to software development. Its main objective is to raise awareness of the social, legal, and professional issues surrounding the use of computer technology. The book is intended as a text for Professional Issues courses but may also be of interest to those already employed in computing or software development.

Three main areas are covered: social, legal, and ethical/professional. These are dealt with in order since the legal issues discussed can be seen as the law's response to the social impacts of computer technology, and the review of professionalism in the final part relies to an extent on material in both of the first two parts. Having said this, there is a large degree of independence between the three parts and between the individual chapters themselves. Many courses will deal with topics in a quite different order and, to facilitate this, each chapter contains, near its beginning, an outline of its relationship to other chapters. The topics covered in each of the three parts are as follows:

1 The first part covers the impact of information technology and some of the problems and difficulties it has brought in its wake. Since this technology really represents the combination of three related but distinct areas – computers and software, data storage, and telecommunications – we consider the issues raised by each of these in turn in the first three chapters before looking at some more general implications:

 (a) In Chapter 1 several software-related disasters are discussed and we consider the factors which distinguish software from previous technologies. We also look at the difficulty of producing reliable and effective software.

 (b) In Chapter 2 we review the development of data storage technology, the ways in which this has been used, and the implications of this for privacy and personal liberty.

 (c) In Chapter 3 we consider the progress in telecommunications and some of the consequences of digitalization, including Calling Line Identification, the Internet, and the current debate over encryption standards.

 (d) Chapter 4 then covers several general issues: the debate about software ownership, the impact of computer crime, the disappointing pay-off of computerization, and the impacts of digital technology on working conditions.

The range of the social and economic impacts of computing which could be discussed is enormous, so inevitably some topics have had to be missed out. In particular we do not consider issues such as the 'Information Society' or the possible use of digital money; in these and other areas it is too early to tell if any of the many predictions made might one day be realized.

2 The second part focuses on legal issues – particularly ones raised by computer technology. It comprises five chapters as follows:

 (a) Chapter 5 gives a general overview of British law. Since the law is a major subject in its own right, this account is inevitably somewhat simplified but it introduces the main terminology and background which are needed for the following four chapters.

 (b) Chapter 6 covers intellectual property law, in particular copyright law, as it applies to software.

 (c) In Chapter 7 we cover those areas of the law which may give rise to liability for software developers. We look specifically at contract law, the law of negligence, health and safety, and consumer protection.

 (d) In Chapter 8 the scope and implications of current data protection law are reviewed and we also look at possible alterations to the law which may come about as a result of EU directives.

(e) Lastly, in Chapter 9 we look at the legislation which has been passed to make it easier to prosecute hackers and virus writers and consider some of the legal issues which are raised by the Internet.

Note that this middle part only aims to include brief outlines of some legal issues relevant to computing. It is not intended to be an appropriate source for resolving specific legal questions. Indeed the relative novelty of computer technology means that some legal issues relating to computers are, at the time of writing, still unresolved.

3 The last three chapters are concerned with computing and software development as a profession:

(a) In Chapter 10 we consider whether software development can be properly considered an engineering discipline, and if not, what developments may be required to make it so. We argue that attention to quality is a key factor here and discuss quality issues in some detail.

(b) Chapter 11 covers the development of professional societies and the role of the British Computer Society in setting standards of training and practice.

(c) The last chapter, Chapter 12, is concerned with the ethical issues that computing professionals may have to confront in the course of their career and how professional codes of practice are used to set standards of behaviour. Particular attention is paid to ethical dilemmas, and the main ideas of moral philosophy are briefly discussed to show how these can be helpful in clarifying dilemmas.

Each chapter follows a similar structure, beginning with a short introduction which highlights links to other chapters and ending with suggestions for further reading and a number of issues to consider. If the book is being used as a course text these issues can form the basis of seminar discussions or essay topics.

There are two major difficulties in writing a book on professional issues, especially one which is intended, as this one is, to give an overview of the field rather than cover every topic in depth. First, there is no clearly defined core of material and, given the space available, not all topics can be covered. One area which is not addressed is that of management issues: controlling and determining the use of computers, managing projects, running companies and so forth. These have been left out since they could easily form the basis of another book and will often be covered in a separate course on project management or general management issues. The other main problem is that the area of professional issues is not static. Some aspects of this book will soon be out of date: data protection legislation is likely to be amended before the end of 1998, other areas of the law can be changed by a judicial decision, and the Internet in particular is still growing so quickly that it is impossible to predict what new issues may arise from it in the next few years. This problem has no solution: if only those issues which are relatively stable were to be addressed then substantial and important topic areas would be ignored.

Finally, many of the topics discussed in this book are open to a variety of interpretations or responses. The intention has been, so far as is possible, not to present answers but to attempt to raise awareness of the issues. Such awareness is surely necessary given the far-reaching impact and implications of modern computer technology.

Acknowledgements

I would like to thank both the British Computer Society and the Institution of Electrical Engineers for permission to reproduce their Code of Conduct and Rules of Conduct respectively.

I would also like to thank all those friends and colleagues who gave their support while this book was being written. I would particularly like to thank my wife for her help and patience.

CHAPTER 1

The nature of software

- In 1982 the computer-controlled Therac-25 radiation machine for the treatment of cancer was introduced in North America. Between 1985 and 1987 three people are known to have died due to radiation overdoses administered from a Therac-25. These overdoses resulted from errors in the machine's controlling software.
- Much software currently running cannot cope with dates after 31 December 1999. Many organizations are, at the time of writing, involved in a race against the clock to correct their software before the turn of the millennium. No-one is sure what the consequences will be if large numbers of organizations fail to make the changes in time.
- In October 1992 a computer-controlled dispatch system went live at London's ambulance service. The system was soon overloaded resulting in delays of up to 3 hours in ambulances arriving at emergencies. It has been claimed that these delays may have led to the deaths of as many as 20 people.

Overview

Software is increasingly the most important component of computer-based systems since it is software which adapts general-purpose computers for specific applications. But the characteristics of software and how best to develop it are still only poorly understood. Many systems have proved not to be reliable and many more have been abandoned before completion, their developers seemingly unable to stem a tide of errors or to complete the system on time or within budget. Nevertheless, modern society has come to place an enormous reliance on software and software development is now a major industry.

Some of the social, legal, and ethical issues which arise from this dependence on an immature technology are considered elsewhere in the book. In this chapter we are primarily concerned with reviewing the impact of software and the difficulties in developing it successfully. We start by outlining how dependent society has become on software and discussing cases where software has been found wanting, including the Therac-25 cancer radiation machine and the year 2000 date problem.

We then consider just why it is so difficult to produce reliable software. We look first at the nature of software and how it differs from traditional technologies and then consider the additional problems of developing software in an organizational context, using the London Ambulance System development as a motivating example.

Relation to other chapters The enormous reliance on software is reconsidered from a social and economic perspective in Chapter 4 where we look at the impact of computer technology on working conditions and assess the economic impact of computerization. Issues arising from the ease with which software can be copied or modified are also considered in Chapter 4 when we discuss software ownership and computer crime.

The difficulties of developing reliable software give rise to many issues: who is (legally) responsible for faulty software (discussed in Chapter 7)? Can software development be considered as an engineering discipline (Chapter 10)? What role do professional societies have in improving the current standards of training and practice (Chapter 11)? Finally, what ethical issues are involved when developing software which is potentially harmful if it fails (Chapter 12)?

1.1 Reliance on software

The degree to which everyday activity is now dependent on computers is unprecedented. Besides the obvious and widespread PC-based applications such as word processors and spreadsheets an enormous range of tasks are now entrusted to computers, among which are:

- The management of virtually all financial applications including payroll calculations, billing customers, credit card accounts, bank accounts and investments, automatic teller machines, and so forth
- Controlling telephone networks – old telephone exchanges are now almost entirely replaced by computer-controlled ones
- Distribution of goods – the use of barcode readers allows shops to automatically reorder stock from suppliers (these same readers also allow shops to monitor the work rates of their cashiers)
- Running booking systems for everything from squash courts to theatre seats and from plane tickets to hotel rooms
- Processing images and graphics – it is now common for pictures and films to be enhanced or subtly changed using computer-based technology. The use of computer-generated animation is also becoming widespread
- Controlling domestic appliances such as video recorders and microwaves

- Assisting with the design of everything from radios to skyscrapers – civil engineers, for example, now depend on computers to carry out the structural analysis of most building designs
- Maintaining the environment in large buildings – heating, air conditioning, security systems, and even lifts are now routinely managed by computer software.

Moreover there is an increasing reliance on software to automate tasks which are safety-critical. This has been the case in military and defence applications for some time but there are now many non-military systems which rely on computer or software control. These applications include air-traffic control, train signalling systems, process control for manufacturing and power generation (including nuclear power) as well as on-board computers for airplanes, trains, and cars.

As a result of the widespread use of computers, it has become almost impossible to go about one's daily business without, knowingly or unknowingly, relying on computer technology. One consequence of this, discussed further in Chapter 2, is that companies and governments now hold enormous amounts of information on individuals.

Another consequence is that we have become very dependent on the correct working of all this software. This is particularly so with safety-critical systems where any error can lead to a major accident or even disaster. However, as we shall see next, software developers have a far from perfect record in the provision of reliable software.

The Therac-25 disaster

For a long time one of the most common treatments for cancer has been to kill the cancerous growth by exposing it to radiation. However, the radiation also damages normal tissue so great care is taken when treating patients in this way. The radiation is, as far as possible, directed only at the affected areas and the dose is carefully controlled to keep it at the minimum required to be effective.

When this kind of treatment was first used a radioactive material (such as cobalt) provided the source of radiation but in the 1960s an alternative method was developed. This relied on a linear-accelerator (or linac) to produce a beam of electrons. This beam could either be used directly to treat surface tissue or, by placing an iron plate in its path, it could be converted to X-rays to treat deeper tissue. When X-rays were used the beam's intensity had to be greatly increased since the iron plate absorbed much of the radiation. The potential danger with such machines was that the patient could be injured or even killed if the plate was not in place when the high-energy beam was used. To avoid this danger, linac-based machines were fitted with interlocks – mechanical connections which prevented the high beam intensity being produced when the plate was not in position.

In 1982 a Canadian company, Atomic-Energy of Canada Ltd (AECL), introduced a new radiation therapy machine, the Therac-25, which was entirely computer controlled. The Therac-25 was a development of an earlier model, the Therac-20, which had also featured computer-based control but only as a convenient supplement to purely mechanical control features; the Therac-20 could still be used without computer control. In the Therac-25 all the mechanical controls of the Therac-20, including safety features, were incorporated into software. This had the advantage that the controls contained no moving parts which would wear out or need replacing. There were additional benefits: it was quicker to carry out the treatment and the dosage could be more accurately controlled.

The Therac-25 was successfully used to treat thousands of patients but, unfortunately, turned out to be unsafe. There were a number of incidents in which patients were injured as a result of receiving incorrect doses of radiation. Nevertheless the machines were kept in service. Then, in 1986, in separate incidents at a clinic in Texas two patients received fatal overdoses. They both developed radiation sickness and died within months of their treatment. The control software had fired a high-intensity electron beam when the iron plate was not in the correct position. It was estimated that the patients had received doses of radiation which were at least a hundred times higher than they should have been.

The operators in both these incidents had made a mistake and at first incorrectly selected electron-based radiation, then, realizing the error, they had changed the treatment to X-ray. A flaw in the software meant that if the operator made this change quickly the machine did not respond properly and the iron plate was not in position before the radiation was generated, thus directly exposing the patient to a high-energy beam of electrons.

Once the problem was understood AECL recommended that the users implement a temporary fix to prevent operators editing dose details after they had been entered. This 'fix' consisted of disabling the up-arrow key on the keyboard, forcing an operator to re-enter all the treatment details from the beginning if he or she had made a mistake. The machine continued in service in several clinics.

However, in January 1987 yet another patient received a fatal overdose from a Therac-25. This time the cause turned out to be a completely different error in the software. Shortly after this further incident Therac-25 machines were taken out of service until modifications could be made – including the addition of mechanical safety features.

An investigation into the series of Therac-25 accidents (Leveson and Turner 1993) brought to light a number of problems besides the faulty software:

- The operator interface produced cryptic error-messages which did not obviously distinguish very serious problems from relatively minor ones. Since many error messages (indicating that, for example, the beam was slightly below intensity) were produced the operators came to ignore them.

- It appears that the manufacturer did not have adequate procedures in place to check the safety of the equipment it was producing. Early safety analyses which were carried out assumed that the software would not fail and concentrated on the hardware, even though safety features had been transferred to the software. Later analyses seem also to have concentrated on the hardware though making assumptions about how often the software might fail.
- There was a tendency to assume that correcting one software error meant that the machine then became safe. However, software errors are rarely isolated and eliminating one error does not mean there are not others still present.

Furthermore when the Therac-25 problems were being investigated, it was found that the same faults were present in the software control of Therac-20 machines. Since mechanical safety features had never been dispensed with in these earlier machines the software errors had not resulted in accidents.

The year 2000 problem

At the time of writing the expiry dates on most credit and bank cards are represented with a two-digit year – 'February 1998' is written as '02/98' for example. What happens at the end of the century? This two-digit year becomes '00' and the software in many ATM machines and point-of-sale terminals, interpreting '00' as corresponding to the year 1900, will reject the cards as no longer valid. This kind of problem appears to be so widespread as to affect most software except that developed very recently. Already there are reports of some banks having problems issuing credit cards with expiry dates in the twenty-first century (BCS 1997), and some supermarkets have also had difficulties. Their stock-control software has interpreted sell-by dates such as '00' on some tins as meaning 1900 and so reported the items as being over 90 years past their sell-by date. These problems pale into insignificance alongside predictions that problems with financial software may bring about global economic collapse or that errors in navigation software may lead to air or sea disasters. Many of these predictions are grossly exaggerated or plain fanciful but it does seem inevitable that a large number of software bugs will appear up to and after the millennium.

The roots of the problem go back to the 1960s and 1970s when many large systems were developed for business applications such as payroll or accounting. These systems were often developed in COBOL or even Assembly languages where the programmer has to specify the number of bytes of storage used to hold a number. Almost universally the convention of using two bytes to represent the year in a decimal form was adopted. Hence years in the range 1900 to 1999 could be catered for. When these systems were developed the turn of the century seemed very far off and file storage space was expensive so it was regarded as wasteful to store the year as, for instance, 1967 instead of 67.

Once this practice was established it became the norm and continued to be followed until recently. This in spite of the fact that the turn of the century was no longer far off and experience had shown that large application systems, once developed, tend to go on being used for decades rather than years. Moreover, there were not the constraints on storage that there had been in the earlier computers so there was no longer the need to be economical with storage space.[1]

The problems associated with the two-digit date format were not widely recognized until the mid-1990s and few large companies have yet managed to do all the alterations required to ensure that their systems will work correctly in the year 2000. Since most programs make use of the date, if only in printing reports (though many will perform calculations involving the date), resolving the problem requires large amounts of software to be inspected, changed, and tested. Year 2000 changes often turn out to take much longer to carry out than anticipated because of problems due to incorrect or missing versions of source code; in effect all the problems of a set of programs not having been properly managed come home to roost.

Many users are hoping that they can make software suppliers liable for problems relating to the year 2000. This is unlikely to be the case and in any event software suppliers do not have the resources to correct all the problems or to compensate for their effects.

Just what does happen at the turn of the century remains to be seen. From a technical perspective the year 2000 problem is not difficult to correct; it is the enormous scale of the work which may be required which gives rise to concern that it will not be addressed in time. That such an intrinsically trivial issue can have been allowed to develop into a major problem with potentially disastrous consequences must call into question the competence of software developers as a professional group.

Other software failures

The Therac-25 incident and year 2000 problem discussed above are far from being isolated cases. Indeed the number of errors or failures in computer-based systems is far too large to allow more than a small fraction to be mentioned in a single book. These range from minor errors, such as formatting problems in

---

1 As an aside, it is worth noting that the saving was never necessary to start with. Dates were being stored in the form dd/mm/yy using 6 bytes of storage when they could have been stored as a day count from a base date (1 January 1900, for example) in a 32-bit binary number. This would have used less storage and catered for dates far beyond the end of the millennium. That such an approach was not used could be due in part to the fact that many software developers had little formal training and may have been unaware of all the design possibilities open to them.

word processors or the apocryphal £0 electricity bill, to more serious errors, like incorrect interest calculations, to potential disasters, such as failures in plant or transport control.

Most of these incidents are never recorded and it is only the occasional error which attracts publicity and is consequently documented in any detail. A small selection of recent software failures includes:

- An error in the software of the Bank of New York in November 1985 caused the bank to become overdrawn by $32 billion on the American Federal Reserve. The software was quickly fixed but the bank nevertheless lost about $5 million in the interest payments it had to make (Forester and Morrison 1990)
- Problems with switching software installed by the American telephone giant, AT&T, caused a 9-hour lock-up on American telephone networks. Some 5 million calls are believed to have been blocked (Neumann 1995).
- Problems with the signalling system on the Docklands Light Railway in London, where there were several teething problems when the line was first built, led to a crash when a driver took over manual control of one train (*Software Engineering Notes* 12(4) and 16(3)).
- A software error at the British Nuclear Fuels' Sellafield reprocessing plant in 1991 resulted in safety doors being inadvertently opened on a container holding highly radioactive material. The error is thought to have occurred after a change was made to control software which had originally been considered safe (Neumann, 1995).

There is little reason to suppose that there will be fewer such failures or disasters in the future. Software often stays in production for decades so even if development techniques were to improve dramatically there would still be a risk from older software.

In addition to the risks from, as yet, unrevealed errors in old software there is the further risk which comes from the increasing reliance on software control. One example of this is the so-called 'fly-by-wire' systems used in modern aircraft such as the A320 Airbus. In these systems there is no direct mechanical linkage from the controls to the wings of the aircraft; a computer monitors the pilot's movements at the controls and then activates motors to move wing surfaces. The weakness in this system is that if the software to interpret the pilot's commands is faulty the pilot can lose control of the plane.

Software systems are not and may never be entirely error-free, but many people seem to assume that such systems cannot produce incorrect results. This in itself is a problem since it leads to over-confidence in the reliability of software. A more insidious problem may stem from human perception of risk. Making a system safer tends to have the effect that its users, believing that errors will be caught by the system, become more careless or reckless – a phenomenon known as 'risk compensation' (Adams 1995).

Nevertheless, in spite of these human factors which may exacerbate some computer-related problems it remains the case that there is clearly a major problem with computer software itself. We discuss why this should be so in the following sections.

1.2 Characteristics of software

Computer software has several unusual characteristics: it is difficult to fully understand and reason about its behaviour, even simple applications result in complex software, and it is highly malleable. These characteristics make the problem of designing and developing software systems quite different from anything encountered before. As a consequence there is no set of design methods or techniques which can be simply adapted from another engineering discipline to be used in software development.

Reasoning about software

Most systems which engineers have built in the past have been largely predictable in their behaviour: they have been systems for which small changes do not have large or unpredictable effects. For example, when a car drives onto a bridge the bridge sags slightly under the weight. A lorry driving onto the same bridge will cause slightly more sag due to its greater weight. Likewise small changes to the design of the bridge are unlikely to produce a bridge which will not stand up: it may not be able to carry as much weight, but we would expect it still to function in a similar way.

Of course, all systems will show erratic or unpredictable behaviour beyond a certain point. If too much stress is put on a bridge it no longer sags but fails altogether and collapses. However, this has not usually been a problem since bridges, and other buildings, are built with a large safety factor. The bridge is designed to take far more weight than it is ever likely to bear. This means not only that the bridge is safe but also that, for the amounts of stress to which it will be subject, its behaviour is largely predictable.

Computer-based systems do not, however, behave in the same way. Digital computers are, in essence, made up of an enormous number of interconnected switches. In early machines these switches were constructed from valves or transistors; in modern machines millions of switches can be implemented on one microchip. At any moment, each one of the switches in a computer will be set either on or off: a particular combination or setting of all the switches together is called a 'state' of the machine. Thus if a machine has a million switches, which we could number from 1 to 1 000 000 say, then if all the even-numbered switches are set on and all the others off this is one state of the machine. The first ten switches on and the rest off is another, distinct, state.

Any given computer has an enormously large (though finite) number of states and these states are 'discrete'. By this we mean that the machine will always be in one or other of its permitted states.[2]

What does a state correspond to? Once entered into a computer, both programs and data are represented the same way: in binary notation as a sequence of 0s and 1s, or switches set on or off. Hence a machine state corresponds to a program and its data at a particular point in its execution. The computer switching from one state to the next corresponds to the program taking one small step in its execution.

The execution of a whole program will involve the computer following a sequence of steps specified by the program. Many of these steps, or state changes, are dependent on the data with which the program is being executed. Some steps will result in blocks of program instructions being repeated or omitted. The same program executed with different data is unlikely to follow the same sequence of steps. For a program to execute correctly, that is, to do what its author wanted it to, each individual execution step must be correct. This in turn depends on the programmer having written a program which specifies a correct sequence of steps for each and every set of data with which the program might be executed.

It is extremely difficult to write programs which are entirely correct but, worse still, the fact that the program may give correct results with one set of data is no guarantee that it will give correct results with a different set of data. The *slightest* change to an input, perhaps corresponding to an unforeseen eventuality, can produce incorrect or totally unexpected results, even program failure.

It is this fragility of software which underlies many of the difficulties encountered in developing and testing systems. It makes it very difficult to reason about programs or to be confident of their correct (that is, desired) operation in all circumstances. This situation is quite different from that faced by an engineer building a bridge, say. The engineer in this situation can be confident that if the bridge can support the weight of a lorry then it can also support a car or motor cycle. However, the nature of software means that a programmer can never, from the fact that a program works with one set of data, be certain that it will work with any different set of data.

In traditional engineering disciplines uncertainty of behaviour is (usually) avoided by building in large safety factors: making a bridge much stronger than it needs to be, for example. But, since programs can behave completely differently with two sets of similar data it is not generally possible to build safety factors into software systems. One approach which has been used for applications where correct functioning of software is vital is to have three

---

2 Of course, there will be instants when it is switching between two states but the machine will always move to another one of its permitted states: that is, to a particular setting of all its switches.

versions of a system developed, usually by completely different development teams, and then incorporate them into a program which compares their outputs. If at least two out of the three systems give a particular result, it is this result which is taken to be correct. This approach is not absolutely safe, however, since many errors arise from oversights or misunderstandings when systems are first specified. Building several different versions of a piece of software does not protect against errors in the specification since they will all share the same design flaws.

Complexity and the difficulty of testing software

Given the difficulty of being sure how software will behave, developers might try to check its correctness by thorough testing. But they run into another problem: all but the very simplest systems are far too complex to test thoroughly. For example, a program which reads in 5 numbers, each between 0 and 99 has $100 \times 100 \times 100 \times 100 \times 100$, that is, 10^{10} or 10 billion, different possible inputs. Even if the program could be tested in 1 second for each of these input cases it would take over 300 years to test the program for every case. This is assuming, of course, that there are no mistakes in the tests themselves and that we do not need to bother about incorrect inputs (such as someone entering an invalid number, like 112).

Moreover, every time an error is found and corrected there is the danger that other errors may be introduced, so the whole testing process needs to be repeated after any changes are made. It has been estimated that as many as one in five attempts to correct an error in a program introduces a new error (Adams 1984) and that with very large systems (those containing hundreds of thousands or millions of lines of code) it becomes very difficult to correct any error without introducing new ones.

Given the high probability of introducing errors every time a change is made it is easy to see that the development of a large software system can be like trying to paint the Forth Bridge: the bridge is so large that there is never a section which does not need repainting. In fact it is worse, since any changes tend to make the system more rather than less complex.

The impossibility of thorough testing means that a different approach to verifying the correctness of a program is desirable. However, here we come up against the problems discussed above. It has turned out to be extremely difficult to reason about the behaviour of software, and research into so-called 'formal methods' (the use of mathematical techniques in the development of computer-based systems) has not yielded methods which have yet found wide acceptance, though there have been some notable successes (Hinchey and Bowen 1995).

Malleability

Another distinctive feature of software is its extreme malleability. To change a traditional engineering artefact, such as a bridge or an engine, once it has been built is usually very expensive and often requires partial or complete redesign. This results in comparatively more effort being put into design since later change is so hard. Software, however, is very easily changed or copied.

Given the ease of altering programs, requests by users for slightly different interfaces or new features can often be quickly accommodated. But the risk with such changes is that, as discussed above, they can easily introduce bugs or errors (this ease of change is also exploited by writers of software viruses to introduce unwelcome behaviour). There are other consequences: versions of programs quickly proliferate and controlling and tracking the program versions which make up a full system can itself quickly become a complex task. A further implication is that it is a considerable temptation to start building a system before its design has been properly verified.

1.3 Practical difficulties in developing software

Problems also arise from the context in which software is produced. It is almost always developed by teams rather than individuals and, if it is to be successful, must find favour with users. The consequent organizational problems and possibilities of misunderstandings further complicate the development process. Indeed many projects fail ever to deliver working software or deliver systems which are almost immediately abandoned. One study, carried out in the United States in the early 1980s, estimated that about three quarters of software development projects did not manage to deliver a system which was then put into use (Gladden 1982). And, over a decade later, there is little reason to believe that the situation has improved (Gibbs 1994). One well-known development project where the software had, in the end, to be abandoned involved a system for dispatching London ambulances.

The London Ambulance Service Dispatch System

The London Ambulance Service (LAS) is the world's largest ambulance service covering an area of just over 600 square miles and a population of around 7 million people (though the daytime population is much larger due to the influx of commuters). The service is divided into two sections: one providing routine patient transport, the other an accident and emergency service. In 1992 the emergency service was typically dealing with up to 1600 calls a day. It had a target of dispatching an ambulance within 3 minutes of a call and attending an incident within 14 minutes.

At that time the service used manual methods for controlling the dispatch of ambulances. The details of a call, such as the location and type of an incident, were noted on paper and sent to a central collection point where duplicate calls (resulting from more than one person calling about the same incident) were eliminated. Call details were then given to an allocator who selected which ambulance to send. The details were next passed to a dispatcher who contacted the ambulance driver by radio or telephone. Once the ambulance was dispatched all communication was by radio. There were problems with this system: paper details could easily get lost, and if a member of the public called back (to ask why an ambulance had not yet arrived, for instance) it was difficult to trace how the original call had been dealt with. The paper-based system meant that, in 1992, an ambulance was dispatched within 3 minutes in less than half of the emergencies handled; an ambulance attended the scene within 14 minutes in only 55% of calls (Classe 1997).

In the autumn of 1990 the LAS decided to commission the development of a computerized dispatch system in order to improve its performance. A requirements specification was prepared and an invitation to tender for the development was issued in February 1991. A large number of companies responded though many commented that the proposed implementation date of January 1992 made the timescale extremely tight. Nevertheless a supplier was selected who offered to meet the deadline. This supplier had carried out work for the emergency services before but had not had experience of developing this kind of system. From subsequent investigations it is clear that price was a major factor in selecting the winning bid.

There were many problems during the development of the new system. Software was frequently late, there was no proper project management and no one involved with the project had experience with PRINCE, the project management methodology which had been adopted for the development. Moreover the software developers made *ad hoc* changes to the software in order to please users. The users themselves were not adequately trained, and were sceptical about the benefits of the system. As a result of such problems the implementation was put back until late in 1992 but, as it turned out, many problems were still not resolved in time.

The computerized dispatch system finally went live at 7.00 a.m. on 26 October 1992. Initially, while there were few calls to deal with, the system worked satisfactorily and staff were able to sort out any problems. However, as the number of calls built up, it became clear that there were major problems. The system was often failing to eliminate duplicate calls, so that sometimes more than one ambulance would attend a scene. The tracking of ambulance status did not work well either. Ambulance crews were meant to radio back their status by pressing various buttons on a special control panel fitted to their vehicle. But this system did not work as well as hoped and crews became confused about what to do. This exacerbated the problems so that the system did not have a true picture of the ambulance fleet's status and made inappropriate allocations of ambulances to incidents. The delays in ambulance response had the further effect that people at incidents would call again asking why no ambulance had come, so increasing the load on the system. Eventually it became clear that the service had lost control of its fleet and on the afternoon of the following day it reverted to a semi-manual-system, using only part of the original software: that for taking calls. On 4 November, this failed as well due to a program error, and the system was then abandoned altogether.

The failure of the LAS system attracted widespread publicity and caused an outcry. There were allegations that as many as 20 people had possibly died as a result of delays of up to 3 hours in ambulances arriving at incidents (*Software Engineering Notes* 1993). However, a later inquiry did point out that there was no evidence of deaths due to ambulance delays. This inquiry also reported that neither the system nor the users were ready for the implementation and that, in any event, the system contained design flaws, in particular an unrealistic reliance on perfect information about ambulance location. The report also stated that the project timescale had been too short.

The problems faced by software projects

The failure of the LAS dispatch system, though dramatic, is not an isolated case. Other recent, major development setbacks include the Taurus system for the London Stock Exchange which was abandoned after £400 million had been spent (Neumann 1995), a computerized baggage-handling system for Denver airport whose problems delayed the opening of the new airport (Gibbs 1994), and a fingerprint-recognition system for the police which was not used because it was too slow and unreliable (Boyle 1995). These failures are well known because they were large projects. Countless smaller developments have also been abandoned.

Why do so many software projects fail? One reason is the inherent difficulty in developing and verifying software, as discussed in the previous section. But, as is clear from the LAS case, there are other problems which can arise, such as unrealistic timescales, inadequate management, uncommitted users, and so on. What seems clear is that the process of developing a large software system, one with many users and developers, is quite different from the kind of small-scale developments undertaken by individuals for themselves or for one or two users. Large-scale development projects have to overcome the additional problems of understanding and addressing user requirements, and ensuring that those working on a project know what they are required to produce. This communication dimension greatly complicates software development.

We shall not discuss all the issues which arise from large-scale developments but highlight some which will be revisited later in the book. These are: the problem of determining what to build, the organizational context of software projects, the need to understand the development process, and the lack of training and standards.

Determining what to build

When engineers construct a bridge to cross a river the problem they must address is clearly defined. They will know what loads the bridge must support and roughly where it should be situated. Studies of the banks and river bed may further constrain the siting of the bridge, leaving the designers with a small set of alternatives from which to choose.

This is not the case for most software projects, especially those intended to automate administrative tasks. The constraints within which a new system must operate may not always be clear to its designers. For example, the design of the LAS dispatch system did not allow for the difficulties in getting accurate information on ambulance locations and statuses. Furthermore software designers must decide which tasks and procedures should be automated and which should be left to administrative staff to carry on doing. This decision is difficult since the very introduction of the system is itself likely to change the way people work. There is no doubt that many developments fail simply because the wrong system is built or because some major feature which should have been incorporated is omitted.

The partiality of many software developers for providing features can be a further problem. Often too little attention is paid to the core facilities which the users really require. As one commentator on the LAS system remarked: 'You should design from the individual people outwards, rather than imposing a solution and getting people to drive it.' The same person commented that most computer systems were 'too complicated, with too many bells and buzzers' (Arthur 1992). This phenomenon of software developers getting bogged down in providing features rather than addressing requirements may be one reason for the apparently low pay-off from computerization (discussed in Chapter 4).

The organizational context

A further difficulty is that producing software in response to a set of requirements is only one component of a development project. Users must be motivated to switch to a new system and adequately trained in how to operate it. Furthermore, users' attitudes to a new system often depend on circumstances outside software developers' control; it is not uncommon for software to be designed and implemented against a background of scepticism or even hostility.

The switchover to using a new system is also problematical, especially if the functionality it provides is critical. It is not easy to carry out trial implementations or to organize the transition. The initial period after implementation is particularly difficult; this is the time when errors which were not caught by testing can surface and when inexperienced users are likely to make mistakes, possibly increasing the load the system must cope with.

Problems arising from the organizational context of software development appear to have been particularly acute with the LAS Dispatch System. User motivation and training were clearly factors in the system's failure as was the premature implementation.

The software development process
The most common approach to verifying the correctness of software relies on a combination of project control and software testing. The former means ensuring that each stage of a project (requirements analysis, specification, design, coding, and testing) is carried out to a high standard and verified before the next stage is started. Even though exhaustive testing of software is, as discussed above, impossible, some testing to check a system's functionality and eliminate obvious sources of error is still essential.

There is, as yet, only limited understanding of the best ways to organize large software developments or how to estimate the effort which is needed. The time and resources provided are thus frequently inadequate, as was the case with the LAS system, which was developed against a tight timescale and without sufficient management control. Even when adequate time and resources are available managers may be uncertain what proportion to devote to design as opposed to coding or how much testing should be carried out.

One reason for this lack of understanding is that an engineering approach to software development, where the process is rigorously controlled and monitored, has rarely been adopted. Without a precise picture of what has happened during previous projects it is difficult to know how to improve.

Just how bad the situation is can be seen from figures published by the Software Engineering Institute, an American software research centre. The Institute has developed a model of software development, the Capability Maturity Model (discussed in Chapter 10), which describes five levels of sophistication in development practices (Herbsleb *et al.* 1997). Level 1 projects are essentially chaotic; higher levels reflect superior degrees of organization and control. A level 5 project will be well managed and monitored enabling people to learn from mistakes. According to surveys carried out by the Institute about 75% of organizations are at level 1 with most of the rest at levels 2 or 3. Only a very few organizations (about 1%) are operating at level 5.

Training and standards
The general absence of a clearly defined software development process is one example of how generally unstandardized software development is compared to other engineering disciplines. This lack of standards appears in several areas: the training of software developers, the standards to be used in documenting designs, the management of different versions of programs and associated documentation, interfaces and subroutines and so on. Below we consider two particular areas: training, and the lack of reusable components.

Currently there are few standards of knowledge or experience for software developers. Some companies certify people as having expertise in their products but such certification is generally obtained for being superficially familiar with a product or interface rather than for competence in software design and development. The British Computer Society (BCS) does set a minimum standard, through its membership examinations, which would ensure a core of common knowledge among software developers. However, most people working in software development are not members of the BCS. Nor do most have computer science degrees (at least in the UK) so there is little guarantee that personnel on a project will share any common core of professional training. This was a problem on the LAS project where the intention had been to use the PRINCE Project Management Method but staff turned out not to be familiar with it.

Software developers also work in an environment where there are few if any standardized components or interfaces. Few manufacturers would envisage designing all the components in a new car. Instead they reuse components from other models or industry standard ones. This option is not available to software developers, who do not have access to a pool of tried and tested subroutines to perform certain functions (such as date-manipulation routines, for instance). Instead these components are redeveloped time and time again in many different systems.[3] There is a growing awareness of the wastefulness of such practices and the prospect of reusing software components is one of the driving forces behind the interest in object-oriented programming methodologies.

However, imposition of standards, though desirable, does have potential drawbacks. Computer and software technology is moving very rapidly so there is the danger that a standard, once determined, may soon be made obsolete by new techniques or technology.

1.4 Summary

In this chapter we have reviewed the increasing reliance which society now places on software for managing everything from bank accounts to air traffic. There is little reason to be confident in the reliability of much of this software, as was shown by considering two particular cases: the Therac-25 cancer treatment machine, and the problems expected to surface at the end of the century due to date-handling deficiencies in much software. We then reviewed the reasons for these problems, which fell into two main categories: those arising from the inherent nature of software, and the difficulties faced by software projects. The inherent characteristics of software we considered included its complexity, the difficulties in testing it, and its malleability. With regard to organizational problems, we considered the example of the LAS Dispatch System development. This project displayed many common problems: inadequate project control, design errors, user scepticism, and so forth. We discussed some of these issues in more detail: in particular the problems of deciding what to build, the organizational context of software development, lack of understanding of the software process, and general lack of training and standards.

---

3 Avoiding the wastefulness of this practice is one of the arguments used by the software engineer Stallman against copyrighting software, see Chapter 4.

Further reading

There are a number of books which discuss the problems of software development and software-related problems or disasters. Two of the most comprehensive are Forester and Morrison (1990) and Neumann (1995).

A detailed source of information on the London Ambulance Dispatch System is the report of the inquiry (Page *et al.* 1993). The British Computer Society has published a study of the year 2000 problem (BCS 1997), and a comprehensive account of the Therac-25 accidents is given by Leveson (1993).

The classic discussion of the problems of large software development projects is Brooks (1982).

Points to consider

1 When someone buys a software package, they cannot inspect the source code since they are only ever given the compiled version of the software. Thus software buyers are forced to accept delivery of what is, in effect, a sealed box. Would it be better to oblige suppliers (by law if necessary) to deliver both source and executable code? Among the points to consider are:
   - Would this enable software buyers to form a better idea of the quality of product that they were buying? It is worth noting in this context that the suppliers of the Therac-25 were unwilling to let their users have a copy of the machine's code even after problems had become apparent (Leveson and Turner 1993)
   - Users could amend the software to fix bugs or add new features – could this give rise to problems?
   - Would software suppliers be put off developing new software by the knowledge that it could be easily copied? Would it still be possible to enforce copyright protection of programs?
   - Would the resulting situation be so very different from that which exists in the PC world where many different suppliers produce very similar products and can easily look at the internals of competitors' offerings?
2 The interfaces and functionality of much software (such as operating systems and common packages) are not currently stable: any supplier can change any aspect of the software they supply with impunity. Should there be standards (again possibly legally enforced) to stabilize the interfaces or functionality of software? Points to consider might include:
   - Is there really a competitive market at present for key software components such as operating systems? If there is not, does it matter?
   - Would such enforced standards hold up progress to the eventual detriment of users?

3 Is the concern about safety-critical software misplaced? After all, there
   have been accidents due to software errors but not nearly as many as due
   to human error. Could one argue that given the enormous number of
   tasks now undertaken by software, the number of accidents is very small
   compared to the advantages obtained?
4 Should software developers be liable for every fault in the software
   which they deliver? Among the issues here are:
   • Suppliers of other products such as cars are liable for the safety of
      the goods they supply, why not software suppliers?
   • It may not be possible to produce error-free software – should
      suppliers be liable nevertheless? If it is not possible to guarantee
      safety of a product, should it not be sold at all, or should the supplier
      take out insurance to cover against problems?
   • If suppliers are not liable, will they ever try to improve the quality of
      the software which they supply?
5 Should software suppliers be obliged to correct errors due to the year
   2000 problem? What implications might the time at which the software
   was developed have for this issue?

CHAPTER 2

Data storage and technology

- Applications for credit cards are now vetted by credit rating agencies. Few people are aware of the existence of these agencies, the data they hold, where they obtain it from, or the vetting criteria they use. Moreover there is evidence that the records of as many as one in three people may contain incorrect information.
- As a result of a comment about his political sympathies, made in a reference when he applied for a government post in the United States, the journalist Peter Kimball was classified as an undesirable citizen. His file was maintained over a period of 30 years and resulted in his being rejected for government jobs and having difficulty in obtaining a passport. When it was finally released the file turned out to contain no substantive evidence of anti-government activity of any kind.

Overview

The enormous capacity of modern data storage technology and the speed with which it can process data make it quite feasible for relatively small organizations to collect and collate large amounts of personal information. What are the implications of this for people's privacy and freedom?

We first look at the tremendous advances that have been made in data storage technology over the last 100 years, from early card-based systems to modern magnetic storage media. Next, we consider the collection of personal data by private organizations for the purposes of assessing creditworthiness and for direct marketing. The implications for privacy of such practices are also discussed.

Finally, we review the extent of information now held on individuals by government agencies and consider cases where such data has been misused either by the government or by public employees. In particular we look at data matching – the practice of comparing information on people from different sources to uncover significant inconsistencies.

Relation to other chapters Many of the issues of data privacy and how data is used are revisited later in the book. In Chapter 8 we review the current UK data protection legislation to see how it limits the way in which personal data can be collected and used.

One issue which is closely concerned with data privacy, and which we do not cover in this chapter, is the current debate about encryption standards. Since this issue also arises in telecommunications we discuss it in the next chapter.

2.1 Development of data storage technology

During the last 100 years there have been phenomenal improvements in the technology for storing and processing data. These improvements mean that information can now be queried and collated in ways which were unimaginable just a generation ago.

The first time that technology was used for larger scale data processing was in the 1890 US census. The results from the 1880 US census had taken 7 years to produce and the rapid increases in the US population meant there was a need to find quicker ways of analyzing census data. The inventor Herman Hollerith devised a system in which census information, such as sex, age bracket, marital status and so on, was represented by holes punched in cards. Once these cards had been prepared they could be rapidly processed by electromechanical sorters and tabulators (machines which counted the number of cards fulfilling certain criteria). Using Hollerith's machines the census data was transferred to some 63 million cards and a first count of the population (about 62.6 million) was produced in 6 weeks; the full 1890 census was processed in just 2 years.

Punched cards were to remain the main form of storage for bulk data right up until the early 1960s though, of course, the machines which processed them became much faster. In the 1950s researchers began experimenting with the use of magnetic media to hold data, and in the 1960s tape and disk drives began to replace cards for bulk storage. Devices such as magnetic disks took up less space, were more reliable, and provided much faster access to data. Moreover, they made it possible to access files at any given point without needing to read through from the beginning.

Magnetic storage media have continued to develop in capacity and access speed. Now it is quite standard to find disk drives which fit into a box about the size of a large dictionary with storage capacities of 2 gigabytes (that is, 2000 megabytes) or more. To put this in perspective, a page of A4 text typically requires 2 kilobytes of storage, and the whole of Tolstoy's novel *War and Peace* probably requires no more than 3 megabytes (even without data compression). Multimedia data requires more storage: 1 minute of sound may take several megabytes, a simple black and white picture as little as 10 kilobytes, but a complex colour picture several megabytes. Video data stored as frames probably requires about 1 megabyte per frame, so a second of video may require 25 megabytes (though compression techniques can reduce this considerably) (Khoshafian and Baker 1996). All the data collected from the 1890 American census could probably be accommodated on a single 2 gigabyte disk – the original census data would have required a stack of cards some 10 km high.

Terabyte databases (containing 1000 gigabytes, that is, 1 000 000 megabytes of data) are now quite feasible. These sizes are indeed required for applications such as storing image data from satellites. In commercial or administrative applications the largest databases are probably required for so-called data warehousing – the storage of large amounts of archive data. Data warehouses may reach sizes of 200 gigabytes and are often used by retailers to hold a record of sales over a period in the hope that subsequent analysis of the data will yield useful marketing information.

Besides the ability to hold enormous quantities of data on disk drives and tapes there is now also the facility to hold smaller amounts of data in highly portable formats. The most significant technology here is that of smart cards: credit card-sized cards which incorporate a microchip. Currently such cards can hold about 12 kilobytes of data (equivalent to a few pages of A4 text) but their capacity is growing. At the time of writing there are over 600 million smart cards in use around the world, a number expected to rise to several billion in a few years. These cards are already being used to hold personal information. In Germany people carry smart cards with their medical insurance details; in South Korea there are plans for them to be used to hold all the relevant data on an individual including pension entitlement, driving licence, and military service record (Grayson 1996; Arthur 1996). In theory it should be possible to use encryption to control access to the data and to prevent the production of fake cards. In practice, such security has been overcome in the past. For example, the satellite broadcaster BSkyB used a system which relied on smart cards to decode scrambled television broadcasts, but is believed to have lost millions of pounds due to pirates producing equivalent cards (Arthur 1995).

Given the vast storage capacity of modern databases and the extent of computerization, it is now impossible for people to go about their daily lives without leaving a trail of data. Reserving plane tickets, paying with credit cards, using supermarket loyalty cards, withdrawing money from bank accounts, or making telephone calls are all actions which leave a record on a database somewhere. Combining the information from several such databases gives a very detailed picture of individuals' circumstances and lifestyles. In the following sections we look at the reasons why such information is collected and the ways in which it may be used, or misused.

2.2 The data business

When a 32-year old lawyer, Jaz Stichaw, applied for a Barclaycard he was turned down because he was believed to have debts of £32 000. But Jaz

Stichaw had never been in debt. The erroneous information had been supplied by Equifax, a leading credit reference agency. Mr Stichaw sued the agency and eventually settled out of court (Cooper 1996).

Techniques used for credit assessment were originally developed by mail order companies who wished to reduce the risks of offering credit to potential defaulters. These techniques involved characterizing neighbourhoods by using census information. House-holders' creditworthiness could then be estimated on the basis of their address. In the UK the postal code system (which divides the country into about 1.3 million postal codes) provides a simple basis on which to link addresses to neighbourhoods.

These organizations used their credit-rating expertise to set up agencies providing banks and credit card companies with information enabling them to assess whether a potential client was a good risk. Two leading credit reference agencies in the UK are CCN Credit Systems and Equifax Europe. They each hold information on most of the adult population of the country, CCN for example is reported to have files on about 44 million people, 3 million businesses, and 50 million vehicles (Givens 1995; Cope 1996).

Typically such companies start with the electoral register as their first source of information. This gives the names and addresses of everyone over the age of 18 who is eligible to vote. This is then supplemented with County Court judgments on debt and bankruptcy. Further information may be supplied by the credit reference agency's clients themselves. CCN, for instance, has more than 200 clients including credit card companies and other financial institutions who supply it with details of loans and customer credit accounts.

The information supplied by such agencies is typically used by lenders in conjunction with some kind of credit scoring system. This involves assessing the creditworthiness of individuals on the basis of their personal profile, taking into account such factors as age, whether they own or rent their residence, type of job, post code, telephone number (not having one is viewed dimly) and so forth (Halstead 1996).

Although the information supplied by credit reference agencies is primarily used for assessing whether to extend credit, it may be used for other purposes. These include investigating the personal finances of company directors, and checking out the details of job applicants. Credit reference agencies have even been used by police forces to help in tracking down suspects (Burke 1995).

Given the number of people who now apply for or use credit cards, and the many different types of card in existence, reference agencies have a wide sphere of influence. How accurate is the information they hold? Clearly there are sometimes errors, as Jaz Stichaw found out, but how common are they? It is very hard to be sure; one survey carried out for Channel 4 Television found that more than one in three files held by credit reference agencies contained errors. Some of these errors were serious, such as incorrectly attributed court judgments (Cooper 1996).

Other commercial uses of personal data

Assessment of credit risk is not the only activity in which commercial organizations make use of databases of personal data. Marketing is another area which is being strongly influenced by database technology.

Until recently the main way in which large companies marketed their goods was to run promotional campaigns (often involving advertising on television) to develop 'brand awareness' among consumers. Profiles of typical customers were drawn up and promotions were targeted accordingly. The main problem with such campaigns was that they were very expensive and it was not possible to be sure how effective they would be.

With the advent of computer technology it became possible to target promotional campaigns much more precisely through direct mail, and to measure the response obtained from the consumers targeted. The main objective when using a database as the basis for marketing is to try to establish 'buying patterns' so that promotions can be very specifically targeted. For example, if a wine company discovered that people who buy expensive clothes are more likely than others to order expensive wines, it could use this knowledge, coupled with a database of consumers, to focus its promotions more profitably.

It is such database-driven marketing techniques which lead to the large amounts of junk mail that many people now receive. In the UK, an adult can normally expect to receive some 50 pieces of junk mail a year, though this is a lot lower than the average for some continental countries – the typical Swiss receives well over 100 pieces a year (Turpin 1995).

To be effective, direct mail campaigns need to be well targeted, and for this they require as much detailed information on consumers' habits and preferences as they can get. One way to obtain this information is the so-called 'lifestyle' questionnaire, containing detailed questions (perhaps as many as 200) on habits and beliefs. This is posted out to consumers, usually with some kind of incentive to fill it in, such as entry into a prize draw. Apparently about 15% of people do complete and return these questionnaires. Given that questionnaires have at some time been sent to most of the 24 million or so houses in the UK, the companies which send them out hold vast amounts of data on consumer preferences and behaviour. Such data, once analysed, enables marketeers to infer the preferences of people who have not completed forms and to target promotion campaigns very precisely (Fisher 1997).

One of the most recent techniques for obtaining information about consumers is the issuing of loyalty cards by supermarkets. The use of barcodes and scanners to automatically price items at the check-out became widespread in the early 1980s. The information gathered was first used to automate and improve stock control but suppliers came to realize that, potentially, it also gave them the means to find out about the habits of individual customers. The only problem was how to associate particular customers with the various purchases that they made. This was the impetus behind the loyalty card – by recording who bought what it became possible to build up detailed profiles of the purchasing habits of customers and to determine who the most 'loyal' (high-spending) customers were. This information can be used to target special offers at particular groups of customers. The supermarket chain Tesco, for example, has a database of well over 5 million customers. Sending a mailshot to all of these is expensive, but having detailed knowledge of spending habits enables the company to target high-spenders, or those who spend a lot on particular products. Loyalty cards also mean that supermarkets now know a great deal about people's private lives – it is quite easy to determine whether someone is an alcoholic by analyzing their purchases, for instance (Green 1995; Sharpe 1996).

Non-commercial uses of data

Commercial organizations have not been alone in using modern database techniques to target particular groups of people. The use of such techniques has also become common in political campaigning.

The United Kingdom has a constituency-based parliamentary system in which each constituency returns a single MP. At election time it is fairly easy to predict, on the basis of past results, the winning parties in most of the 650 or so constituencies. There are, however, about 50 marginal constituencies where such predictions are unreliable. In each of these, the loyalty of the majority of voters is fairly evenly divided between two parties and the outcome depends on the preferences of a relatively small group of 'floating voters'. These are voters who are not sure which way to vote and who switch their allegiance from one election to the next. There are estimated to be some 200 000 floating voters in marginal constituencies in the United Kingdom, and their preferences are critical in determining the outcome of an election (Fisher 1997).

Using direct-marketing databases it is now possible to locate the bulk of these floating voters. Newspaper reports at the time of the 1997 election put the cost of buying a list of 1000 likely floating voters in the region of £50–150, depending on the supplier and how the list has been compiled. On this basis the names and addresses of all the floating voters in marginal constituencies would cost about £10 000–30 000. The extent to which the major political parties make use of such techniques in general elections is not clear. However, both the Labour and Liberal Democrat Parties are reported to have used direct marketing lists to try to build up membership.

One way database technology definitely was used in the 1997 election campaign was for recording the comments made by opposing politicians. Such databases could then be analyzed to reveal inconsistencies or the occasional gaffe. The Labour Party also used databases to record voting intentions from canvas returns. Concern has been expressed that such databases can easily be misused. One Labour councillor is reported to have voiced the fear that they could be used to vet applicants for jobs in Labour-controlled councils, and so help prevent activists from other parties being employed (Gosling 1996).

Privacy issues

Does the collection of personal data by private organizations compromise privacy? This depends on just what one means by privacy.

Most writers who have discussed privacy stress the importance of control. Thus at the most basic level, privacy is an issue of controlling who one sees or deals with. An extreme example of this might be a millionaire who buys a large secluded residence and bars entry to all but a small group of people. At the other extreme, imprisonment generally entails a severe and degrading loss of privacy – a prison inmate usually has no private space to retire to, and little control over his or her environment.

Another important dimension of privacy is the amount and intimacy of information which people choose to reveal about themselves and to whom. In this regard, what most of us reveal to colleagues at work differs enormously from what we reveal to family and friends. Exactly what information is seen as being private is to an extent arbitrary; many people (in the United Kingdom at least) are quite happy to tell a casual acquaintance where they were born, but are less happy about revealing their age, for example.

Given that people like to have control over what is known about them (we shall not go into the reasons for this) does the collection of personal data result in a loss of privacy? To the extent that people supply such data voluntarily (because they are asked or offered a minor financial inducement) it is hard to maintain that it does. What people do lose when information is recorded about them is their anonymity – that is, the freedom to go about their lives unnoticed and to choose how they present themselves to other people and, especially, to organizations.

Before the Industrial Revolution people lived almost entirely in small communities and could have few secrets from one another. Industrialization brought greater mobility and the development of large urban areas whose occupants could, if they wished, live unknown and unrecognized. It is this anonymity of urban life which large-scale information storage has undermined. Now everyone has a history stored on a computer somewhere.

What are the implications of this? First, the way in which information about us is passed around is largely out of our control. We do not know who buys such information, whether it is accurate, or how it is used.

Second, the presence of databases limits the way in which we can present ourselves to others in daily life. A common argument is that this is a good thing, and that it is only those who are up to no good who present themselves falsely in their dealings with other people. There is much support for this view. Parents are very keen to know, for example, whether anyone with a record of sexual offences against children has moved into their area. (It has also been pointed out that if wrongdoers cannot wipe the slate clean at some point and start afresh, they become trapped in their past.)

Third, databases can be seen as undermining people's individuality. Clients of supermarkets may now be labelled as 'status-conscious high-spenders', (less valued) 'low-income bargain hunters', or 'eco-conscious vegetarians'. Each type of organization, from banks to retailers to political parties, is adopting its own classifications and treating people according to where they fit in these. This rise of what has been called the 'dossier society' in which decisions about individuals are made not as the result of face-to-face contact or personal acquaintanceship but on the basis of computer files and statistical profiles (Laudon 1995) may have some benefits. Applications for loans or credit may be assessed more impartially by software comparing people's details against statistical profiles than by bank managers who, in the past, might have discriminated against some customers for fairly arbitrary reasons. The danger comes when this process is taken to its logical conclusion. What if the status-conscious high-spenders of the supermarket chain are seen by the police as being likely criminals or tax-evaders?

The circumstantial evidence is that most consumers are not concerned about commercial organizations holding data on them. One study reported that only 9% of people are reluctant to fill in forms asking for personal information – the majority are happy to give personal information to marketing surveys or for loyalty cards in exchange for some kind of reward or the promise of better service (Cooper 1995).

The main danger of abuse of personal information comes perhaps not from commercial organizations but government authorities. They know more about people and obtain information, such as income data, which people would probably choose not to reveal if they did not have to. We discuss the use of data by governments in the next section.

2.3 The uses of data by government authorities

In the autumn of 1945 Penn Kimball, an American journalist who had just completed over 3 years in the Marines, sat an exam to join the US Foreign Service. He passed the exam but by the time he was eventually offered an appointment he had already started another job. He asked to postpone his appointment but when, a few years later, he applied to take it up he was turned down. He was eventually told that his appointment had been 'disapproved'.

Over the following years Kimball pursued a journalistic career and became a professor of journalism at Columbia University. During this time he applied for a number of government appointments and an overseas scholarship, but was always rejected. In 1975, however, the American Freedom of Information and Privacy Act was amended giving Americans the right to request copies of government files held on them. Curious about what might be held on him – especially after the mysterious rejections he had received when applying for government posts – Kimball requested to see his US State Department file.

When he finally saw the file he was amazed to discover that he had been classified as a dangerous radical and a security risk. His file also stated that he was 'too clever' to be caught carrying a Communist Party membership card.

These conclusions were the result of the original security clearance investigation which had been triggered more than 30 years earlier when he had applied for the Foreign Service post. The investigation had been carried out by FBI agents who talked to former colleagues of Kimball as well as people who had known him as a child.

It was not easy for Kimball to determine the identities of many people who had been interviewed since their names had been blanked out. It appeared that because he had once signed a petition supporting a strike at an aircraft factory (which the FBI had classified as 'Communist inspired') his past had been more thoroughly investigated than would normally have been the case. One or two remarks by informants who said he was 'left-leaning' or that he had once been spotted 'drinking with Communists' seem then to have tipped the balance, resulting in his being classified as a security risk.

Kimball discovered that there were not only State Department and FBI files held on him, but also a CIA file. Over a period of years, through repeated requests, he obtained more than 250 pages of his files – and even then some pages were withheld. He eventually managed to get his State Department and FBI files destroyed, but was unable to get the CIA file removed.

The contents of the files held on Kimball appear to have prevented him from obtaining several jobs and at least one scholarship. The most worrying aspect is that there seems never to have been any hard evidence that he was a security risk. Kimball had been so classified on the basis of odd comments by people whose relationship towards him or impartiality had not been verified. Moreover he was never officially informed of how he was viewed and so was never given an opportunity to challenge or refute any of the allegations made against him.

Use and misuse of official data

Kimball's file was entirely paper-based but his case shows how easily information can be distorted or misinterpreted and how damaging this can be for an individual. With computer technology the dangers are even greater. Computer-held data has an aura of infallibility but is not necessarily accurate. Moreover, the ease with which text can be searched for particular words probably increases the dangers of information being misinterpreted. Using computer technology, for instance, an agent could have searched through hundreds of testimonials looking for occurrences of the word 'Communist' and given undue weight to these while ignoring comments which might show things from a different angle.

There is now an enormous amount of data held on individuals by government authorities. In the United Kingdom most adults are likely to appear on at least some of the files held by the Department of Social Security (DSS), the National Health Service (NHS), the Department of Employment, the Inland Revenue, the Driver and Vehicle Licensing Centre (DVLC), and the TV Licensing and Records Office. This is not an exhaustive list and it does not take into account the databases held by local organizations.

Information held by the police or health services can be particularly sensitive. But it is not necessarily accurate. Police forces regularly compile and collate intelligence information on individuals living in their area. Much of this information will comprise reports of sightings of known criminals but it will also contain gossip and unsubstantiated or malicious allegations. One estimate is that more than one in five adults may appear in police intelligence databases (Campbell and Connor 1986).

The inaccuracy or misuse of data held by police or health authorities can have disastrous consequences for an individual. There have been several incidents of wrongful arrest due to inaccurate computer information, including one tragic incident in France where a hospital worker was shot dead by police. The shooting incident occurred when police stopped his car which their computer had erroneously identified as being stolen.

Criminal records and other information on people in England and Wales are held on the Police National Computer (PNC). Cases have been reported of police officers who have obtained information from the PNC for personal reasons or who have passed it on to private investigators or journalists. In one case in 1996 two Metropolitan Police officers were fined for using the PNC to obtain information on the boyfriend of the former wife of one of the officers (Bennetto 1996). In a far more serious incident, a police officer accepted bribes from a drug dealer to obtain his police file and to destroy an incriminating surveillance log (MacDonald1996).

Currently, in the United Kingdom, NHS data is held locally. One disadvantage of such a system is that if a person is hurt in an accident a long way from home, it can take doctors a long time to get hold of the patient's medical records. This has led to government suggestions for creating a computer network to cover the whole of the NHS. However, health data is often extremely sensitive. In one case in the United States a banker who also served on the board of a local Health Maintenance Organization (similar to a health authority in the United Kingdom) managed to obtain the health records of bank clients. The banker then called in loans from people who had suffered from cancer (Hunt 1996).

Besides the problems which arise from inaccuracies in data, its mis-interpretation, or its misuse, a separate set of issues arise from the computer analysis of data.

Data matching

There is an apocryphal story of a priest at a party who is asked by one of the guests if he has ever heard any unusual confessions. 'Well, in fact', replies the priest, 'the first confession I heard was by someone who had committed a murder.' A while later a man comes over to join the group. When asked whether he knows the priest he replies 'Oh yes, I made the first confession he ever heard.'

This story illustrates the essence of data matching, how collating information from different sources can reveal more than was originally meant to be divulged, or can turn up inconsistencies. Data matching on computer files is primarily used for the detection of fraud. Typically, two files containing information given in different circumstances and to different authorities are compared to find inconsistencies. For example, a file of students who collect grants from an education authority and another file of people claiming unemployment benefit might be compared to find anyone who was fraudulently collecting both grant and benefit.

Of course, data matching often produces suspects erroneously, either because the data is wrong or because it may be impossible to be certain whether two records on different files actually refer to the same person. One example is the incident which occurred in California in 1984 when a curt letter was sent to an 18-year-old boy accusing him of being several months late in registering for the draft. It transpired that there was no boy of that name at the address and that the name itself was fictitious; it had been made up by two teenagers a number of years earlier when filling in a form at an ice cream store which was offering free birthday treats to children. The data collected by this company had been sold to a direct mailing company and had in turn found its way to the draft authorities. The data on this file was then regularly matched with records of draft registrations. When the non-existent boy's eighteenth birthday came up and he had not registered for the draft the warning letter had been automatically generated (Roszak 1994).

Data matching has been used by local councils in the United Kingdom to try to reduce benefit fraud. Files from neighbouring boroughs may be compared to find people who are simultaneously claiming benefits in more than one borough. However, it is often difficult to match information such as addresses. One report claims that a data-matching exercise which was begun in 1995 produced over 7500 matches but that only one of these led to a conviction (Walker 1997).

Public interest versus state control

The proponents of the use of data matching by government authorities claim that it is a legitimate way to protect taxpayers' money. They point to the high cost of fraud and the difficulty of effectively combating it by other means. They also argue that data matching does not involve any operation which could not have been done by manual comparison before the advent of computer technology.

The detractors argue that it completely inverts the normal investigation process in which the checking of a person's records would be triggered by some evidence or suspicion. With computer matching, they argue, people whose names are produced by a match may effectively be under suspicion until they can establish their innocence. This is, of course, particularly dangerous if the data is unreliable or the matching criteria are imperfect. They also point out that before computerization it simply was not practicable to carry out large trawls of files to find suspicious cases. Hence, they say, it is simply misleading to claim that data matching does not set any new precedent.

Of course, from the perspective of those who carry out data-matching exercises, many of the problems arising from incorrect matches can be resolved by using personal identification numbers on as many files as possible. This would ensure that only correct matches would be uncovered and avoid the danger of innocent people being put under suspicion. To follow this approach automatically leads to the requirement for some kind of identity card, to ensure that people cannot make claims under different identities.

The danger that many people see with such a situation is that it results in the effective existence of a national database, since all the information held on an individual by the state can then be very easily retrieved. They are afraid that such comprehensive databases might be abused by central authorities – ultimately, perhaps, in helping to stifle political dissent. There is also the problem that even if such databases are not misused, the fear of possible misuse may make some people more cautious about expressing opinions freely.

2.4 Summary

The development of data storage and processing technology over the last 100 years has now made it possible for organizations to hold and process enormous amounts of information. In the commercial world this has led to the rise of database marketing, with individuals increasingly being classified and targeted according to their lifestyle. These techniques have also been exploited by political parties and pressure groups.

The main impact of this technology on individuals has, we have argued, been a loss of anonymity. People's past and current lifestyles now colour their dealings with every large organization they come into contact with and decisions about individuals are increasingly made on the basis of computer-based data and statistical profiles. This can have advantages, as dealings may be more rational and less coloured by the personal prejudices of those in positions of authority or power. On the other hand, people can be categorized purely in terms of profiles which they then become unable to escape from.

As the Kimball case demonstrates, there have always been dangers for individuals when governments keep erroneous information on them or misinterpret correct information. Governments can now hold and process enormous amounts of data on their citizens and the dangers of these powers being abused are a perennial cause for concern in some quarters.

As we have seen, the pressure to reduce fraud leads to information being collated by central authorities. This can be beneficial in eliminating gross abuses of public funds. The danger is that it might lead to a central database on citizens and that this could, at some stage in the future, be abused by the authorities.

Further reading

There are a number of books covering database marketing techniques. One which gives a general introduction is *Direct and Database Marketing* by Graeme McCorkell (1997).

Penn Kimball's experiences of investigating the contents of his own file are detailed in his book, *The File* (1983). The use of computer technology by government agencies in the United Kingdom is extensively discussed in *Big Brother* by Simon Davies (1996), and in *On the Record* by Duncan Campbell and Steve Connor (1986).

The collections of papers *Computerization and Controversy* edited by Kling (1996), and *Computers, Ethics and Social Values* edited by Johnson and Nissenbaum (1995) contain sections on data privacy issues. In particular they contain articles by Richard Kusserow and John Shattuck which argue for and against allowing data matching exercises.

Points to consider

1 What is privacy? Is it important and, if so, why? In the light of your response to these questions, would you consider your privacy to be compromised if:
   - One of your neighbours kept a log of all the times you came home and went out?
   - Details of everything you bought from the shops was made publicly available – on the Internet, for instance?
   - You received direct mail from a supermarket where you shop saying that it had analyzed your purchases and that you appeared to have an unhealthy diet, consequently it was advising you to eat more fruit and vegetables?
2 Are there problems with political parties using database marketing techniques? Is this good for democracy, ensuring that politicians are more aware and sensitive to public mood and opinion? Or does it debase political debate by treating policy as merely part of a political 'marketing

mix' and result in large swathes of the electorate being ignored because they are not floating voters?

3 How many computer files or databases do you expect there are which hold information on you? If all these files were merged would the resulting information give an accurate picture of the kind of person that you are or could it be misleading? Would you be concerned if there were inaccuracies in the data held?

4 'If you are honest, you have nothing to hide' is a common comment made about people who are investigated by the police. Is this always true? What about data matching – presumably only people who are claiming benefits fraudulently or who are evading taxes need to worry about having their records on different files compared.

5 Is there a good argument for the introduction of identity cards in the United Kingdom? They are common in Europe and would reduce fraud and other forms of crime. Is it possible that identity cards could actually reduce the need for authorities to carry out data-matching exercises since fraud would be less likely to occur in the first place?

CHAPTER 3

Telecommunications and networks

- Using modern digital telephone technology companies can find out and record the telephone number of anyone who makes a call.
- When the McDonald's hamburger chain sued two green activists for distributing a leaflet criticizing the company, information on the trial was made available worldwide on an Internet Web site which was accessed by millions of people.
- An American programmer, Phil Zimmermann, lived under the threat of imprisonment for several years for having written an encryption program which produced messages which could not be decrypted by codebreakers.

Overview

In this chapter we are concerned with the impacts of telecommunications technology and the issues it raises.

We start by reviewing the progress of telecommunications technology: the development of computer networks, the vast increase in data transfer rates, and the future potential of the technology. Next we look at the impact that telecommunications technology has had and consider three issues in particular. The first of these is 'Calling Line Identification', the facility with modern telephone networks to determine the number from which a call is being made. We then look at the way modern communications technology, in particular the Internet, makes it much harder for governments or large organizations to control what information is made available to the public. Lastly we consider the debate which is currently in progress over data encryption, that is, how and to what extent individuals should be able to protect the information which they send over a communications network.

Relation to other chapters The impact of modern telecommunications technology is also discussed in the next chapter, where computer crime and the effects of computer technology on modern working conditions are considered. The legal issues which relate to the use of the Internet are considered in Chapter 9.

3.1 Advances in telecommunications

One of the earliest systems for long-distance communication was developed by the Frenchman Claude Chappe in the 1790s. Chappe's system was visual; semaphores were placed on the top of towers spaced at about 10-kilometre intervals. In an early demonstration a message was sent from Paris to Lille (about 200 kilometres away) in a few minutes. This system was extensively used in France, reaching a high point in the 1850s when about 30 cities were 'connected'. However, by this time the system had been superseded by the electric telegraph, first demonstrated by Samuel Morse in 1835. The electric telegraph had the enormous advantages of not being affected by weather conditions and of a much faster transmission rate. Using morse code, operators could send about 30 words (approximately 150 characters) per minute; an enormous improvement over the 20 characters per minute rate of Chappe's visual system.

It was with the development of the telephone by Alexander Graham Bell in 1876 that it first became possible to send an analogue signal, such as the sound of the human voice. Early telephone subscribers were connected to manually operated exchanges and had to ask an operator to connect them to a particular line. In the 1890s Almon Strowger developed an automatic switch which allowed a caller to dial a number and be directly connected. The Strowger switch was electromechanical and wear of the mechanical parts caused occasional problems such as crossed lines or poor sound quality. These problems led, from the 1960s, to a move towards fully electronic exchanges in which switching was carried out by a special-purpose computer.

It was also in the 1960s that engineers began investigating how to link computers together over wide areas. Much of this research was funded by the American Defence Department which wanted to develop a command and control infrastructure which could survive a nuclear war. The experimental network which was developed, the ARPANET, was revolutionary in using 'packet switching', a technique where messages are chopped up into fixed-length 'packets' and independently routed through a network of leased telephone lines by computers placed at each node. Packet switching is analogous to sending a book to someone by posting each page separately; individual pages may travel by different routes and arrive at different times; it is up to the receiver to reconstitute the book. Packet switching made it possible to send much more data than with the 'circuit switching' then used in telephone systems, where a direct connection is established between sender and receiver.

The telephone as it was originally developed worked well for transmitting the sound of the human voice but was poorly suited to digital data. With the development of digital microprocessors it became apparent that it would be more efficient to convert non-digital signals to digital and send everything in digital form. This results in a much higher capacity network and the ability to carry many different kinds of data – voice, video, digital, and so on – in so-called Integrated Services Digital Networks (ISDN). The move from analogue to digital encoding has also been accompanied by a move from copper wire to fibre-optic cable as the preferred transmission medium. These changes have led to enormous increases in capacity: using the older technology typical rates for sending digital data over a telephone line might have been as low as 2400 bits/second and data was transmitted over the ARPANET at 56 Kbits/second. With the advent of fibre-optic cables rates of 1 Gbits/second (where 1 Gbit is 1000 Mbits, a Mbit being 1000 Kbits) are now possible. And this is far from the limit of what is feasible. It is claimed that using current fibre-optic technology, it should be possible to achieve data rates of 50 000 Gbits/second.

Probably one of the most widely talked about applications of tele-communications technology is the Internet. The Internet itself is simply the result of many independently developed networks being linked together. There was no point at which the Internet became officially recognized as such, though the term Internet became common in the early 1990s. Initially the main applications for the Internet were electronic mail, newsgroups, file transfer, and remote login. It was the development of the World Wide Web, effectively a distributed hypertext system, and associated browsers in the early 1990s which led to the Internet becoming much more widely used. The growth of the Internet has been phenomenal; by 1992 there were over 1 million hosts connected and the number of World Wide Web sites went beyond 1 million in the mid-1990s.

3.2 Calling Line Identification

A young child is watching television, when an advertisement comes on showing soft toys. The child is entranced. 'Would you like your mum and dad to get you one of these?' comes a soft voice, 'Pick up the telephone receiver and hold it near the television.' A sequence of dialling tones is played over the television and, picked up by the receiver in the child's hand, dial the toy manufacturer's computer. There the calling number is identified and recorded. This number is then used along with a 'reverse telephone directory' (a directory listing subscribers by number rather than name) to find the address where the child is living. Shortly afterwards the family receives a personalized offer for soft toys.

This kind of marketing has not yet been used but is now technologically feasible. Indeed combining the use of television advertising with the demographic data used by direct marketing agencies, it would be quite easy to tailor the size and price of the toys offered in the mailshot to the probable income of the household.

Identifying calls

It is the new digital telephone systems which makes scenarios like the one outlined above possible. It is now possible to identify the number from which an incoming telephone call is made and telephone companies in America and Europe have, over the last decade, been offering customers services which exploit this facility.

This service, 'Calling Line Identification' (CLI), has caused considerable debate wherever it has been introduced. There has been concern that there are many instances where the knowledge that the receiver of a call can determine the number from which it was made would deter people from calling. Among the examples used have been:

- Police information lines which allow people to telephone and give information anonymously
- Telephone counselling services which people can call without needing to give their name. Conversely, counsellors who are dealing with disturbed patients may wish to be able to telephone their clients from home without revealing their own telephone number
- Battered wives or estranged children may wish to contact their husband or parents without saying where they are
- When people make a simple enquiry to a commercial organization, such as a double-glazing supplier, they want to be sure that they do not risk being pestered ever afterwards by sales calls.

On the other hand, it has been pointed out that there are situations in which CLI is highly desirable. For example:

- CLI helps to reduce nuisance or hoax calls. Before the introduction of CLI it was estimated that there were some 25 million obscene telephone calls made in the UK every year (Edwards-Jones 1991).
- CLI can be essential for the emergency services since it allows them to quickly find the address from which a call is made. This is particularly important if the person calling is badly injured or confused and not able to give the address clearly. In one incident in Massachusetts a young woman who had been stabbed died when the emergency services were unable to understand the address she gave over the telephone; had CLI been in operation she might well have been saved.

When CLI was introduced in the United Kingdom research indicated that the majority of people were not concerned about their number being available to the person on the other end of the line (Jackson 1994). Most people, it seems, wanted the benefits. For example, many financial institutions can have the caller's details up on-screen even as an operator answers the telephone. Likewise there are many potential benefits for businesses, especially sole traders; an electrician or a painter would be able to call back potential clients who called while he or she was out, for example.

Introduction of CLI

The first CLI system was introduced in 1987, in New Jersey, by the Bell Atlantic Company. It caused considerable controversy there, and in other states where it was later introduced. One reason for the controversy may be that there are some states where over 50% of telephone subscribers pay to be ex-directory (this may, in part, be due to the fact that reverse directories, listing subscribers by number, are much more common in America). For such people, not being able to control when their number was disclosed was clearly anathema. Some states reacted to CLI by outlawing it altogether. In Pennsylvania, for example, a court determined that CLI broke the State's Wire-tap Law.

When British Telecom introduced CLI in the UK there was less controversy. This may be due to a cultural difference or because BT, having seen the problems in America, trod more carefully. The service was introduced with the facility to block the giving out of the calling number on all calls (the subscriber had to request the local exchange to do this) or it could be blocked on individual calls (by prefixing any number dialled with the digits 141). Before the introduction of the service in 1994, there was a large advertising campaign to raise people's awareness and the introduction was even delayed for a few weeks because of concerns about the lack of public awareness.

The service is now extensively used by companies and emergency services. There are also telephone receivers available to show the numbers from which incoming calls are being made. Nevertheless, it is not clear that most subscribers are aware that these facilities exist or how they may be used by companies.

Who owns a telephone number?

The issues around CLI are closely related to some of the issues of privacy and anonymity discussed in the previous chapter. CLI represents, above all else, a loss of anonymity. With the older telephone systems people could make calls without revealing their identity. This has now changed.

Some people argue that there is no real problem with this. A telephone user, they argue, is not unlike someone driving a car. It is generally accepted that cars should have registration numbers to ensure, as far as possible, the accountability of drivers for any reckless or dangerous driving. Otherwise there would certainly be more accidents on the roads. In the same way someone making a phone-call is using a public service and should be accountable for the way he or she uses it. Thus hoaxers or people making abusive calls should not be able to hide behind a cloak of anonymity.

The opposite view is concerned with the loss of the subscriber's control over his or her number. Telephone users cannot be sure that their number is not being noted at the other end, nor how that number will be used in the future.

The difficulty posed by CLI is to strike an appropriate balance between the right to anonymity and the right not to be subjected to abusive or irritating telephone calls. Where exactly this balance lies may be determined differently in different countries; what is clear is that digital telephone technology has permanently changed the relationship between caller and the person called.

3.3 The Internet and information exchange

In 1990 the hamburger chain McDonald's issued writs for libel against two London activists, David Morris and Helen Steel, for having distributed a leaflet entitled *What's Wrong With McDonald's*. This leaflet, first distributed a few years earlier, alleged that McDonald's was responsible for, among other things, the destruction of large areas of rainforest, selling food which was unhealthy, exploiting children in its marketing, cruelty to animals, and behaving badly towards its employees (Davies 1997).

When the case finally came before a High Court judge in June 1994 it was to become the longest running trial in English legal history, lasting for 313 days.

The case is interesting for another reason as well. In February 1996 an Internet site, 'McSpotlight', appeared which publicized the trial and contained over 1700 pages of information about the company. The original document, *What's Wrong with McDonalds*, was reproduced translated into a number of languages so that it could be downloaded. A considerable amount of further information was also available from the site including scientific papers, witness statements, a video of an interview with the defendants, and even a quizz about McDonald's. The danger for the organizers of legal action was avoided by setting it up on a computer in the Netherlands where the libel laws are less stringent (Freedman 1996).

When the judge finally gave his verdict it took him over two hours to read out a summary of his judgment. The judge found in favour of the company and awarded McDonald's £60 000 damages. In his ruling he said that the company had been libelled by many of the allegations, including those that McDonald's was responsible for destruction of rainforest, and serving unhealthy food. On the other hand, he found that the defendants had shown that the company's marketing exploited children and that it was responsible for some cruelty to animals.

The judgment was, however, a Pyrrhic victory for McDonald's. While the trial was in progress the McSpotlight Web site had been accessed over 13 million times. A leaflet which had originally been available from a few protestors outside one or two McDonald's branches in the UK had now been distributed worldwide. Of course, the case was also reported in the press and on television. What makes the Web site significant is the vast amount of detail that was made available. This included not just copies of the original document which was the object of the case but also many pages of court transcript and other information. It has never been practicable for conventional media to make this quantity and detail of information available.

The impact of the Internet

What impact is the Internet likely to have on people's lives in the next 5, 10, or 20 years? The development of such a communications infrastructure was unforeseen by most people even in the late 1980s (by which time the Internet already existed with a user community numbering tens of thousands). The rapidity of its development makes it very difficult to assess for how long the Internet will continue to grow, the ways in which it will come to be used, or the kinds of effects it may have on society. Clearly it has already had a substantial impact; setting up a Web site allowed activists campaigning on the behalf of the defendants in the McDonald's case to publicize and distribute information on the case to an extent which probably would not otherwise have been possible.

Below we shall discuss three areas relating to the impact of the Internet: the potential effect on politics, the availability of information, and electronic commerce. A fourth topic, teleworking, is discussed in the next chapter since it is a phenomenon which has already developed and involves more than just telecommunications technology.

Political decision making

In the 1997 British general election all the main parties had Web sites to publicize their policies. Likewise, in the previous American presidential election the two contenders had also had sites. Such sites do not, however, appear to represent any significant change in political decision making. Internet sites were used, in much the same way as advertisements in other media, to promote one particular political message.

Potentially more significant in the longer term are the numerous forums for the exchange of views which the Internet supports. These include mail lists (where messages posted to the list are automatically distributed to all the list's subscribers) and newsgroups which are usually accessed though the Internet. Newsgroups are essentially bulletin boards to which users can submit articles; some have a moderator who vets the articles and filters out irrelevant, duplicate, or offensive submissions.

Mail lists and newsgroups make it possible to support continual debate on issues of contemporary concern. There are thousands of such lists and groups with a (combined) regular readership numbering millions. If it is possible to support debate in this way, then the question arises whether the role of legislative assemblies might change in the future. Such assemblies developed to provide forums in which representatives could debate and legislate on issues of contemporary concern. Formerly there was no other mechanism available for a democracy to work – it was simply impracticable for everyone to have a say on every issue. With mail lists and newsgroups, however, anyone with a home computer and a modem can, in principle, participate in debates on contemporary issues. Indeed it is easy to envisage a situation where referendums could be frequently held on issues of concern, electors voting by e-mail.

This scenario has its attractions. It appears to be closer to the true ideal of participative democracy: people can influence the way in which policy or legislation is formulated in areas of particular concern to them. Also, one of the weak links in representative democracy – the representatives themselves – would be removed or at least reduced in importance.

But there are also problems. Although debate over newsgroups can be well informed and pertinent, there is no guarantee of this. Debate in unmoderated newsgroups can get sidetracked, or even degenerate into so-called 'flaming' – the posting of emotive or abusive comments and articles. Some of these problems are addressed by having a moderator but then there is the issue of whether or not the moderator manages to strike the correct balance in ensuring that a representative range of articles are posted. Those who feel that a particular strand of opinion is not properly reflected in a newsgroup can, of course, always set up an alternative newsgroup. This, though, leads to a situation where there is not a real debate about issues.

Perhaps a more significant stumbling block is that those connected to the Internet are far from representative. Currently, for example, university staff and students are over-represented in terms of their actual proportion of the population. If a democracy is to be truly representative then care must be taken to ensure that no group is excluded. Until everyone is connected to the Internet (and this may well never happen) it will be hard to justify its use for participative democracy.

The information super-highway

One of the most persistent claims for the Internet is that it will give people easy access to vast amounts of information. There is also a widely held view that economic success in the future is going to depend on so-called 'information workers' (people whose jobs are primarily concerned with manipulating information) and that access to communications infrastructures is critical for such people. Such beliefs have led to a considerable drive in many countries to develop the Internet and to ensure that schools, universities, and businesses are connected.

There are problems with this view of the Internet and its importance, which are often not considered. One major problem is that there is no guarantee of the quality of the information available. There is no editor to ensure that the contents of Web pages are correct or clearly expressed, for example. Nothing prevents someone setting up Web pages which are completely inaccurate or misleading. Of course, the ease of propagating information on the Internet has also been used for more sinister motives, such as distributing child pornography and even information on how to make bombs.

Moreover, the ease with which online information can be accessed and copied means that many people are reluctant to publish on the Internet. Doing so is likely to result in loss of royalty if the material they have developed is copied. It is true that many papers and magazines have Web pages, but these are usually samples of their publications rather than complete copies. Indeed the current situation is probably somewhat misleading – if Internet access becomes very common, and they are not able to find a way of charging for access, many of these sites may reduce the information they make available.

Online information gives rise to a more insidious problem: the ease of accessing it leads people to ignore other sources of data. It is, of course, far more work to go and look for information in libraries, but these nevertheless represent more reliable sources. What is available on the Internet is rather arbitrary and certainly issues of copyright and the vast difficulty of digitizing older documents or data means that it presents a distorted picture in many areas.

Electronic commerce

There is much speculation about the development of commerce over the Internet. Already there are some Internet-based sales outlets though, as yet, they sell little in comparison to conventional retailers. Of course, products and services vary in the degree to which the Internet provides an appropriate sales medium. Software can be ordered, paid for, and transmitted over a communications network; normally, however, some kind of delivery will be necessary.

Electronic commerce has not developed as quickly as many people thought it would. Nevertheless, there are still predictions that it will become much more significant. The advantages for traders of using Web sites to promote their goods is that they can trade from anywhere and can avoid the expense of a large investment in premises. The advantages for the consumer are the ease of shopping around to find the best bargains, and not needing to visit shops in person.

There has also been speculation that if electronic commerce does take off, it could become much harder for governments to raise revenues through taxation. It would not be clear where the transactions were taking place, and in any event it would be very difficult for taxation authorities to track the flow of money in order to tax it.

However, there are reasons for questioning whether electronic commerce will develop to become as significant as has been predicted. First, it is not clear that customers always consider price to be the absolute priority when purchasing. If they do, it is not clear why companies which sell by catalogue have not already displaced more conventional retail outlets. It is unclear that the Internet makes it possible to sell or market things in ways which are significantly different from the techniques long used by mail order companies. Indeed it seems that shopping is, for many people, a leisure activity which has a social dimension that could not be reproduced over the Internet.

A completely different set of problems relates to security and confidence. It is easy to set up a Web site, and a person who buys a product over the Internet has no real guarantee that the site from which he or she purchases is genuine until the article arrives. If it is not, the defrauded consumer probably has no way of getting the money back. Likewise there is considerable uncertainty as to how safe it is to send a credit card number electronically. These are factors which clearly put many people off buying over the Internet. Consequently, secure communication over networks is now an issue of considerable concern and, as we see in the next section, much debate surrounds the kind of encryption algorithms which should be made available to users.

3.4 The encryption debate

In February 1993 two American customs agents visited Phil Zimmermann, a computer programmer living in Colorado. For the next few years Zimmermann was to be under investigation for exporting munitions, an offence for which he would almost certainly have gone to prison if he had ever been convicted. The 'munition' in question was a computer program called PGP (Pretty Good Privacy). PGP encrypts e-mail and other files with an algorithm (RSA) which produces output that is beyond the capacity of even government agencies to decrypt. According to American law anyone wishing to export munitions must first obtain an export licence, and encryption software is classified as a munition.

Zimmermann had first developed PGP in the late 1980s. He had not managed to market it successfully, and in the early 1990s was working on an improved version. The catalyst for the widespread distribution of PGP came in 1991 when the American Senate was debating new legislation, known as Anti-Crime Bill S.266. One of the provisions of S.266 was that providers of electronic communications equipment and services should ensure that it was possible for the government to be able to obtain plain (non-encrypted) versions of any text or other data sent. These provisions provoked an outcry in America. A friend of Phil Zimmermann determined to make PGP widely available before the bill could be passed. He is reported to have driven round in his car with a laptop computer and acoustic coupler, stopping at public telephone boxes every few miles to upload a few copies of PGP to Internet FTP sites before rushing off to another pay-phone.

Once it was available on the Internet, PGP was soon to appear in Europe in contravention of American export regulations. It was this which was to result in Zimmermann coming under investigation two years later (by which time the contentious clause in S.266 had been altered). Zimmermann lived under the threat of prosecution and possible imprisonment until the start of 1996 when the investigation ended without his being charged.

The Zimmermann case is all the more strange for the fact that the techniques he used were already in the public domain. If a programmer working largely on his own was able to develop encryption software using these techniques, there was certainly nothing to stop any foreign power doing the same. Indeed many people saw the Zimmermann case as symptomatic of governments' desire to prevent private individuals, rather than hostile powers, from making use of powerful encryption techniques.

The importance of encryption

The encryption of messages first became widespread in the Renaissance; governments wished to be able to communicate secretly with their ambassadors and, given the ease with which messages could be intercepted, they could only do this by using encryption. From the Renaissance onwards most Western governments maintained so-called 'black-chambers' – offices which systematically intercepted diplomatic correspondence in order to try to decipher it.

The development of new communications technologies in the nineteenth century led to the widespread adoption of encryption by the military. In the American Civil War both sides made systematic use of wiretapping to intercept their opponents' telegraph communications. It was the later advent of radio that perhaps gave the biggest impetus to the development of cryptography. Radio transmissions are easily intercepted and so encryption is essential if they are to be kept secret.

As the codes used became more sophisticated, so the techniques for breaking them began to require some kind of automation. In the Second World War efforts to break the German Enigma code led to the development of proto-computers by Allied codebreakers, including Alan Turing. Modern cryptography makes extensive use of computers. The encryption of messages is more securely carried out by a program running on a computer or even by specially developed hardware. Likewise efforts to break the more sophisticated codes now require enormous computer power. The National Security Agency (NSA), the American agency responsible for codebreaking and developing new codes, is one of the world's major users of computers.

Until recently the use of encryption techniques was largely confined to diplomatic and military use. Now, however, the Internet has made the development of secure encryption systems of enormous importance. At one level users of e-mail who wish to ensure that their messages cannot be read require some kind of encryption system. There are also strong commercial pressures for the development and adoption of encryption standards. If electronic commerce is to take off then there have to be secure ways to transmit sensitive credit-card details over networks. There are other requirements as well, for example the ability to verify that messages are from the person or organization they purport to come from.

To be sure that their communications are safe, commercial and private users wish to use the most secure encryption techniques available. This brings them into conflict with central governments since the most secure techniques are widely believed to be beyond the capacity of even governmental agencies to decode.

The development of encryption methods

Traditional encryption methods, or ciphers, all worked on the same principle. A piece of text (the plaintext) is manipulated by an algorithm which comprises a series of substitutions and transpositions to produce a scrambled output (ciphertext). This process is parameterized by a single key which is needed both to encrypt the plaintext and to decrypt the ciphertext. Such ciphers are known as 'secret-key' ciphers since they rely on the key used to encrypt a message being kept secret.

With the advent of computer technology these algorithms have to be much more sophisticated to be effective, since computers make it possible to try out large numbers of keys very quickly. The security of secret key ciphers relies on the cipher algorithm itself and the length of the key – measured in bits. If too short a key is used the cipher becomes vulnerable, however well the enciphering algorithm has been designed.

An important factor that must be taken into account when designing modern encryption algorithms is that they may be hard-wired into microchips for use in communications appliances, such as fax machines. Consequently it may be possible for someone who is trying to decrypt a message to devise new messages and to see how they are encoded.

One well-known secret-key algorithm which was standard for many years is Data Encryption Standard (DES). DES was derived from a cipher developed by IBM in the 1970s and was adopted by the American government in 1977 as an encryption standard for unclassified information. DES uses a 56-bit key which was believed to make the cipher sufficiently secure in the 1970s but is now generally felt to be inadequate.

A major weakness of all secret-key ciphers is the need to distribute the key to anyone who is going to encrypt a message. This means there is always a danger of the key being found out by a third party. This weakness led, in the 1970s, to a proposal for ciphers in which the key used to encrypt data was different from the key required to decrypt it and where the latter would be extremely difficult to discover even if one knew the former. The advantage of these, so-called, 'public-key' algorithms was that the key for encrypting could be made public without compromising the contents of messages encrypted with the key.

Perhaps the best-known public-key algorithm is RSA (so called after the initials of its inventors Rivest, Shamir, and Adelman). To encrypt messages using RSA a user must first make a public and private key. These keys are derived from a pair of very large (at least 100, and maybe 200 digits long) prime numbers. The security of the cipher derives from the fact that it is extremely difficult to factorize numbers obtained from multiplying large primes together.

One of the drawbacks with public key systems, such as RSA, is that, because they rely on doing multiplication and exponentiation with very large numbers, they generally run much more slowly (as much as a hundred times slower) than secret-key methods. This is important where large streams of data need to be quickly encrypted or decrypted during network transmission. Because of this, public-key algorithms are generally used to encode a one-off session key for a message which is then encoded in a conventional secret-key cipher such as DES. For example, PGP generates a random session key to use for each message; this key is used to encode the message using IDEA (a secret-key cipher developed in Switzerland), the session key is then encrypted using the RSA cipher, and finally the RSA-encrypted key and IDEA-encrypted message are sent together. Such an approach makes PGP encrypted messages effectively unbreakable given the current state of cryptology.

The politics of encryption

Recent advances in cryptology have meant that so-called 'strong' encryption[1] can, potentially, be used by anyone with a computer. The reaction of governments has been to try to limit the availability of strong encryption technology or to control its use. The policy of the United States is particularly significant in this context since, through the NSA, it employs large numbers of cryptologists and probably funds more research into cryptology than any other government.

Under US law companies exporting products which include encryption technology must have a licence. Traditionally only systems using weak encryption were granted export licences. The consequence of these restrictions is that any software, such as e-mail packages or Web browsers, which is imported from the United States will not use a secure encryption algorithm for protecting information which it sends. It was because the encryption program PGP did not have an export licence (and would almost certainly never have been granted one) that Phil Zimmermann became the object of an investigation when PGP appeared on computers in Europe.

It became obvious, however, that such export restrictions are largely ineffectual in limiting the availability of strong encryption. The approach which

---

1 A distinction is generally made between 'strong' and 'weak' encryption. The distinction is somewhat vague but in this context strong is generally taken to mean not easily broken by government agencies.

has since been suggested or adopted is to ensure that governments can get hold of the keys. France, for example, has adopted a policy which obliges users of ciphers to disclose the keys to the government (Doyle 1994). Other countries have proposed policies which are commonly referred to as 'key escrow' in which the keys to decrypt messages are held by some agency to be released only in particular circumstances.

One of the first proposals for a key escrow system was that of the American Clipper chip. The Clipper chip is an encryption-decryption chip for use in digital telephones and fax machines. It was proposed by the US government in 1993 and immediately caused controversy. One source of concern was that the encryption algorithm used had been designed by the NSA and was classified. The chip was designed to be tamper-proof so that the encoding of the algorithm would be destroyed if anyone tried to reverse-engineer it. Consequently no-one could be sure how effective the encryption algorithm was, though the US government claimed that it was very much more secure than DES (which was commonly felt to be becoming obsolete).

The real opposition to the Clipper chip, however, was centred about the proposal for keeping a database of keys. Each chip was to hold a serial number and an encryption key (the encryption algorithm involved chips exchanging keys to generate a key for a session). Each chip would send a copy of its serial number along with every encrypted message. The US government would keep a record of the serial numbers and keys of all Clipper chips and a key would be released on production of a warrant. Thus police investigating an individual would be able to decrypt his or her communications if they were granted a warrant to obtain the key of the chip encoding them.

There was enormous opposition to the Clipper chip. Civil rights campaigners were concerned that it meant that individuals had no absolute right to privacy. Many commercial organizations were worried that foreign customers would be reluctant to buy products which included Clipper chips. Companies would not be obliged to use the Clipper chip in their products but would not be eligible for government contracts unless they did (the idea being to make the chip a *de facto* standard). Many detractors argued that the idea was ill conceived, those engaged in criminal or subversive activities would simply use additional encryption to circumvent the chip so it would not be of any use against those people who were being presented as posing a threat.

The intense opposition to the proposal led to its being shelved in late 1994 (Connor 1995) but key escrow was to reappear in proposals put forward by the British government two years later. The British scheme, outlined in a discussion document called *Licensing of Trusted Third Parties for the Provision of Encryption Services* (DTI 1997), was that only companies licensed by the government would be allowed to provide encryption services. These so-called 'Trusted Third Parties' (TTPs) would be obliged to hold the keys used in encryption algorithms and to release them to the appropriate authority on production of a warrant. A warrant might be obtained by the police investigating a suspected drug-dealer, for example, or by the close relatives of a deceased person who had left some encrypted documents. The proposed measure was intended, according to the government, to balance the need for secure communications to underpin the development of electronic commerce with the requirements of law-enforcement agencies to decrypt the communications of criminals and terrorists.

The British proposals met with similar criticisms to the American ones. Why would criminals use encryption methods which they know that the authorities can decode when they have access to other, absolutely secure methods. Moreover how can users be sure that the TTPs can always be trusted? It would only take one dishonest employee of a TTP to compromise the whole scheme. What will happen to these proposals is, at the time of writing, not clear. There was a change of government shortly after their publication and some reports suggest that the new government favours a policy in which suspected criminals could be legally obliged to reveal the key of any cipher they had used (Sabbagh 1997).

3.5 Summary

The development of telecommunications over the last 100 years has been even more dramatic than that of computer technology and has, in recent years, completely changed the ways in which the telephone network can be used and the facilities that it provides.

From a purely technological viewpoint this technology makes enormous changes possible in people's everyday lives and in society as a whole. These range from the relatively minor, such as Calling Line Identification, to potentially tremendous impacts on democracy and the ways in which people live and work. What permanent changes actually come about will depend on the reactions of the majority of people to the technology. It remains to be seen whether people will wish to carry out many of the activities of life, from shopping and working to voting or meeting their spouse, through an electronic communications medium.

Encryption, which we discussed last, has come to prominence recently for two main reasons: it is a key component to making the Internet an appropriate medium for commerce or, in the longer term, electronic voting and, second, advances in cryptography itself have changed the balance between those sending secret messages and those wishing to decode them. This poses a dilemma for many governments. On the one hand, they wish to promote electronic commerce and the use of the Internet which they see as a spur to economic growth. On the other, they are concerned that such technologies also favour criminals and terrorists or, in repressive regimes, political dissenters. One approach which has been tried is key escrow but this looks unlikely to succeed. Whether there are further attempts to control the spread and use of strong encryption remains to be seen.

Further reading

The books by Tanenbaum (1996) and Beauchamp and Poo (1995) give good introductions to telecommunications technology. The site http://www.mediahistory.com is a good starting point for looking at material on the Web about the development of telecommunications.

Calling line identification and its introduction are discussed from an American perspective in *Who Owns Information* by Anne Wells Branscomb (1994).

There are now many books which discuss the Internet and its potential impacts on society. Among these are *The State of the Cybernation* by Neil Barrett (1996), *Silicon Snake Oil* by Clifford Stoll (1995), and the collection of papers *Cultures of Internet* edited by Rob Shields (1996).

A good guide to PGP with some background (though not up to date on the outcome of the investigation) is the book *PGP: Pretty Good Privacy* by Simson Garfinkel (1995). A comprehensive guide to cryptography is *Applied Cryptography* by Bruce Schneier (1996).

Points to consider

1 What rights should people have over whether and when their telephone number is disclosed? Is the universal introduction of CLI the only way to stop nuisance calls?
2 Might current communications technology undermine news broadcasts and papers as they currently exist? Someone receiving the news in electronic form would be able to filter it, so leaving only the articles which he or she was interested in. Would this be a good thing or might it lead to a fragmentation of society with people unaware of each other's concerns?
3 Does the ease with which one can make information available on the Internet mean that most of what is available is unreliable? How could information obtained on the Internet be guaranteed to be accurate?
4 Some people believe that the Internet will completely change the way in which people live, but many of the facilities it offers are no different in principle, though much faster, than those provided by the postal service. For example, one can already shop through mail order catalogues – what does the Internet provide that is fundamentally different? If mail order has not replaced conventional shopping expeditions, why should shopping from a Web site be any more successful?
5 Is it necessarily a bad thing if governments are no longer able to monitor private communications now that encryption technology has become so effective? Does the answer depend on the kind of government which is in power?
6 Can key escrow cryptographic systems be justified? Is there any way to be sure that keys are never compromised?

CHAPTER 4

The computerized world

- According to one software industry association over $15 billion was lost to suppliers in 1994 due to illegal copying and distribution of software.
- Already EFT (electronic funds transfer) represents over 80% of all monetary transactions in Britain. Foreign exchange markets transfer many billions of dollars daily, all by EFT. The potential for fraud or disruption is now enormous.
- In spite of massive spending on information technology by many Western countries there is little evidence that computerization has brought about any significant increase in productivity in these countries.
- Most check-out cashiers in supermarkets now have their work rates – how many items they scan, how many mistakes they make – monitored by computer.

Overview

In this chapter we look at general issues raised by computer technology and consider some of its social and economic effects.

There is considerable discussion in the software industry about software piracy and illegal copying of software. But this discussion largely ignores the debate which has gone on in the background concerning the kind of rights which developers should have over the software they produce. We consider this debate first. We then discuss how computers have created whole new areas of (what have come to be recognized as) crime such as virus creation and hacking. The next issue we consider is the real pay-off of computer technology. Many studies seem to show that the impact of computers – in economic terms, at least – has been quite marginal. We review some of the explanations which have been advanced for this phenomenon. Finally we look at the impact of computer technology on working conditions and whether computers have liberated workers from drudgery or whether they have, on the contrary, made working conditions increasingly stressful.

Relation to other chapters Issues concerning the ownership of software are considered again in Chapter 6 where we look at the current legal position in the United Kingdom. The law relating to computer crime and misuse is presented in Chapter 9. Several of the issues considered in this chapter, such as the debate on software ownership, will be looked at again in the final chapter from an ethical viewpoint.

4.1 Do programmers own their software?

The software industry has formed more than one association dedicated to preventing people from copying software. One of these, the Business Software Alliance, claims that 'software theft' resulted in losses of over $15 billion to the software industry in 1994. Such figures rest on the assumption that people can own software in much the same way that they might own a car or a house and that such ownership gives the right to control absolutely the use and distribution of software. There has in fact been much debate over the kinds of rights that should be accorded to the developers of a piece of software.

Superficially, property rights are a simple matter; property is disposed of as its owner wishes. In practice, the enjoyment of virtually every kind of property is restricted in some way. For instance, a house owner may be prevented from altering the house or grounds by conservation or planning laws, and many other laws or regulations constrain the use of the property. Such constraints are designed to prevent people's untrammelled enjoyment of their property interfering with other interests. Thus listed buildings cannot be lost to future generations because of a whim of a current owner; suburban dwellers can (sometimes) prevent the construction of buildings which would spoil a neighbourhood, and so on.

It is not immediately obvious what kinds of property rights, if any, should apply to software. Someone who copies software does not deprive anyone else of its use (unlike someone who takes a car). On the other hand, software is a vital component of modern industry and commerce and, increasingly, the expertise or capital of companies may be tied up in the software they have developed to provide a service or run their business.

The debate about software ownership is relatively simple to the extent that most people tend to adopt one of two main positions. The first, which is promoted by the software industry, is that all copying of software is wrong and that the law should reflect this. A diametrically opposed position is that programmers should never be able to prevent their software being modified or copied. This latter position has been forcibly promoted by Richard Stallman, the original developer of the UNIX Emacs text editor and the founder of the Free Software Foundation, a charity which has developed a copyright-free implementation of UNIX.

Below we briefly review why ownership of software has become an issue, before discussing the main arguments put forward by those who wish to prevent the copying of software and by their opponents, in particular Richard Stallman.

A short history of software ownership

In the early days of computing in the 1950s and 1960s, software such as operating systems or compilers was supplied free with the computer. It was seen as an indispensable and, compared to the hardware, cheap component.

However, in the late 1960s computer suppliers began to sell hardware and software separately. This development was a result of American anti-trust laws designed to prevent commercial practices which militate against the operation of a competitive and free market. This unbundling led to the growth of software houses, companies specialising only in the development of software, some of which developed and marketed software packages.

Until the 1980s computers were expensive and used only by large organizations which either developed their own software or bought large, specialized packages which were then customized for the buyer. This simply was not an environment in which there was much scope or incentive to copy software.

With the advent of the personal computer things changed. For one thing, most of the software, such as word processors or spreadsheets, was in package form and could be used by anyone with the right machine. Another factor was that many of the early users of small computers were hobbyists who found it quite natural to swap programs and modify each others' code. Indeed some companies, such as Apple, actually encouraged their users to write and exchange software in an open manner.

An environment in which software was freely exchanged was anathema to companies which depended for their income on the sale of packaged software. For these organizations there was the further problem that the legal status of software was not entirely certain. At one stage software companies experimented with the use of 'dongles', small plugs containing a microchip which were plugged in between the computer and its printer. Without the appropriate dongle fitted, a package would simply not work. This strategy was not popular with users and was eventually abandoned. Dongles could, in any event, always be circumvented by someone determined enough to analyze the executable code of the package.

The package software industry nevertheless thrived and came to use copyright laws (discussed in Chapter 6) as the main way to prevent its packages being copied. More recently the industry has formed lobbying groups to campaign for particular legislation and to prosecute those who infringe software copyrights.

Some arguments around software copying

One of the most common arguments advanced against software copying is that it is theft. Indeed, this is how many of the statistics provided by associations of software producers describe unauthorized copying. There are problems with this. For a start, copying software without authorization is simply not theft, it is copyright infringement. But, more importantly, to call the copying of software theft is no argument at all. It presupposes that those who develop software have an absolute right to control where and when it is copied. Should they have? A person who, for instance, takes a car without permission is obviously stealing since the owner is deprived of the use of the car. Someone who copies a piece of software, however, is not directly depriving anyone else of anything.

Why then should software developers be able to restrict the copying of software? The main justification given is that it ensures that developers are rewarded for their labour since they can earn money from licensing their software. And, furthermore, that these rewards are important incentives which motivate developers to produce innovative software. Copying of software, it is argued, is wrong because it undermines these incentives and so harms everyone by retarding the development of new software.

A number of objections to this argument have been made. First, it relies on a simplistic supposition of 'more software, good; less software, bad'. In reality, the utility of software depends more on how it is deployed and whether it is used appropriately. Second, it presupposes that the only incentive for people to develop software is financial reward. However, this ignores the fact that an enormous amount of software (such as the GNU software of the Free Software Foundation or the Linux operating system of Linus Torvalds) has been developed in the absence of financial incentive. Critics, such as Stallman, maintain that it is quite feasible for programmers to earn a living even if they cannot make money from licensing their software (they just don't make such a good living). Finally it is not clear that, in the long run, preventing copying actually helps software production or innovation. New software is often best developed by adapting or changing existing software. Restricting copying results in programmers making programs different simply to avoid claims that they have copied particular features. The resulting (artificial) differences make it more difficult for users to move from one program to a better one.

A further argument against unauthorized copying is that it results in software being more expensive for those who do pay. This argument has been criticized for assuming that people who copy a software package would buy it if they were not able to copy it. This seems unlikely; much software is copied because users cannot afford it or because it is the only way to evaluate a package without having to buy it. Copying, some maintain, may even help the software industry in making it possible for new users to try out different packages before buying the one they like the most.

Stallman's position against software ownership

One of the fiercest opponents of software ownership is Richard Stallman who has campaigned against software copyright for over a decade. His main argument is that software ownership, controlling the distribution of software, and withholding source code obstructs the use, adaptation, and development of software.

If software is licensed then fewer people will use any particular program, Stallman argues, because having to pay automatically raises a barrier to use. This actually makes software production less efficient because the same amount of time is required to develop a program regardless of the number of users. This is, of course, true but critics may argue that many businesses have requirements for software which captures key aspects of the way they do business. Such organizations will naturally want to restrict the distribution of their software because its value for them goes far beyond the resources required to develop it.

Furthermore, according to Stallman, software which is owned by particular individuals or an organization will only be distributed in object-code format. This means that it is effectively impossible for users to correct bugs or to adapt software to particular environments. On the other hand, critics may argue that bug-fixes or modifications often introduce errors or cause existing users problems. Restricting the distribution of source code does have the advantage that it prevents a situation where there are vast numbers of slightly different and unreliable versions of a piece of software.

A second problem with software whose source code is not available is that it cannot be used to instruct new programmers on what large programs look like. Moreover, development of new software is most simply and efficiently carried out by adapting existing software. Consequently, Stallman maintains, withholding source code makes it harder to educate new software professionals and inhibits the development of better software. Critics may, of course, point out that new developers only need to see the source code of one or two large programs, not every large program. So long as there are some programs whose source code is available it is not important if the source of many others is not. It is true that it is often useful to reuse some existing code or features, but critics would contend that control of source code does not necessarily inhibit this. If there is a real need for many reusable components there is nothing to prevent a software house from marketing libraries of subroutines or (for object-oriented languages) classes.

In conclusion

To some extent the argument over software ownership reflects the backgrounds and aspirations of its participants.

Arguments against copying tend to be favoured by people who consider software development from a business perspective. They want to be sure that if they invest time or money in software development, their investment will not be lost because the system they have supported is copied and widely distributed by someone else.

In contrast, there are many people working in software development who have a university research background. Their interest in software centres around the intellectual challenge of developing new or exciting systems. The idea of keeping their code secret or controlling the distribution and use of their software runs counter to a research culture in which ideas are openly and freely exchanged.

It may be, of course, that either approach is quite viable and can be made to work equally effectively.

4.2 Computer crime

In August 1986 Clifford Stoll, a new system administrator at the Lawrence Berkeley Laboratories (LBL) in California, was asked to investigate a 75 cent accounting discrepancy on one of its computers. By painstakingly tracking down the source of the discrepancy Stoll discovered that the computer had been infiltrated. The intruder used an obscure bug in the GNU Emacs editor to obtain privileged access to the computer and to use it as a stepping stone for accessing other machines.

Rather than prevent the hacker from gaining access again, it was decided instead to monitor his activity in the hope of locating where he was calling from. This monitoring was to last for almost a year and was done by directly tapping the incoming telephone lines. In this way there was no danger that the intruder could find out that he was being monitored. After a while it became clear that the LBL computer was being accessed from Germany by someone who seemed to be interested in computers on the military network, MILNET. Unfortunately the hacker was very cautious and rarely stayed connected for more than a few minutes – not long enough to allow the calls to be completely traced.

Stoll then concocted a set of fake files on the Strategic Defence Initiative (President Reagan's Star Wars space programme) in the hope that the hacker would stay connected for a longer period to look at and download them. The hacker 'took the bait' and technicians were finally able to trace the connection to the residence of a West German, Marcus Hess. But this was not the end of the story. One of the concocted files included instructions for defence contractors on how to get onto a mailing list for further details on SDI. Stoll and his colleagues were amazed when, a few weeks later, a letter arrived from a small American company asking to be added to the mailing list. Stoll's hacker, it now appeared, was actually engaged in espionage, using networks to obtain military information.

The 75 cent accounting error had by now snowballed into a fully fledged security investigation with both the FBI and the CIA involved. The evidence collected on Marcus Hess's activities was to result in his being arrested by German police in June 1987. Investigators believed that Hess had sold information to the Russian KGB but were unable to establish this when he came to trial. Nevertheless he received a 20-month prison sentence for his activities.

Hess's case is significant; not only is it one of the best documented hacking incidents but it is a striking illustration of just what a determined hacker can achieve. There have been many other reported cases though these have usually been motivated by simple curiosity or financial gain.

The potential impact of computer-based fraud or of hacking is tremendous because of the almost total reliance which is now placed on electronic computers and networks for managing and transferring money. It is estimated that over 100 million electronic messages and hundreds of billions of dollars are transferred over the world's networks every day.

Not only has computerization led to new forms of crime and new ways of committing old crimes but computers are often used incidentally in the commission of other offences. A blackmailer may draft letters using a word processor, a paedophile ring may distribute child pornography over computer networks, or a drug dealer maintain a computer database of contacts. The use of computers in crime has given rise to a whole new area of forensic investigation. Commonly called forensic computing, this involves using knowledge about the organization of file systems or the operation of particular processors to produce evidence for court cases. For example, the recovery of information which users believe they have deleted is one common requirement.

The use of computers in crime is extremely diverse. Below we briefly review two main areas of computer crime: conventional crimes, such as fraud, which are now often committed by modifying computer information, and completely new crimes, such as breaking into computers (hacking) or virus writing. The distinction between these two main areas is not absolute in that skills and techniques used by hackers to break into systems for fun may later on be used by those same people to commit fraud.

Old crimes in a new medium

There is an apocryphal story of a programmer at a bank who tampers with a program which calculates interest on accounts. Interest calculations do not usually produce a figure which is a whole number of pounds and pence – very often there will be an additional fraction of a penny interest. The programmer modifies the program so that each fraction of a penny is added to his own account. Given that interest may be calculated on millions of accounts, removing a fraction of a penny from each one soon produces a significant amount of money. The programmer waits for this to build up, changes the program to stop extracting money, closes the account, and leaves the bank.

Whether or how often this kind of fraud, sometimes called 'salami fraud', has been successfully perpetrated is hard to gauge. Nevertheless it illustrates how computers have created new opportunities for crime. Many other so-called computer crimes only rely on computers incidentally. So-called 'data diddling' involves changing the information entered or stored on a computer. Thus a clerk may switch overtime hours from one payroll record to another so redirecting the payment for overtime.

These kinds of crimes often go undetected, allowing the perpetrator to get away without anyone even realizing what has happened. A further problem with many computer crimes is that the victim, usually a large organization, often does not wish it to be revealed that they are vulnerable to computer-based fraud or vandalism. Consequently it is impossible to gauge the extent of such crime.

Virus writing and hacking

In October 1987 a rogue program appeared at the University of Delaware and infected hundreds of diskettes. For the most part it did no harm but data was lost from a small proportion of diskettes and one student even lost a draft thesis. This was the first appearance of a computer virus which was later to become known as 'Brain' (after Brain Computer Services, a Lahore-based computer store run by two brothers who had written the virus). The Brain virus worked by overwriting part of the 'boot sector' of a PC diskette – the boot sector contains code which is automatically executed when a PC is turned on. The virus would also infect other diskettes and so propagate itself. The authors of the virus, who had written it about a year before, were astonished at the speed with which it had spread from Pakistan to America.

Brain was the first computer virus to appear 'in the wild', that is, to infect machines without their users being aware. Programs which behaved like biological viruses had already been developed by computer scientists a few years before. The Brain virus was relatively harmless (data was only lost in the event of a diskette being almost full) but other, more destructive viruses were soon to appear. The computer virus problem mainly affects personal computers which were originally designed to be used by single users and so do not have the security and memory management features of larger multi-user systems. Consequently computer viruses and software to detect them have become commonplace.

Another form of program which has been used for criminal purposes is the so-called 'logic bomb'. This involves modifying a program in such a way that once some triggering condition occurs (usually a particular date being reached) the program fails to operate or even causes damage. Typically this technique is used by disgruntled employees to wreak revenge on their employer, or by people who have written a piece of software and wish to ensure that they get paid or even hope to be rehired to fix the problem.

Viruses and logic bombs are not the only form of malicious software. Networks have been brought to a standstill by 'worms', programs which are designed to spread and multiply through a computer network. In one of the best-known incidents, in November 1988, a worm was released which is believed to have infected thousands of machines on the Internet. The worm caused havoc for about a day but was relatively quickly neutralized.

Another new kind of crime, that of breaking into computers, has also received much attention. Enormous numbers of computers are now connected to the telephone network and can be accessed from anywhere in the world. This has led to hackers[1] breaking into machines. Often this is done for its own sake but in some incidents hackers have copied sensitive information, such as credit card numbers, or even modified data held on the computer. A common technique used to obtain telephone numbers of computers, sometimes called 'scanning', involves programming a computer to automatically dial a sequence of numbers and make a record of those where a computer modem is attached. The hacker can later try to gain access to these computers by guessing logins and passwords. Some hackers will even search rubbish outside offices to find user names and sometimes passwords.

More sophisticated techniques rely on a good knowledge of Internet communication protocols. These include faking the origin of message packets to gain access to a machine or developing 'sniffer' programs which inspect packets passing through a node on the network and look for login and password information.

Discussion

It is extremely difficult to determine the current scale of computer crime. A survey carried out by the FBI's National Computer Crimes Squad (quoted in Icove *et al.* 1995) suggests that, at most, only about one in six computer intrusions are even noticed. Such low rates, coupled with the reluctance of many organizations to acknowledge that their computer security has been compromised, makes the extent of the damage caused by computer crime and hackers impossible to estimate.

The future scale and impact of computer crime is no less easy to assess. Society is coming to place greater reliance on networked computers, especially for money management and transfer. This increases vulnerability to hacking and other computer crimes; there have even been suggestions that computer viruses or worms could be developed by military organizations to wreak havoc on the information infrastructures of hostile nations.

On the other hand, it is clear that hackers and others have often relied on weak security to gain access. Poorly chosen passwords are a perennial problem; it is quite easy to write programs which will try a sequence of dictionary words, place names, and personal names as passwords. Since users commonly choose

---

1 People who try to gain unauthorized access to computers over a network are often referred to as 'crackers'.

passwords which fall into one of these categories an exhaustive trial of the alternatives often yields results for the intruder. Moreover, past hacking incidents and the publicity which has surrounded them may well lead to organizations adopting more rigorous security which will make them less vulnerable – at least to outside intruders.

Of course, computer systems will always be vulnerable to people within organizations who abuse their position of trust. However, here one is looking at the broader problem of white-collar crime. In this context the scale and impact of the worst computer-related offences are still quite minor compared to the wave of white-collar crime which has swept through, for instance, the financial services industry in recent years (Coleman 1994).

4.3 The disappointing pay-off of computerization

There has been an enormous increase in computer power over the last 40 years. Since the invention of the integrated circuit in the early 1960s the performance of computers, in terms of computing power per pound, has been doubling approximately every three years. Moreover, computer technology has been widely adopted and there are few spheres of activity which have not now been affected by computers in some way.

However, there is little evidence that the enormous investment made in computer technology over the last few decades has paid off. Many studies by economists fail to find any link between spending on information technology and business success or productivity. This holds true both for studies of groups of companies and for those made at a national level. For example, during the 1980s American investment in computers grew at a rate of about 24% per annum but there is no evidence of increased productivity in the American economy in this period (Baily 1989). One economist, Steven Roach, has even coined the term 'productivity paradox' to describe the apparent failure of computerization to improve economic performance (Attewell 1996).

Is it really possible that computers do not pay their way? On the face of it such a claim seems absurd. Computers have become indispensable for applications ranging from payroll calculation and ticket reservations to engineering simulations and seismic analysis. Consequently some critics have argued that the 'paradox' results from inappropriate ways of measuring productivity or the protracted learning time needed to absorb the new technology (Baily 1989; King 1996).

Other commentators have taken the productivity paradox as being indicative of real problems with computers. They argue that many of the benefits from earlier computerization do not extend to the more recent applications of computer technology, especially the personal productivity software available on PCs. They also point out that much software is poorly designed and that potential benefits may be lost in an organizational setting.

We shall not consider the debate over how productivity should be measured but look in more detail at the arguments advanced by some commentators for believing that the economic benefits of computerization may be smaller than generally supposed. Such arguments are not well known among computer professionals but are worth considering, if only to bear in mind when designing new systems. We start by looking at one particular example – word processing.

An example – word processing

Word processing is one of the principal applications of personal computers. Among the obvious benefits provided by word processors are: the ease of making changes or correcting mistakes, the ability to save documents and use them as drafts for other documents, spell checking, and the ease of formatting documents to a high standard (possibly using different fonts or layout styles).

Most of these advantages relate to the actual production of a document. Word processing software does little to help with the more difficult aspects of writing such as working out the structure or producing clear prose. This is borne out by studies which indicate that there is little increase in efficiency when word processors are used in document preparation (Gould 1981; Card *et al*. 1984). One of the main problems appears to be that people make many more revisions when they are using a word processor, yet these revisions do not improve the quality of the final document. One executive has been reported as commenting that with word processors reports can go through as many as 40 drafts though without seeming to improve the quality of the end document (Baily 1989).

The temptation to make ineffective revisions may, of course, disappear as people gain experience with word processors. But there are other problems.

Word processors are difficult to master (at least for the average user), they have a large number of features (many of which are only very occasionally required), there are frequent changes of version, and there is little compatibility between different packages. Some idea of the time required to fully learn how to use one of these packages can be gauged from the large manuals which typically accompany them.

Many features provided by word processors are of less utility than they first appear. A good example here is spell-checking. A user can never rely on a spell-checker to spot all the spelling mistakes in a document; it cannot spot that the word 'there' has been misspelt as 'their', for instance, or deal with names of people and places. In fact, spell-checking is extremely difficult to automate effectively. Consequently spell-checkers do not obviate the need to read through a document to eliminate spelling mistakes.

Computers are generally very reliable, but the losses which can occur when they do go wrong or when the user accidentally deletes a document may be enormous. Of course, users are advised to make frequent backups of their data but most probably do not. In any event, backups are of no use if a document has only been recently created.

The problems outlined above do not mean that word processors are not useful, but they do imply that their utility may not be as great as it first appears. If account is then taken of the money and time spent on computers and software then the benefits may become more marginal than one might expect.

Similar arguments can be applied to many kinds of software package. And some have further problems of their own. For example, estimates suggest that anywhere between 10% and 95% of spreadsheets contain errors (Howlett 1997). Given the reliance which is placed on spreadsheet calculations in business the impacts of such errors can be enormous. One recent report suggests that a company overspent by £10 million when buying another company because of a spreadsheet error (Marshall 1997).

The problem with computer software

If one accepts the argument that computers and software are often not as effective as they appear, then the question arises as to why this should be so. The speed and accuracy of computers is such that one might think that using them to help with tasks would inevitably bring enormous benefits. However, although computerization brought clear benefits in many of its early applications (managing large databanks or performing lengthy engineering calculations), software for later applications (particularly for personal productivity) may suffer from a number of problems. Among those we discuss below are issues of usability, usefulness, and reliability.

Usability

Software usability is a perennial problem. Many users have difficulties learning how to use packages and even very experienced computer users can spend hours trying to transfer data between different packages or work out how to use a new feature.

Why is this so? One reason (advanced by Landauer 1995) is that most software is designed by programmers. Because they are very familiar with computers and software, programmers lose sight of the problems which a novice user encounters or the ways in which such a user interprets instructions and explanations.

A different source of usability problems is the large numbers of versions of packages which suppliers release. Each new version tends to add new features or to change the interface in some way. Users often end up buying upgrades to packages such as word processors or spreadsheets before they have fully mastered the software which they already have.

Usefulness

Usefulness is perhaps a more significant problem. Much software facilitates tasks which are irrelevant or marginal, or seeks to automate and control activities which people are highly resistant to having automated.

An example of the former is the use of computerized databases by many small businesses who would be better served by old-fashioned card-files. The amount of data they need to hold simply does not justify the use of computer technology. A further example is the widespread use of spreadsheets, not just to analyze results but to experiment with different scenarios. It has become common to develop spreadsheet models to show the impacts of different factors (varying rates of growth, inflation, market share and so on) on business forecasts. The utility of such exercises has never been established.

An example of software which people are reluctant to use is that of diary managers and schedulers. There are many such programs which purport to keep a database of people's availability so that meetings can be easily scheduled. These packages are rarely used in practice since most people are highly resistant to losing control of their time.

Reliability

The last main problem is that, as mentioned before, although computers are, on the whole, very reliable they are not nearly as reliable as older paper-based systems. Moreover, when they do go wrong (due to hardware failure or, more likely, a software error) they can cause absolute chaos. Examples here include the London Ambulance System and the year 2000 problem discussed in Chapter 1.

Organizational effects

A second set of reasons which have been put forward for explaining why computerization may not give rise to increased productivity relates to the way computer technology is used in the workplace. Many of the potential efficiency gains due to computerization may, it is argued, be lost because people end up spending more time writing, more time making things look good, or become obsessed with producing information for the sake of it (Attewell 1996).

Speaking directly over the telephone is an extremely efficient form of communication. It may be that the ease of producing memos with word processors or sending e-mail messages leads to less direct communication. It takes much longer to draft an e-mail than to talk directly to someone. Thus there may be an effect whereby computer technology actually encourages people to adopt less efficient forms of communication.

Furthermore, with computer technology people are tempted to spend a lot of time making documents look good. This may be worth while for the person doing it since making a good impression is often important in bureaucratic organizations. But making internal documents look good does not actually make an organization more efficient or productive.

Finally, organizations now collect and analyze far more information than in the past. Much of this information and the analyses which are made of it may be of little real value and largely a waste of time.

To summarize the argument, because of the nature of organizations and the pressures on individuals within them to make a good impression, many of the potential benefits of computerization are not realized. Instead, they are diverted for other purposes which do not actually help to increase productivity.

In conclusion

The discussion above reflects some of the criticisms of computer systems which have been made by a number of critics, especially HCI (human–computer interaction) researchers. How valid are they?

Clearly there are often problems with computer software, especially where usability is concerned. These may arise from the recency of the technology; some commentators argue that society is going through a period of learning how to use computers effectively and that, once this has been done, there will indeed be significant productivity gains (Baily 1989). Others have contended that computers have now been around too long for this argument to still be plausible (King 1996).

It is also difficult to quantify the benefits of computers. The technology has progressed so rapidly and made so many new facilities available that it is not clear that the effects on people's quality of life can be measured in simple economic terms. How does one assess the worth of being able to do desktop publishing or to access the Internet from one's home, for example?

The real question then becomes one of what society wants and expects from computer technology and whether it gets it or not. For those who enjoy using computers their use is an end in itself; for those who do not a more careful assessment of their costs and benefits may be in order.

4.4 Impact on working conditions

Bill Gates, in the book *The Road Ahead*, recounts how, when he was dating a woman who lived in another city, they would have 'virtual dates'. This involved finding the same film showing at approximately the same time at cinemas in both the cities. Mr Gates and his virtual inamorata would each drive to the respective viewings, talking on their mobile phones. At the end of the films they would drive home in their different cities, discussing the film, again over the mobile. In the future, Mr Gates explains, it will be better because the virtual couple could hold a private video-conference as well.

To some people Mr Gates's vision is not so much unappealing as simply incomprehensible. For them choosing to carry on a relationship in this way seems indicative of a curiously ordered set of priorities. Such reactions illustrate a major problem in predicting how computing will affect people's lives. There are the things that the technology will make possible (these alone are difficult enough to predict). But, importantly, there is also the issue of how much people will be prepared to use technology. Clearly there are people for whom 'virtual dating' appears to be a reasonable reaction to physical separation, but there are many for whom it is not.

Because of such difficulties in making general predictions, we shall concentrate on just one area where computers may have an impact – working conditions. There are two main reasons for looking at working conditions in particular. First, over the course of most people's lives work occupies a greater proportion of time than any other single, waking activity. Consequently changes to working conditions inevitably affect the quality of life. Second, it is in the workplace that the effects of computerization are most advanced It is at work, therefore, that some indication may appear of the kinds of effect that computers may have more generally on the quality of life.

We look at two particular aspects of the way computerization affects work. First, does computerization deskill work and make it easier for employers to monitor and control the workforce? Or alternatively, does it remove much of the drudgery of work, allowing workers to concentrate on more interesting and challenging activities? Second, we look at the way in which computing and telecommunications obviate the need for work to be done in an office and consider some implications of this – the rise of working from home and the increasing globalization of the world economy.

Such dramatic changes must inevitably lead to a redistribution of work away from the unskilled to the computer-literate. At present it is not certain whether more jobs have been lost than gained in this way (though it seems likely) so we shall not consider impacts on levels of employment.

Effects on the quality of work

At Electronic Banking Systems the work is tightly controlled and monitored. Rows of workers sit at desks inside a building whose windows have been covered up to eliminate distractions. No personal possessions or pictures are allowed on the desks; no talking is permitted either, unless it is necessary for the job being done. Supervisors sit at raised desks at the front and back of the room. Overhead video cameras are mounted allowing an operator in another office to watch employees and to zoom in on what particular people are doing.

In one room workers open letters and sort them according to contents, in other rooms they do data entry or accounting work. The work rates are specified and carefully monitored. Those opening letters must deal with three a minute, those typing must maintain a rate of 8500 keystrokes per hour.

Statistics on the work rates and error rates of each person are compiled on computer and reviewed by a manager.

Electronic Banking is an American company in the 'lockbox processing' business. It provides a service of opening and processing letters for companies or charities. Workers may handle large amounts of money in the day so the atmosphere of orderliness and tight security reassures clients (Horowitz 1996).

However, it is not only in environments where money is being handled that electronic surveillance and computer monitoring of work is being used. Some security experts claim that so-called 'time thieves' – employees who spend too much time talking and having breaks, or who leave early – cost American industry over $100 billion each year (Cook 1995). Consequently many American companies are turning to surveillance and monitoring to ensure that employees stay on the job.

Surveillance is easy when workers use computers. It is easy to monitor the number of keystrokes and errors made by a data-entry clerk. Likewise the rate at which check-out operators in supermarkets scan items of shopping, or the time that help-desk staff spend answering calls, are routinely monitored. Modern security systems, where people have to use swipecards to open doors, provide detailed information about an employee's movements in the course of a day. More sophisticated systems have also been developed such as so-called 'active badge' systems which can track the location of each individual within a building.

Close monitoring makes work more stressful and creates an atmosphere of mistrust. Ironically it may, in the long run, not even produce the effects that employers want. The stress of being closely monitored and always maintaining a particular work rate is likely to show through in higher sickness and absenteeism as well as a more rapid turnover of staff. Another factor is that workers who are closely monitored have an interest in keeping their rate of work at the minimum acceptable level, for fear that to do better will simply result in the minimum level being raised making the job still harder. There is evidence also that monitoring work rates reduces the level of cooperation among staff, making people reluctant to help others even with problems that they could easily resolve (Grant and Higgins 1991).

Such problems can lead to computerization being handled differently. For example, in the mid-1980s at the Manitoba Telephone System, a Canadian public corporation, operators reported receiving 'shock-like' sensations from the computerized switchboards which they used. At that time the working conditions were highly controlled and operators were expected to deal with each customer call in an average of 30 seconds. Inspection of the equipment did not reveal any faults but eventually the operators walked out and an independent inspection was made. The inspectors' report indicated that the equipment was safe but that the highly automated and closely monitored nature of the work had led to severe stress among operators. As a result the monitoring of call-time was stopped and a project was initiated in which operators became directly involved in respecifying their jobs and making suggestions for improving service. These led to operators being reorganized into work groups and being given greater responsibilities. The changes resulted in less absenteeism, and in greater satisfaction among users of the operator service. (Clement 1994).

Although it can be used to increase the level of monitoring it is also clear that many jobs can be significantly enhanced by computer technology. Much of the drudgery of bookkeeping has been removed by computers. This frees up accountants to perform more sophisticated analyses of the financial data or to develop financial models. Likewise people in many other jobs can have their work enhanced by the ease of storing and analyzing information on computers. Workers who control production processes, such as in steel mills or chemical plants, may spend less time operating machines but more time analyzing the performance of the process to fine-tune it or to spot problems.

The use of computers for monitoring is just the latest of a long line of techniques for controlling work which go back to the nineteenth century. It was in the 1890s that the American F. W. Taylor began to carefully study many work processes. Taylor's 'science of work' involved dividing all jobs into component tasks or actions which could be separately timed to determine how long the job should take and to see whether it could be redesigned to be done more quickly (hence the term 'time and motion' study). Taylor advocated setting up production systems where jobs were defined by formal procedures, and complex jobs were split into separate, simple tasks. The advantage of Taylor's approach, from a management perspective, was that jobs were simplified and could be carried out both more efficiently and by less skilled labour.

Taylorism, as it is often called, results in extremely tedious and dispiriting work. It is an approach to production in which human 'operators' are merely seen as units in a process to be measured and controlled in the same way as raw materials or components. Taylorism is an essentially dehumanizing approach to organizing work, and it also appears to be fundamentally flawed.

The most famous demonstration of the inadequacies of Taylor's approach came in the so-called Hawthorne Studies. These took place in the late 1920s in an American telephone company when a group of women were assembled to test the effects on output of varying working conditions. The women worked in a special room and the experimenters varied particular conditions such as the amount of lighting or the duration and time of rest periods. They were surprised to find that with each variation in the conditions the performance of the women improved, even when they returned to their original working environment. The experimenters were forced to the conclusion that more subtle effects were at play than the immediate physical conditions of work. They explained their results in two ways: the very fact of knowing they were part of an experiment had affected the workers' performance, and the women had formed a social group which improved the quality of their work and imbued it with new importance.

The Hawthorne Studies lasted for over ten years and gave rise to a completely new way of considering work. This, the human relations approach, stressed the importance of social relationships and conditions on performance. From the human relations perspective improving performance at work consists of organizing work in such a way as to motivate people and to allow them to fulfil their desire for social contact and achievement.

It would seem that it is the way in which computerization is used and introduced, rather than computerization itself, that is important. Thus computers can be used to closely monitor staff and their performance in accordance with the approach advocated by Taylor. Alternatively they can be introduced more sensitively and in a way which enhances the interest of a job. Whether the impact of computers in the workplace is benign or not may ultimately depend on which approach is more effective. If companies which use computers to monitor and control manage to perform more effectively than their competitors, then the possibility of computers improving work conditions for most people will become less likely.

Effects on the location of work

A further effect of information technology has been to make it feasible for some types of work, such as programming or answering enquiries, which involve just the use of a computer or telephone link, to be carried out at virtually any location. Callers to telephone help or information lines are unlikely to realize that their call is being answered by someone in a different country or even on the other side of the world.

One consequence of this is that a lot of work is now contracted out to offshore or Third-World companies with cheaper labour costs. For instance, many American organizations send data-entry work to Caribbean offices employing low-paid local staff. Perhaps the most dramatic example of overseas contracting is the rise of the Indian software industry. Based primarily in Bangalore, it has grown in 10 years from virtually nothing to become a $1.2 billion industry with hundreds of companies employing some 100 000 software developers. These companies now carry out the development of whole systems for large companies as well as many software conversion projects (Taylor 1996). Of course, only certain kinds of work can be contracted out in this way. Software development and data entry are easily done remotely, many other kinds of work are not. Even much work which is primarily knowledge-based is specific to particular countries – for example, legal or auditing work depends on knowledge and experience of particular legal systems and sets of regulations. Language also raises a barrier in many areas.

Computer technology also makes possible many innovative working practices which are usually motivated by organizations' desire to cut the costs of maintaining office space. One of these is 'hot-desking' where workers have no fixed desk or office. Instead they keep all their work and any personal belongings in their briefcase or in a small, movable filing cabinet. They can then use any desk which is vacant for as long as they need it, having calls rerouted to where they are.

Another, more common practice is that of 'teleworking' where someone with a computer, communications link, and maybe photocopier works from home. There are now believed to be about 25 million teleworkers in America alone (Black 1993). For such people home-working can be a mixed blessing. They are freed from the need to commute and are able to work in more pleasant surroundings, but they often find it difficult to combine work and home life and feel obliged to remain available for work during longer periods. As with hot-desking, there is also the problem that most people work better as part of a group and much work is not easily partitioned into separate tasks for individuals.

Although it seems clear that computers are having a significant impact in globalizing many industries and opening them up to worldwide competition the effects on individuals' places of work are harder to assess. There has been a considerable amount of experimentation with teleworking but there is evidence that it is often abandoned with staff reverting to previous working patterns. Although teleworking may appear attractive for a while, in the longer term people start to feel isolated. It may be that such schemes are often implemented too hastily since it is easy for companies to calculate the cost of maintaining office space and desks but the value of people working together rather than separately is much harder to judge – especially over a protracted period of time.

4.5 Summary

This chapter has considered just a very few of the issues raised by the advent of computer technology

Property rights for software were discussed because this is an issue which affects the kind of software that will be available and, over a longer period, is likely to have a significant impact on how useful software really is. Critics of the present framework of software ownership may have a point when they claim that the current norms do not actually help to bring about the production of effective software. In any event the claims of the software industry that all software development must be encouraged do not seem to take into account the serious doubts being raised by economists and many others about the utility of much software.

If a common conclusion can be drawn from the other issues that have been discussed – computer crime, the economic impact, and impact on work – it may be that the impact of computerization is not and may never be as significant as many people claim. Computer crime has, so far, been more dramatic than significant. The idea of computers transforming work and lifestyles seems hard to reconcile with the debate going on in other quarters about why no-one can detect a positive contribution to productivity from computer technology. Finally, computers have dramatically affected working conditions for many people, but most of those affected are concentrated in low-skill clerical work or in particular professional jobs. Whether changes to working styles can spread across a greater range of jobs remains to be seen.

Further reading

Much material relating to software copyright is available on the Web. Both the BSA and Free Software Foundation maintain Web sites which are at:

> http://www.bsa.org/
> http://www.gnu.ai.mit.edu/

A good overview of the various kinds of computer crime which may be perpetrated and ways to protect against them is given in the book *Computer Crime* (Icove *et al.* 1995). Accounts of the activities of hackers are given in a number of books: *Cyberpunk* by Hafner and Markoff (1991), *Approaching Zero* by Clough and Mungo (1993), and *The Hacker Crackdown* by Bruce Sterling (1994). The tracking down of the German hacker Marcus Hess is described in the *The Cuckoo's Egg* by Clifford Stoll (1989). The collection of papers *Rogue Programs: Viruses, Worms and Trojan Horses*, edited by L J Hoffman (1990), is good source of technical information on computer viruses and similar programs.

The discussion of the apparently disappointing payback from computerization is largely based on the arguments presented by Thomas Landauer in his book *The Trouble with Computers* (1995). Many assumptions about the utility of computers are also questioned by Theodore Roszak in *The Cult of Information* (1994) and by Clifford Stoll in *Silicon Snake Oil* (1995).

The impact of computerization on working conditions is discussed in many books including the collections *Computerization and Controversy* edited by Rob Kling (1996) and *Information Technology and Society* edited by Heap *et al.* (1995). A critique of the assumption that technology improves working conditions is given in *Architect or Bee* by Mike Cooley (1987). Good general discussions of the nature of work in organizations are *The Individual, Work and Organization* by Robin Fincham and Peter Rhodes (1992) and *Understanding Organizations* by Charles Handy (1985).

Points to consider

1 As much, if not more, effort can be expended in testing software and eliminating bugs than in the original development itself. Suppose a company copies a piece of software (assuming they can get hold of the

source code) and then spends a lot of time testing it and correcting the errors. This can greatly increase the utility of the software yet the differences in the actual code of the new version and the old version might be quite small. Currently this would be regarded as simply an infringement of copyright and the second company would be liable for damages. However, could one argue that they have done just as much to produce a usable piece of software as the original developer? Points to consider include:

- It is often easier for people who are not involved in developing software to test it since they are more detached and are less likely to assume that the software is correct. Are there significant advantages in having testing and development done by completely different companies?

- What if the testing company found no errors? Might they nevertheless be justified in claiming that they have done useful work in enabling users to be more confident about the software?

2 How might one go about estimating an accurate figure for the amount of money lost to the software industry from copying and piracy? How could the following factors be accurately reflected in the figure:

- differences in levels of copying or piracy between countries,
- many pirated copies of packages may be used by people who would not use them at all if they had to pay for them (in other words their using the package does not represent a lost sale for the software supplier),
- many of the copied versions may hardly ever be used beyond some initial experimentation with the package?

3 Given the apparent vulnerability of computers to crime is it appropriate for ever greater reliance to be put on computers?

4 How useful are measurements of productivity when considering the use of computers? For example, would international air transport or photography necessarily show up as improving productivity if analyzed in a similar way? One particular point to consider is:

- There were not enormous queues at public reference libraries before the advent of the Internet, so can one argue that the Internet is not providing any major benefit in making information more readily available?

5 There are now software packages available to help convert dictation directly into text. Does such software necessarily bring about improvements in productivity – what benefits and drawbacks may it have?

6 One of the problems faced by employers when introducing computerization to the workplace is that not all its effects are easily measurable. For example, with hot-desking it is relatively easy to calculate the reduction in office space which can be made and the

resulting savings that this will give. On the other hand, workers in a hot-desking office may feel more isolated and find it harder to build up a network of people from whom to ask for help or whom they are happy to help. This drawback is much harder to quantify than the space saving.

- How could such social and psychological effects of technology be taken into account and measured when taking decisions on the use of computer technology?
- What kind of timescale is required to assess whether a particular form of working is more efficient? For example, a working environment which is more stressful may seem more efficient to begin with but its drawbacks may not become apparent until higher levels of absenteeism and staff turnover are reached – this may not happen for months or even years.

CHAPTER 5

An overview of the law

Laws are basically formalized sets of rules for regulating the behaviour of individuals and organizations in society. Individual legal systems have evolved in different ways and adopted varying approaches and conventions. Thus the English legal system is 'adversarial' and a 'common-law' system; cases are either 'criminal' or 'civil' in nature. What does all this mean?

Overview

In this chapter we give a general introduction to the law. Our overview concentrates on English and Welsh law and is intended to answer the following questions:

- In what way is English law distinctive? How are the legal systems of Scotland and Northern Ireland different?
- Where does the law come from? What are the main sources of legal rules?
- What are the differences between so-called 'criminal' and 'civil' law and what are the implications of these differences?
- How do the courts operate? What procedures are followed in civil and criminal cases.
- What is meant by the concept of a legal person and how are legal persons formed?

Finally, we consider the current scale and complexity of the law in order to demonstrate that it is neither simple nor, necessarily, predictable. We shall also discuss some of the problems which have arisen when the law has been applied to computer-related disputes or wrongdoing. It is such problems which have, in part, led to some of the legislation which we shall look at in the subsequent chapters.

Note that the discussion in this and the following chapters is only intended to raise awareness of the legal issues in computing and not to serve as a reference in determining the legal position in a particular case or incident.

Relation to other chapters The overview of the law given below forms the background for the next four chapters which discuss how the law relates to particular aspects of computing: Chapter 6 is concerned with ownership of software, Chapter 7 with responsibility for faulty software, Chapter 8 with data protection, and Chapter 9 with computer misuse and other offences.

The concept of legal personality, which is introduced here, is also relevant when we discuss professional societies in Chapter 11.

5.1 British legal systems

The legal system of the United Kingdom is really three separate systems – England and Wales share one system, Northern Ireland and Scotland each have separate ones.

The English system, along with those of America and many former British colonies which take English law as their source, is a **common law** system. Broadly speaking, this means that the law developed, at least in its early stages, by using the decision of a judge in a particular case as a guide, or precedent (the relevant precedents in an area are sometimes referred to as **case law**), for how similar cases should be decided. Subsequently, of course, the law developed through parliamentary legislation but the use of precedent is still of fundamental importance.

Another feature of the English legal system is that its trials are adversarial; one side (the prosecution) accuses the other (the defence) in front of a judge and, in more serious cases, a jury. The judge (and sometimes the jury) listens to the two sides and then decides the case on the basis of the arguments and evidence which have been presented. Thus court proceedings are primarily concerned with deciding between two arguments or cases rather than finding out the truth as such. The judge does not independently call or question witnesses; decisions and judgments are made solely on the basis of what the two sides present in court.

The English system is quite different from the Romano-Germanic (or 'civilian') systems which are prevalent in Europe. These systems of law derive ultimately from that of ancient Rome and are much more influenced by the writings of legal experts than is English law. A further difference is that trials in Continental systems are inquisitorial in nature with the judge effectively conducting an investigation to find the truth behind an incident or claim.

The Scottish legal system is, like the English one, adversarial but is distinctive in that it has features of both English and Continental systems. After Scotland gained its independence from Britain at the beginning of the fourteenth century, its lawyers tended to be trained on the Continent and so Scottish law was influenced by Continental practice. This influence continued until after the union with England in 1707, finally ending when the Napoleonic wars made it impracticable for Scottish lawyers to train abroad. In this chapter we shall not discuss Scottish law separately since the laws relating to computing are embodied in Acts of Parliament which have effect throughout the United Kingdom. It should be noted, however, that there are significant differences of procedure in Scotland and that some of the issues relating to contracts may differ.

The system in Northern Ireland is much closer to that of England and Wales. The differences here are more in the court procedures than the nature of the law itself.

5.2 Sources of English law

English law has evolved over hundreds of years and still bears many traces of that evolution. Because of this the simplest way to explain the sources of law is to look at them in their historical context.

Courts

One tends to think that the courts would have no existence were it not for the law but it would be quite possible for courts to function in the absence of any formal law – deciding each case on its merits probably in accordance with some general notions of fairness.

This is much the situation which pertained after the Norman Conquest in 1066. The early law derived from the rules and practices of the community which were reflected in judges' decisions. These decisions and the principles they embodied formed what is called the **common law**. From very early on judges tried to be consistent and to avoid giving judgments which conflicted with **precedent** – that is, with the judgments already made in similar cases.

The practice developed of recording judicial decisions so that they could be circulated among judges. This evolved into a system of recording important cases in **Law Reports**. 'Important' in this context means that a case sets a precedent in some area of law which was hitherto uncertain, rather than that it is concerned with a large amount of money or a particularly notorious crime. Law reports have now existed for some 400 years and are still being published to this day. They constitute a major source of law.

One drawback with the common law was that it evolved into a rather inflexible system which did not always result in judgments which were considered to be fair or reasonable. People who had not achieved a satisfactory result through common law were occasionally allowed to petition the sovereign. Such petitions were generally dealt with by the sovereign's chancellor who, later, came to preside over a separate court called the Court of Chancery.

The Court of Chancery was able to enforce rights which were not available in common law and was generally more flexible in its judgments. The separate body of law which stemmed from the Court of Chancery was known as **Equity** (literally 'fairness') and, in time, itself became bound by precedent. Legal reforms in the nineteenth century reorganized the courts so that all courts could apply both common law and equity, though equity took precedence where there was a conflict. This blurred the distinction between the two kinds of law but lawyers still refer to equity as a distinct area of the law.

Parliament

Parliament did not begin making law until the thirteenth century – later than the courts. Parliament passes statutes (Acts of Parliament) which then form part of the law and take precedence over any previous judicial decisions. The Acts passed by parliament may have their origin in political campaigns and lobbying, in the need to fulfil treaty obligations undertaken by the government (as with the 1984 Data Protection Act, discussed in Chapter 8), or to reform the law to remove anomalies or address new problems. There are a number of official bodies, including the **Law Commission**, which have been set up specifically to keep the law under review and suggest such changes. It was as a result of a Law Commission report into computer crime that the Computer Misuse Act, discussed in Chapter 9, was passed in 1990.

In addition, parliament may, by means of a statute, grant to ministers, local authorities or other bodies the power to make regulations or bye-laws which have legal force. This so-called **delegated legislation** is usually concerned with specific areas such as, for example, food safety and hygiene. One example of delegated legislation which we will discuss in the next chapter are the Copyright (Computer Programs) Regulations 1992 which clarify how the provisions of the Copyright, Designs and Patents Act 1988 should be interpreted where programs are concerned.

The European Union

The most recent source of law comes from membership of the European Union. British law must now be consistent with European Union law and where there are differences it is European law which takes precedence.

European laws are passed by the the **Council of the European Union**. The Council comprises one representative from the government of each member state. These representatives are not permanent and which particular ministers represent their countries at a Council meeting depends on the issues being addressed. Recommendations for legislation are made to the Council by the Commission. This is a body made up of permanent representatives (commissioners) from each member country; there are seventeen commissioners, larger countries having two, others just one.

European legislation comes in two forms:

1 **regulations** which immediately become part of the law of each member country and take precedence over existing legislation, and
2 **directives** which are instructions to member states to alter their existing laws to meet particular criteria. For example, the Consumer Protection

Act 1987 (which we discuss in Chapter 7 since it has implications for the liability of software engineers) was passed to bring UK law into line with an EU directive on product liability.

The legislative powers vested in European bodies mean that Parliament is no longer the supreme law making body for the United Kingdom. In practice, however, this only affects those areas of law with which the European Union is concerned such as those relating to economic activity. Hence whole areas of British law are largely unaffected but laws relating to some computing activities such as Data Protection, which we discuss in Chapter 8, are or will be affected.

5.3 Branches of the law

English law has two main branches – **civil law** and **criminal law**. Civil law is mainly concerned with private disputes between individuals or groups. Criminal law, on the other hand, regulates behaviour which is seen as offending against society in general and covers offences such as speeding, reckless driving, theft, robbery, assault and so on. There are other branches of law, such as ecclesiastical or admiralty law, but with the exception of industrial law, which covers trade unions and employment issues, these are highly specialized and unlikely to affect most people.

The differences between civil and criminal law are not absolutely clear-cut and one piece of legislation (such as that relating to copyright) can specify both civil and criminal penalties. Furthermore, a particular action can sometimes be covered by both civil and criminal law so that an individual who, for example, distributes pirated software may be both prosecuted for a criminal offence and sued for damages in civil law by the owner of the software copyright. Another example is the recent case of the American sports star O. J. Simpson who, after acquittal on a criminal charge of murder, had to fight a civil law suit for damages from relatives of the victims; both court cases related to the same alleged offences.

One factor which does distinguish the two areas of law is the distinct, though related, court systems through which civil and criminal cases pass. In the rest of this section we consider civil and criminal law in greater detail. The two different court systems are presented in the next section.

Civil law

Civil law is largely concerned with resolving disputes between individuals or groups of individuals. Civil cases are initiated by an aggrieved party, the **plaintiff**, taking legal proceedings against (suing) another party, the **defendant**. Normally the objective of such proceedings is either to obtain **damages** (financial compensation) or an **injunction** (an order from the court obliging the defendant to do or refrain from doing something).

For example, an author Sarah Jones, say, who finds out that without her permission a company, Smith Publishers Ltd, is about to publish a book with a copy of an article that she wrote might sue the publishers for an injunction to prevent them distributing the book. The case would be referred to as '*Jones* v. *Smith Publishers*'; the plaintiff is always named first. If Smith Publishers had already sold a lot of copies of the book then Sarah Jones might sue for damages, that is, compensation for the royalties she should have received.

Civil law is extensive and is normally regarded as comprising the following branches:

- **Contract law** which regulates both the kinds of agreements (contracts) which people can enter into and disputes arising out of contracts, We shall consider the implications of contract law for software development and liability later.
- **Property law** which is concerned with ownership and transfer of all kinds of property such as land, goods, and intangible property (company shares or patents, for example).
- **Tort** Torts (or wrongs) are acts or omissions to act which have caused harm or injury and which can result in legal proceedings. Areas of tort include negligence, libel, and trespass. Specific torts which we shall look at later include 'passing off' where a trader promotes goods or services when using another trader's name, negligence which allows people to claim damages for injury resulting from the carelessness of others, and libel which now encompasses defamatory remarks made in e-mail messages.
- **Family law** which is concerned with marriage, divorce, custody and welfare of children and so on.

Computer systems and software may be affected by any of the first three areas of civil law. Software development is often undertaken according to a contract, and produces deliverables (programs, design documents and so on) which are affected by intellectual property law. Faulty software (such as embedded software in a domestic appliance which resulted in food being made inedible or dangerous) might give rise to an action for negligence.

Criminal law

Criminal law is generally concerned with acts which can be seen as offending against society at large. It encompasses murder, assault, robbery, theft, drugs offences, road traffic offences, and others. Criminal law also provides punitive sanctions, such as fines or imprisonment, against transgressors.

Criminal cases are normally brought by the Crown. A case brought against Smith, say, will be referred to as '*R. v. Smith*' (R standing for Regina, the Queen) and Smith is said to be prosecuted for the offence. If Smith is found guilty then he may appeal to a higher court and the case becomes '*Smith* v. *R.*', Smith now being referred to as the **appellant**. The prosecution, however, may not appeal if Smith is found not guilty. Hence if an individual is acquitted of a particular offence then he or she cannot be prosecuted again for that same offence.

It is possible for criminal proceedings to be instigated by bodies other than the Crown. Perhaps the most common example of this is the prosecution of shoplifters by the shops themselves. In more serious cases, though, it is almost invariably the Crown that brings proceedings.

5.4 The structure of the court system

The most obvious route for dealing with legal disputes is, of course, through the court system. There are a number of courts and they differ from each other in three main ways: whether they hear civil or criminal cases, the relative importance of the cases they deal with, and whether they are courts of first instance (that is, the first court in which a case will be heard) or courts of appeal. The main courts are:

1 **Magistrates' courts** which deal mainly with minor criminal offences and certain civil cases (primarily those to do with family law or local administration). A magistrates' court typically comprises three justices of the peace (magistrates). Magistrates are usually unpaid volunteers who have not worked as lawyers. There is no jury in a magistrates' court.
2 **County courts** where the bulk of civil litigation is dealt with. There is no jury and jurisdiction is limited to small or non-complex civil disputes.
3 **The Crown Court** which is notionally just one court but which, in practice, sits in about 90 centres around the country. It is here that serious criminal cases and appeals from magistrates' courts are heard. A trial in the Crown Court is presided over by a judge with a jury.
4 **The High Court** which hears appeals from county, magistrates', and Crown Courts as well as hearing complicated or major civil cases. The High Court is split into three divisions:
    (a) **Family Division** which deals with family law
    (b) **Chancery Division** which concentrates on wills, insolvency, and intellectual property rights
    (c) **Queen's Bench Division** which deals with all other areas of civil law.
High Court judges sit alone unless they are hearing an appeal in which case more than one judge may sit in the same court.
5 **The Court of Appeal** which hears only appeals. These may be from the High Court, the Crown Court, or county courts, so it deals with both civil and criminal cases. Normally three judges hear an appeal.
6 **The House of Lords** which is the final court of appeal in the United Kingdom. The judges, peers who hold or who have held high legal office, normally sit in a committee of five.

7 **The European Court of Justice** which sits in Luxembourg. Until recently the House of Lords was the final court of appeal for British citizens but now the European Court of Justice is the highest court for matters which involve EU law. The Court includes a judge from each member country, fifteen in all.

Courts are not, however, the only route for the resolution of legal disputes (though certain kinds of disputes, those involving the criminal law for example, will inevitably end up in the court system). The two other mechanisms which are available are:

8 **Tribunals** which are usually concerned with resolving disputes in specific areas. For example, the Data Protection Act (discussed in Chapter 8) established a tribunal to adjudicate on certain disputes relating to data protection. Tribunals comprise a mix of legal experts and experts from the particular area of concern of the tribunal. There has been a considerable growth in the use of tribunals in recent years and currently there are in the region of sixty tribunals which, it has been estimated, deal with about six times as many cases each year as come before the courts.

9 **Arbitration** which is used in many civil cases and involves appointing an arbitrator to resolve the dispute. The arbitrator is an independent expert with knowledge of the area in which the dispute has occurred. The use of arbitration is particularly common in the business world since it provides a quicker, cheaper, and more flexible way of resolving disputes.

However, the decisions of both tribunals and arbitrators can be overturned in the courts if the decision is not consistent with the law as it stands.

Procedure in civil cases

If an individual or a company, Smith Software Ltd (SSL) say, has a grievance against another party, Acme Computers Ltd (Acme) for example, then if SSL cannot reach an amicable settlement with Acme the next step will usually be to consult solicitors. SSL's solicitors may then try to come to an arrangement with Acme (or their solicitors) but, failing this, they will advise SSL on their chances of a successful court action.

Assuming that SSL decide to pursue their case, the court they will deal with depends on the size of the claim, or the complexity and nature of their suit. Claims for less than £25 000 are normally heard in a county court, those for more than £50 000 in the High Court. Claims for intermediate amounts might be heard in either court.

Assuming that SSL is claiming £80 000 damages then the process which will be followed has essentially three stages:

1 **Issuing a writ** SSL's solicitors will draft a **writ**, basically a short account of the grievance and the damages being claimed. The writ is then

presented to, or **served on**, Acme who have the option of paying or contesting the claim.

2 **Clarification of case** If Acme contests the claim then there follows a period during which the precise nature of the claim and the supporting evidence is clarified. This process is quite lengthy and complicated; its purpose is to ensure that the issues and evidence involved are clearly defined so as to avoid losing time once the trial begins.

3 **Trial** In civil cases there is normally no jury. The case would come before a judge who would decide issues of both law and fact. At the trial, the plaintiff's (that is, SSL's) lawyer will first present the grievance and call witnesses to give evidence. These witnesses may then be cross-examined by the defendant's (that is, Acme's) lawyers. Once the plaintiff's lawyer has finished presenting his or her case, the defendant can submit that there is no case to answer, in which case the judge will then give a decision. It is much more likely, though, that the defendant's lawyer will present a defence, calling further witnesses and producing further evidence.

Normally witnesses are asked solely to state facts and are not allowed to give opinions or judgments. However, in cases where there are technical issues with which the judge or court may not be familiar, as may happen with computer-related cases, it is common practice to call **expert witnesses**. Such witnesses have knowledge and expertise in a particular area and are asked to explain technical points and to give opinions on issues in their field.

After all the evidence has been presented, the two sides make a final statement of their respective cases. The judge then arrives at a verdict, but this may not be given until after the judge has been able to reconsider the evidence and study the points of law raised. In civil cases the verdict is given on the basis of which side's case appears, on balance, the more likely to be true.

This outline is, of course, greatly simplified but the main stages of the process are largely as described.

At any point during the process the two parties can decide to settle outside court and so drop legal proceedings. It is not unusual for cases to be dropped just before they actually come to trial. There is also, of course, the right to appeal to a higher court. Depending on where a case starts appeals could be heard in the Court of Appeal, and the House of Lords. If an issue of European law were involved then appeal to the European Court in Luxembourg is also possible.

Procedure in criminal cases

One of the factors which distinguishes criminal cases from civil ones is that it is usually the responsibility of the Crown to bring the prosecution and to prove guilt. Defendants are presumed innocent until guilt has been proved beyond reasonable doubt. Thus the 'burden of proof' is much more stringent in criminal cases than in civil ones.

The police are responsible only for detection and investigation of an offence. If the police believe that an individual may be guilty then the case is passed on to the **Crown Prosecution Service** (CPS). The CPS then decides, on grounds of likelihood of conviction and public interest, whether to prosecute. A decision by the CPS not to prosecute does not prevent private individuals bringing a prosecution but in practice this is very rare.

There are essentially two kinds of criminal trial:

1 **Summary trial** for minor offences, such as many traffic offences, which takes place in a magistrates' court without a jury. Magistrates are limited in the penalties which they can impose; in general they cannot give a custodial sentence of longer than 6 months nor impose a fine greater than £5000. They have the power, however, to refer a case to a Crown Court if they believe that a higher sentence may be justified.
2 **Trial on indictment** for more serious offences and which takes place in a Crown Court before a jury. The jury decides whether the accused is guilty on the basis of the evidence presented. Points of law are decided by the judge who also controls the proceedings.

Some offences can be tried 'either way' – that is, summarily or on indictment depending on the choice of the defendant.

If found guilty the defendant may be granted leave to appeal either against conviction or against sentence. Generally, few appeals against conviction are allowed though there are many appeals against sentence which are heard each year.

5.5 Legal personality

An important legal concept is that of legal personality. In simple terms a 'legal person' can sue or be sued. As well as people, organizations such as companies, universities and certain statutory bodies are also regarded as legal persons. The mechanism by which a legal person is brought into existence is called **incorporation**. In particular, joint stock companies and chartered bodies are incorporated and we consider these two kinds of body below.

Joint stock companies

Joint stock companies are created by being registered under the terms of the Companies Act 1985. When such a company is created it becomes a separate legal entity with members. These members, called **shareholders**, provide capital and in return receive shares in the company. Shareholders may sell their shares to other people or companies. The shareholders have ultimate control, though day-to-day management of the company is carried out by the directors whom they appoint. A company is liable for all its debts but the liability of the shareholders is limited to any outstanding capital that they may have agreed to provide. Thus limited companies have a legal identity which is entirely separate from the identity of their directors or owners.

There are two kinds of company. **Public companies** have their shares openly traded on the Stock Exchange. The name of public companies is always followed by the phrase 'public limited company' or the initials 'plc'. **Private companies** do not have their shares openly traded and are distinguished by having 'Limited' or 'Ltd' at the end of their name.

Chartered bodies

Chartered bodies are created by a charter from the Crown, normally granted in response to a petition from an organization wishing to acquire independent status. The charter will specify the duties and powers of the newly formed corporation. Universities and many professional bodies are incorporated by charter. For example, the British Computer Society was granted a Royal charter in 1984.

5.6 Scale and nature of the law

Until the twentieth century the amount of legislation passed by parliament was modest and the law as a whole did not change quickly. However, the quantity of legislation has grown rapidly. There are now about 3500 Acts of Parliament (HMSO 1996) and an estimated further 10 000 or so regulations and statutory instruments in force. In addition to this there are a large number of cases which are reported each year. The report of a single case can easily run to 30 or 40 pages and it has been estimated that about six volumes of new law reports appear each year (Atiyah 1995). Nor is this all the legislation to take into account; European directives also affect some areas of English law, further complicating the situation.

As a consequence the law is now extremely complex and most lawyers specialize, since to be reasonably sure how the courts will decide in a particular dispute requires considerable knowledge of the relevant area of law. Furthermore, there are many issues where the law is uncertain since there is no relevant case which may serve as a precedent.

Hence many commercial organizations avoid using the law as a mechanism for resolving their disputes, preferring to go to arbitration or simply to cut their losses. This is also in part due to the way in which disputes are resolved in a court of law. For example, in a dispute between two parties A and B the judge may decide on a balance of probabilities that B has a marginally better case. This being so the judge will declare in favour of B and A effectively loses completely even though both sides may be partially at fault. This makes going to court risky if the case is not reasonably clear.

Particular problems

How well has the law managed to cope with computer technology and computer-related crimes? The rapid development of computer technology and the speed with which it has become established as an integral part of everyday life has not given the law much time to react. There are two problems raised by computer technology:

- Lawyers and more particularly judges develop considerable expertise in the law but were, until recently, largely unfamiliar with computer technology. This means that someone pursuing a computer-related law suit has not simply to establish the justness of his or her case but possibly also to educate his or her lawyers on the technological issues who, in turn, must explain these to the judge.
- Computers and software may make it possible for people to commit acts which many would feel are unacceptable (such as hacking) but which might not be covered by the law.

The first of these two problems is probably receding as more lawyers become familiar with computers and more computer-related cases have come before the courts. The second problem is more fundamental and in the rest of this section we briefly review two cases where the authorities attempted unsuccessfully to use the then-current law to convict hackers for existing offences.

1 In Hong Kong a computer hacker was accused of stealing an amount of electricity which was worth only a small fraction of one Hong Kong cent (*R.* v. *Siu Tak Chee*, discussed in Bott *et al.* (1995)). There are two problems with such an accusation: first, it is difficult to establish that any electricity has been used which would not have been used anyway by the normal operation of the computer and, second, the amount of electricity involved is trivial. In the event the case was dismissed and the defendant not convicted.

2 In another case (*R.* v. *Gold* (1988)) two computer hackers managed to access British Telecom's Prestel Gold computer network and to read an (unprotected) file containing logons and passwords. One of the hackers then used the logon and password of the Duke of Edinburgh to leave a message 'Good Afternoon HRH Duke of Edinburgh'.

   The two were charged with forgery (Figure 5.1) and convicted in the Crown Court. However, on appeal the conviction was overturned on the grounds that words such as 'recorded' and 'stored' implied some permanence. Since the logon and password were only transiently held until being verified this condition was not met according to the appeal judges. The judges also commented that the prosecution was an attempt

In section 1 of the Act forgery is defined:

A person is guilty of forgery if he makes a false instrument, with the intention that he or another shall use it to induce somebody to accept it as genuine, and by reason of so accepting it, to do or not to do some act to his own or any other person's detriment.

Elsewhere in the Act it is stated that an 'instrument' can be:

recorded or stored on disc, tape, sound track or other device

Figure 5.1 The definition of forgery according to the Forgery and Counterfeiting Act 1981.

to use the forgery law in a circumstance for which it had simply not been designed. As a result of this and similar cases new laws were introduced as discussed in Chapter 9.

5.7 Summary

Britain has more than one legal system, there being significant differences between that of England and Wales, and those of Northern Ireland and, especially, of Scotland.

English law developed initially by using the precedent set by judges' decisions – case law. Later parliament became primordial in making the law and Acts of Parliament take precedence over case law. Most recently the European Union has also had an effect on English law since European legislation takes precedence over that of member states. However, the effects of European legislation are largely confined to certain areas, such as company law or health and safety.

English law has two main branches: civil law and criminal law. The former can be seen as being largely concerned with disputes between individuals or groups and the latter with acts which society as a whole condemns and seeks to prevent or punish. Civil and criminal proceedings differ in many respects including which particular courts are involved and the burden of proof required. The burden is much more stringent for criminal trials.

The law has had difficulties in responding to certain computer-related activities, such as hacking, and these have been addressed by changes in legislation or completely new legislation. These are discussed in more detail in the following chapters.

Note that the introduction to the law that we have given in this chapter is inevitably somewhat simplified but it covers the main terminology and concepts which are required for the subsequent chapters on computer-related law.

Further reading

A good introduction to the law, written for the general reader, is *Law and Modern Society* by P. S. Atiyah (1995). A more thorough introduction, aimed at those who are beginning law studies, is *An Introduction to Law* by P. Harris (1993).

A text which gives an overview of each of the legal systems of the UK is *Britain's Legal Systems* produced by the Stationery Office (HMSO 1996) though this text concentrates on legal procedures and the structure of the courts rather than the law as such.

Texts which cover the law from a more practical viewpoint and concentrate on the process of law include *The Administration of Justice* by Robin White (1991) and *English Law* by Denis Keenan (1995).

CHAPTER 6

Ownership of software

Programs and other documentation relating to software development, such as data models or user manuals, are very easily copied. What protection does a software developer have against another individual or company simply copying his or her software and then using it or marketing it as their own?

Overview

This chapter is concerned with the legal protection available to software developers which prevents other parties depriving them of the benefit of their efforts. The area of the law which provides such protection is **Intellectual Property Law** which encompasses copyright, patents, trademarks, and so on.

After a general introduction to intellectual property rights we shall concentrate on two areas: the law of confidence and copyright. The former prevents people passing on or exploiting ideas or information which have clearly been communicated to them in confidence. Copyright law is, as its name suggests, concerned with who has the right to copy something.

Patent law is covered only briefly since it is of much more limited scope than the laws on confidence or copyright. All computer programs are automatically covered by copyright law but only certain kinds of inventions come within the scope of patent law; inventors are, in any event, protected by the law of confidence in the first instance (provided they do not disclose their invention). Moreover, patent law is relevant to hardware rather than software and no more than a relatively small proportion of those in the computer industry are involved in hardware design.

Relation to other chapters The debate about what kinds of property rights are appropriate for software has been reviewed in Chapter 4. The implications of confidentiality and copyright for contracts involving the development or purchase of software are covered in the next chapter.

6.1 Intellectual property

The law distinguishes between three forms of property: land, goods, and intangible property. Land was the first kind of property to be recognized by the law. Consequently land law is very old and has continually developed to reflect changing constraints on land use. Laws relating to personal property developed later and make a distinction between tangible property or goods, for instance cars and household items, and intangible property, such as company shares and intellectual property.

Intellectual property can generally be thought of as comprising the results of intellectual endeavour. Examples include paintings, films, novels, designs, inventions, and trademarks. Such items are covered by a range of laws, each dealing with a particular form of property and reflecting differing balances between the rights of the creator and the general interests of society. Patent law, for example, enables an inventor to control the use of his or her invention by means of a patent. However, it also imposes limits on the protection that a patent provides, otherwise the inventor would have an indefinite monopoly to the detriment of society as a whole. In contrast, concerns about monopolies have not influenced copyright law where the property being protected is primarily artistic.

Confidentiality and copyright are addressed later in separate sections; the other forms of intellectual property (patents, trademarks, and design rights), we briefly discuss below.

Patents

Patent law is concerned with protecting inventions. From the perspective of an inventor a patent is very attractive since it gives exclusive rights over the invention for a period of up to 20 years. The kinds of inventions protected can be thought of as either **product inventions** or **process inventions**; these have been described respectively as either old ways of making something new or new ways of making something old. Examples of inventions which might be patentable would be a new kind of computer interface or storage device (a product), or a new way of manufacturing printed circuits (a process). To be patentable an invention must:

● be novel
● contain an 'inventive step' – in other words, the invention must not be obvious to people working in the field of the invention
● have an industrial application and
● not fall in one of the areas specifically excluded from patent law; these include scientific theories and discoveries, artistic works, and algorithms – in particular, computer programs.

Thus patent law applies to computer hardware but not, in general, to software. However, a computer program could be covered by a patent if it formed part of a larger patentable invention, such as a new computer-controlled manufacturing process.

To patent an invention the inventor must apply to a patent office to have it registered; the registration process is complex and may take several years. The inventor must also be careful about discussing the invention before making his or her application; if the invention becomes known about it will no longer be novel and so not be patentable. Nevertheless, since an invention must have an industrial application to be patentable, the inventor will usually need to discuss it with potential manufacturers or users before applying for registration. In such discussions, the inventor must rely on the law of confidence to prevent general disclosure of the invention.

Trademarks

Trademarks have long been used to identify products or their manufacturers. Well-known examples include Hoover, Coca-Cola, Guinness, and IBM. Trademarks can be registered, effectively preventing competitors from using the same mark. To qualify for registration a mark must be distinctive, capable of being represented graphically, and dissimilar from existing trademarks. Trademarks are registered for particular classes of goods or services so it is possible for two companies to use the same mark provided their businesses are quite different. Thus two companies, one selling fire-resistant clothing, the other producing computer games, could probably both register the name 'FireSoft', for example, since it would be unlikely to confuse consumers. However, when a name becomes very well known this may no longer be the case. A manufacturer of small soft toys would probably not be allowed to register the name MicroSoft even though their business had nothing to do with software.

Trademarks are not restricted to names so, for example, a distinctive form of packaging could be registered. In principle there is no reason why moving images or even sounds may not qualify as trademarks. Hence a particular animated icon or graphic which a company uses in its Web pages could be registered provided it met all the relevant criteria.

Even when a company has omitted to register a name or trademark it may still be able to prevent others from using it. To do this the company has to rely on the law of **passing off**. This derives from common law and prevents others from using a name or mark under which a trader has built up a reputation, that is, from passing themselves off as the original trader. In a recent case champagne producers successfully prevented a manufacturer marketing a product under the name of 'Elderflower Champagne' by arguing that it was an instance of passing off.

One current problem area, which is related to trademarks, is the registration of Internet domain names. Companies are obviously keen to register domains which are based on their name but this inevitably leads to problems since there is no global system of trademark registration and so companies in different countries may share the same name. Also, as mentioned above, the same name may be used by different companies in one country provided they trade in distinct business areas. One recent dispute involved a UK training company,

Prince, and an American sports supplier, Prince Inc. The former registered the Internet domain **prince.com** though it had not registered its name as a trademark; Prince Inc, on the other hand, had registered its name as a US trademark but not sought to register the Internet domain **prince.com** until it had already been taken. There have also been cases of speculators registering Internet domains using the names of well-known companies in the expectation of selling them at considerable profit when the companies finally come to set up Internet sites. However, in one recent case the department store Harrods recovered the domain name **Harrods.com** in a court action (Stammers 1997).

Designs

Designs for attractive yet functional objects can be protected from copying by being registered; the criteria for registration are that a design be novel and that its shape have aesthetic appeal. Thus novel and distinctive designs for a mouse or keyboard could probably be registered; a design for a plain box-like housing of the main unit could not.

Designs of purely functional objects, such as the internal components of a laser printer, cannot be registered. However, such designs may still be protected by what are called **design rights**. These rights are similar to copyright in that the design is protected as soon as it is recorded. A point worth mentioning in the context of computers is that layouts of semiconductor circuits are explicitly protected by separate regulations called **Semiconductor Design Rights**.

6.2 The law of confidence

Under English law when information is imparted in confidence the recipient is under an obligation not to make it public. This obligation is enshrined in the law of confidence, an area of equity which is primarily defined by case law.

The law of confidence can be used to prevent confidential information being disclosed to a third party, or to obtain damages if it has been disclosed. It can protect information ranging from trade secrets, such as recipes for well-known sauces or foods, to new inventions or databases of business prospects. Moreover, there does not need to be a contract between two parties for a duty of confidence to apply. For example, an inventor who discloses an invention to a potential manufacturer, before seeking a patent, can prevent the manufacturer using or divulging the idea even if the two parties have not entered into a contract.

For the law of confidence to be invoked with respect to a particular piece of information there are three criteria which must be satisfied. These are that the information:

- is confidential

- has been communicated in circumstances which give rise to an obligation of confidence and
- has been (or was intended to be) disclosed or used without authorization and, where commercial information is concerned, to the detriment of the party which communicated it.

For example, a programmer might discuss an idea for a PC package with a software publisher, perhaps describing the package's interface and how it would work. If there is nothing new about the proposed software then no obligation of confidence can arise. However, if the proposal is novel then, provided it had clearly been imparted in confidence, the publisher would be under an obligation not to use or pass on the idea. What would be considered as imparting in confidence is clearly a matter of judgement: a casual conversation with a group of friends in the pub certainly would not. A private meeting where the confidential nature of the information was stressed, possibly by writing in advance, would.

The obligation of confidence is not absolute in that there are circumstances where it is acceptable (legally speaking) to break a confidence. For instance, if someone were told that another person had committed a crime and had evaded detection then the recipient would be placed under no obligation not to inform the police. In such circumstances the public interest in apprehending offenders is taken to be more important than keeping information private.

Employees automatically owe a duty of confidence to their employers. A programmer employed by a software house who took a program listing home and showed it to friends to help them develop a competing product would certainly be in breach of confidence. There would still be a breach even if he or she waited until leaving the software house before showing the listing to friends. When in a new job, however, the duty of confidence with respect to what can be remembered about a former job largely lapses, unless there were explicit restraints specified in the former employment contract. It is quite normal to include such restraints but there are limitations on what can be imposed. A software house could not prevent its programmers from taking programming jobs in other companies, for example. It probably could prevent them from working on the development of competing products for a period of a year or two.

A significant point about the law of confidence is that it does not prevent the disclosure of information which has been obtained by other means. If A tells B something in confidence this places B under an obligation not to divulge it but it places no obligation on C, an eavesdropper who managed to hear the conversation without A or B realizing. In effect there is no law of privacy and, under English law, one cannot 'steal information' (see also the case of *Oxford v Moss*, Figure 9.2). Thus it is unlikely that a hacker who obtained confidential information by breaking into a computer could be sued for breach of confidence if he or she were to make the information public. However, the hacker would certainly be liable for prosecution for computer misuse, as discussed in Chapter 9.

6.3 Copyright

Copyright law originally came about in response to the development of printing; laws relating to copying were passed in the sixteenth century and the first modern copyright Act in 1710. Copyright now encompasses the results of just about any creative endeavour including photographs, films, videos, broadcasts, sound recordings, cable programmes, and software. Even computer-generated material is covered, on the basis that things worth copying must also be worth protecting. The latest copyright act is the Copyright, Designs and Patents Act 1988.

The purpose of copyright is to ensure that the author of a work benefits from his or her efforts. There is no formal procedure which needs to be followed; a work is covered as soon as it is written down or recorded in some form. Other people may not then copy or exploit the work without the express permission of the copyright owner.

For a work to be protected by copyright, it must be:

- original, that is, it must have been created by the author and be the result of at least a small amount of skill or judgement and
- it must be recorded in writing or otherwise. A work held on magnetic media, such as computer disks or even computer memory, would be regarded as having been recorded.

Note that, where programs are concerned, copyright protection extends beyond the code itself and covers associated documentation, such as design diagrams and user manuals (provided they satisfy the above criteria). Other computer-based material such as databases or digital pictures is also covered. However, with a database there must have been some skill or judgement exercised in its compilation or design. A simple list of addresses of friends or of a company's customers, for example, would probably not have required sufficient skill in its compilation. In practice, however, almost all databases of any significance are protected by copyright.

Copyright is more general than patent law in that it applies to any original, recorded work, but it is more restricted in that it does not generally protect ideas as such, only their expression. An inventor who obtains a patent for a novel product can prevent other people from exploiting the same invention even if they think of it independently. Under copyright only the inventor's notes would be protected and then only against copying – there would be no redress against someone who happened by chance to produce similar notes or designs. However, the distinction between the expression of ideas (protected by copyright) and the ideas themselves (not protected) is not always clear-cut. A cartoonist who produces a comic book based upon a particular novel can be sued for copyright infringement even though there might be no direct copying involved.

One common misconception is that the Internet is some kind of 'Copyright Free Zone'. It is not. The varying national laws affecting different sites and the ease of downloading data may make it hard for Internet publishers to enforce their rights, but these rights still exist. Of course some material available on the Internet comes with explicit directions as to whether it may be copied or reproduced, but the bulk does not. Users who, for example, copy images from Web sites and include them in their own site could find themselves the object of a copyright suit.

Ownership of copyright

In copyright law the person who creates a work is referred to as its **author**. Hence we talk about a program's author or a photograph's author. Where computer-generated works are concerned the author is the person who operated or owned the computer which produced the work. Thus an organization operating a computer to generate a sequence of random numbers for a prize draw would, from a legal standpoint, be the author of the sequence. This would still be the case even if the organization did not own the copyright of the generating program but was using it under licence.

Initially the copyright in a work belongs to its author unless he or she is an employee, in which case it would normally belong to the employer. Hence programmers employed by a company would not normally own the copyright in the programs that they write. However, for a person who is employed in some other capacity, the situation is different. For example, a clerical assistant who writes a program out of work hours to make his or her job easier probably will own the copyright, since the program was not developed in the normal course of employment. Had the program been developed in the employer's time and using the employer's resources then the situation would be less clear-cut.

The duration of copyright in a work varies according to the kind of work and the author. Copyright in a program and related documentation lasts for 70 years after its author's death. If a work is computer-generated the period is shorter, 50 years from the creation of the work.

The owner of a copyright has essentially two ways available to exploit the copyright. First, he or she can transfer the copyright to another party, possibly in return for a fixed sum or payment of royalties – this is known as **assigning** the copyright. The new owner can then exploit the copyright in the same way as the original author could have done.

Alternatively the author can grant one or more **licences** to copy the work. A licence is essentially a written permission to allow someone to do something which would otherwise be unlawful. With software licences permission is given to copy the software for the purpose of using it and for making essential backups. Licences may be either exclusive or non-exclusive. An exclusive licence means that only the recipient of the licence can carry out certain restricted acts (even the owner is then prevented from carrying out these acts). For example, an author might grant an exclusive licence to distribute a book he or she has written; the author could not then grant a separate licence to another publisher to publish the same book. A non-exclusive licence does not prevent the copyright owner from granting similar rights to other people. In principle copyright assignment and licensing can become quite complex since it is possible to assign or license only part of the rights existing in a copyright.

For some categories of work copyright law also assigns **moral rights** which give the author some control over what may be done with the work even if he or she does not own the copyright. An author of a novel can assert the right to be identified as such, for example. This is the source of the phrase *The right of X to be identified as the author of this book has been asserted etc. etc.* found at the beginning of many recently published books. However, moral rights are not available for software on the grounds that this would hinder subsequent modification and enhancement.

Rights and exceptions

Copyright law restricts what people other than the copyright owner may do with a work. These **restricted acts** include:

- making a copy of the work
- making an adaptation of the work
- issuing copies of the work to other people
- performing, showing, or playing the work in public or broadcasting it.

One consequence of the restrictions on copying is that someone who does not own the copyright in a piece of software does not have the right to use it. Running a program involves loading it from disk into the computer's main memory, so making a copy. This is a restricted act unless the copyright owner gives his or her consent. The normal mechanism for providing consent is by a licence, discussed further in the next chapter. Note that, technically, an Internet user infringes the first of the above restrictions every time he or she accesses a Web site since this always involves copying information from the site. In practice, though, the act of publishing material on the Web gives implicit permission to anyone to make a copy to view it. However, it cannot be taken as giving permission to make copies for other purposes – to distribute to friends, for instance.

The restriction on making adaptations means that only the copyright owner has the right to enhance or modify a program. Translating the source or object code of a program is also considered to be making an adaptation. Taking a program written in C, say, and rewriting it in Java is a restricted act, as is decompilation (the reconstruction of the source code of a program from its executable form). Hence, decompiling software in order to find out how it works infringes copyright except in particular circumstances, discussed below.

Copyright law has always included exceptions, called **permitted acts**, to the restrictions outlined above; for example, to allow some copying for private study or research. The way in which such exceptions applied to programs was clarified by the Copyright (Computer Programs) Regulations 1992 which were passed in response to a European directive. The Regulations specified the following permitted acts for software:

- Decompilation when this is done purely to determine the interface to a program and there is no other way of finding out. Hence someone developing a word-processing package would be entitled to decompile a competing word processor provided it was done with the sole purpose of finding out the format in which documents were saved. This would be done so that the new software could be developed to correctly interpret documents written with the competing word-processor. However, if the suppliers of the other package published details of the format then there would be no justification for carrying out the decompilation.
- Making backups of the software to ensure that a second copy is available in the event of the original copy becoming damaged, lost or corrupted.
- Adapting a program in order to correct an error or bug.

Note that these permitted acts relate to software sold after 1992; they do not affect licence agreements made before then.

Infringement

Someone carrying out a restricted act without the permission of the copyright owner infringes copyright. Infringement is usually a civil matter and it is up to the copyright owner to take action. Typically the owner would sue for damages or for an injunction to prevent further infringement. If the infringer had been selling copied software, for instance, then the owner could also sue for an account of profits made, in order to recoup the royalties which should have been received. The court has the power to award additional, punitive damages if the infringement of copyright has been particularly blatant or caused the plaintiff more than purely economic loss.

Some forms of infringement may also incur criminal penalties. These so-called **secondary infringements** include activities such as marketing, distributing, or retailing pirated items. Someone distributing or selling pirated software may also be guilty of further offences such as forgery, making misleading trade descriptions, or theft, and so risk heavy fines and even imprisonment. These penalties reflect the scale of the perceived problem of software piracy which, organizations in the industry claim, accounts for billions of dollars of lost revenue each year.

For most systems developers there is little danger of becoming embroiled in a copyright dispute with the exception of one relatively common scenario. This might arise when, for example, a programmer who has worked on a piece of software, a stock management system, say, for company A leaves to go and develop similar software for a second company, B. Subsequently, company B starts marketing a stock management system and company A becomes aware, through personal contacts or market research, that company B is selling software similar to its own. Company A then sues company B for infringement of copyright. There are a number of different possibilities as to what has happened:

1 The programmer, let us call him or her P, has simply taken a copy of company A's software and perhaps modified it slightly for company B – changing headings on screens and reports, for instance.
2 P has developed similar software for company B – possibly in a different programming language – but has nevertheless reused or copied some essential element of company A's software, such as the overall structure or the data model.
3 P has developed similar software for company B, but this time starting from scratch and possibly changing the design, the interface, or the overall structure of the system.
4 P has been only marginally involved in the development of similar software – contributing perhaps as a member of a design team – the bulk of the work being undertaken by company B's existing programmers and designers.

How would a court find in these different scenarios? In the first scenario it is clear that there has been infringement of copyright and possibly also breach of confidence. An example of such a case was that of *IBCOS Computers Ltd* v. *Barclays Mercantile Highland Finance Ltd* (Figure 6.1).

In the second scenario, infringement has also occurred since certain key elements of the software have been copied (this also happened in *IBCOS* v. *Barclays*). This kind of copying is sometimes called 'non-literal' copying since the programmer has not directly copied code but higher-level elements, such as the overall design, which do not show up in a direct line-by-line comparison of the programs. There have been a number of American cases of this kind which have been influential in English law. One of the best known of these is *Computer Associates* v. *Altai* (Figure 6.2) in which the judge outlined a method for determining whether non-literal copying had taken place. It should be stressed, though, that this is an American case and there is disagreement amongst lawyers as to whether the test should be used in UK cases.

In the third case there probably has not been any infringement but it might be difficult to establish this. The fact that programmer P could easily have

In this case a programmer, P, had developed a general accounting package and in 1979 licensed it to C who had an agricultural dealership. Subsequently P and C developed the software (written in a version of COBOL) and in 1982 set up a company to market it to other agricultural dealerships.

In 1986 P left the company and signed an agreement recognizing that he had no rights in any of the software that had been marketed. Moreover P also agreed not to sell, or work for a company selling, similar software for at least 2 years.

Immediately on leaving P was engaged as a consultant for a company called Highland and in his spare time developed another software package which would be a direct competitor of the software he had originally marketed with C. This software was also written in COBOL, but a different version of the language. At the end of the two-year period this new package was marketed and the plaintiffs (including C) sued for breach of confidence and infringement of copyright.

In this instance the plaintiffs were successful. In particular, the judge took into account the presence of identical mistakes in the comments and the same redundant code appearing in the two sets of programs. These were taken as indication of direct copying. The judge also ruled that not only were individual programs copied, but the overall structure of the programs making up the package had also been copied and that this was also protected by copyright.

Figure 6.1. *IBCOS Computers Ltd* v. *Barclays Mercantile Highland Finance Ltd* (1994)

copied software puts the onus on the defendants to prove that this did not happen. This is made more difficult by two factors:

- Most experienced programmers tend to have a particular style of coding which gives rise to similar elements in all the programs that they write. Moreover, they might make consistent spelling or grammatical mistakes, in program comments for instance, which could be construed as evidence of copying.
- The application itself tends to dictate the structure of the program or the data model used. Hence structural similarities might arise purely as a result of the consistent use of a particular design methodology.

Consequently in this scenario, there is a risk for the unwary programmer of becoming embroiled in legal proceedings and even being found liable for copyright infringement when no copying actually took place. It is as well to be

The defendants sold a job-scheduling package. One component of this package was an interface called OSCAR which was similar to the interface component of the plaintiffs' competing package. Indeed OSCAR was written by an ex-employee of the plaintiffs who had reused code, copied from his former place of work, without the knowledge of his new employers, the defendants. When they found out they rewrote the scheduler (without the contribution of the ex-employee) to produce a non-infringing version.

The judge found that the first version of OSCAR infringed (and awarded damages) but that the second version did not. The plaintiffs appealed but the decision was upheld.

The appeal court also set out a three-stage procedure to be used in determining whether non-literal copying had occurred:

- The original program is effectively reverse-engineered to determine the structures and designs (at varying levels of abstraction) used in its development.
- These design elements are inspected to determine whether they originate in the public domain, are dictated by the operating environment, or constitute idea rather than expression. This inspection leaves a residue of elements which are protected by copyright.
- The alleged infringing program is assessed to see to what extent it has copied the protected elements.

Figure 6.2. *Computer Associates v. Altai* (1991)

aware of such risks and to adopt an approach which ensures that the eventuality could not arise.

In the fourth scenario above the possibility of infringement has been completely avoided by the programmer not becoming directly involved in work which is too similar and ensuring that there is substantial independent input to the development. It has even been suggested that the only sure way for software developers to avoid accusations of copyright infringement is to adopt a 'clean room' approach. In this approach teams would not contain members who had worked for competitors on similar products and the software would be developed without looking at existing packages on the market.

A different source of copyright disputes, having nothing to do with the copying of code as such, arises when the user interfaces of programs are similar. Most cases of this kind, often called 'look and feel' cases, have so far arisen in the United States (Figure 6.3) where the bulk of packaged software is developed. However, as with *Computer Associates v. Altai* mentioned above, cases decided under American law may influence decisions in the UK but do not set a reliable precedent. As far as English law is concerned it seems likely

There have been a number of cases in America where software developers have been sued for allegedly copying a program's interface. Well-known cases include:

Lotus Development v. *Paperback Software* (1990) Paperback marketed a spreadsheet, VP-Planner, which had the same menu-command system as Lotus's popular 1–2–3 package, but was much cheaper. Users could switch to VP-Planner without the need for further training. Lotus sued for copyright infringement even though no program code had been copied.

The judge ruled for Lotus declaring that the command menu was protected but that the rotated 'L' layout of cell coordinates was not. The judge's reasoning was that there was a wide range of command interfaces which could have been implemented, therefore using the same one as Lotus 1–2–3 infringed copyright. However, using the same rotated 'L' layout of coordinates did not because the ways of specifying these were limited.

Apple v. *Microsoft* (1992) Apple failed when it claimed that the Windows interface produced by Microsoft infringed copyright on its own user interfaces. Apple cited some 150 features which it claimed had been copied, including overlapping windows and the use of icons. The court ruled, however, that the various elements were either not protectable by copyright or failed due to lack of originality.

Lotus Development v. *Borland* (1995) Lotus sued Borland, claiming that the menu system in Borland's Quattro spreadsheet infringed copyright on Lotus 1–2–3. Borland lost but appealed against the decision. The appeal judge ruled for Borland saying that the menu system of a software package was a means of operating the package and, as such, could not be protected by copyright. This decision overturned the precedent set by the earlier decision in *Lotus* v. *Paperback*.

In the early 1990s there was enormous confusion in the United States over whether program interfaces could be protected by copyright. Courts gave contradictory rulings and lawyers often had trouble following the reasoning. Now, it seems that the situation has clarified and that American courts are averse to allowing software vendors to protect interfaces using copyright legislation.

Figure 6.3. *American 'look and feel' cases*

that the degree of similarity would be the most important factor in such a case. A program which presented an identical interface would certainly be in breach of copyright; one which had a similar style of interface but which was nevertheless quite distinct probably would not.

6.4 Summary

In this chapter we have discussed a range of intellectual property rights. The implications of these for computing can be seen by envisaging how they might apply to a computer sitting in an office, as follows.

- The operation of particular circuits, cards, or devices within the machine may be covered by patents and the layout or shape of internal components by design rights. The designs of the semiconductor chips themselves will also be covered by specific semiconductor design rights. Of course, some of the patents or design rights may well have expired.
- Parts of the external design of the computer, a distinctive keyboard for instance, may be registered designs which cannot be used by other manufacturers (at least not without a licence to do so).
- Various names and logos which appear on the computer, its peripherals, or software may be registered marks protected by trademark law.
- The software and data stored on the computer will be covered by copyright legislation. The user or owner of the computer will almost certainly not own the copyright of much of the software installed but will be using it under licence from a software supplier.
- Much of the data, and possibly software, on the computer may be covered by the law of confidence. This would certainly be the case if the computer was sitting in a company's office and contained copies of business plans or sales data, for instance. Some of the data may also be affected by data protection legislation, to be discussed in Chapter 8.

These last two areas, confidence and copyright, are particularly relevant to software developers and were discussed in greater detail.

The law of confidence is the main mechanism available for protecting business ideas, unpatented inventions or other sensitive information. For this law to apply, care must be taken to ensure that the necessary criteria are met. These are that the information is confidential and that it is only disclosed in circumstances which make its confidentiality obvious. Anyone who is given information in such circumstances is then under an obligation not to divulge it to a third party if to do so would damage the originator of the information. An employee may also have further obligations which are specifically imposed by a contract of employment.

Copyright protects material from being copied; it does not protect ideas or inventions but does protect the form in which they are expressed. Copyright is the principal way in which software is protected; the protection it provides covers both direct copying and modification or translation of software. Since similarities in programs may be construed by the courts as evidence of copying, software developers who work on similar products for different employers may need to be careful to ensure that they do not become embroiled in a copyright dispute.

Further reading

Comprehensive texts on intellectual property law include those by Cornish (1996) and by Bainbridge (1994). These texts, both called *Intellectual Property*, are primarily intended for law students and cover much material which is not relevant to computing. There are some textbooks which deal specifically with legal issues for computing, *Computer Law*, by Bainbridge is designed to be accessible to non-lawyers. The collection of articles edited by Reed, *Computer Law* (1996), contains interesting discussions of issues such as the patentability of programs. This book, because it focuses on areas where the law is in a state of flux, contains good examples of how subtle distinctions may be drawn by judges when deciding cases.

Points to consider

1 Copyright protection for software lasts for 70 years from its author's death. Is this too long? Would not a shorter period (5 or 10 years, say) be more appropriate given the pace of progress and also overcome many of the criticisms made by Stallman and others?
2 In practice it becomes impossible for authors of widely performed works to negotiate a licence with every individual who might wish to perform the work. This has led to the existence of **collecting societies**. One well-known collecting society is the Performing Rights Society, which charges a fee to proprietors of shops and other public places who play recorded music on their premises. The collecting society then redistributes these fees to the owners of the copyright and makes a charge for the service it provides.

  Could a similar scheme be made to operate with the Internet?
3 The Copyright (Computer Programs) Regulations allow a user of a program to alter it to correct errors. Does this permitted act have any value when suppliers do not normally supply source code? Is this an area where the law could reasonably be changed, for example to oblige software vendors to supply-source code?
4 As stated in the chapter, the author of a computer-generated work is considered to be the person or organization which operates the computer on which the work is generated.

  Suppose a software house markets a program to generate abstract images, such as Mandelbrot sets and others. The images are generated by the user supplying a few parameters which automatically determine the image produced.

  If the program becomes widely used what kinds of problems might arise when people sue for copyright infringement? Would the situation be different if there was a small (or large) random element in the images generated?

CHAPTER 7

Software contracts and liability

What recourse does a company have when it subcontracts the development of a large application system to a software house and the software later turns out to contain serious errors? How bad do the errors have to be for the company to be able to sue its supplier? What happens if someone is injured as a result of an error in software, for example if the arm of a computer-controlled industrial robot suddenly swings and injures a worker as a result of an error in the control program?

Overview

This chapter is primarily concerned with the legal issues surrounding responsibility for the quality and correctness of software. Probably the bulk of software in operation is developed by software houses, either in specific development projects or as part of generic packages. In order to consider the issues surrounding liability for incorrect software we must first look at the kinds of agreements which cover the development or purchase of software. Such agreements are covered by the law of contract, an extensive area of the law which determines whether contracts (or parts of them) are valid, what happens when a party to a contract fails to meet its obligations, the conditions for terminating a contract, and so on. In passing we also consider the implications of copyright law for such contracts.

We then look at the liability which developers have for the software which they produce. Such liability results primarily from the contractual terms themselves and (where only monetary loss is concerned) from the law of negligent misstatement. Where physical injury results, several areas of law become relevant, including consumer protection law and health and safety legislation. Of course, many software suppliers seek to limit their liability for errors in the software they supply by including so-called exclusion clauses in contracts. But the law restricts the use of such clauses and we look at some recent cases where suppliers failed to limit their liability. We also consider some of the legal implications of software faults as a result of the year 2000 problem.

Relation to other chapters Copyright law was discussed in the previous chapter and its implications for software contracts are considered below. Similarly, the problems of faulty software were covered in Chapter 1, and in this chapter the legal position is considered (in particular with respect to the year 2000 problem). Issues of liability also provide reasons for membership of professional societies, described in Chapter 11.

7.1 Contracts

A contract is basically an agreement which is enforceable by law. It sets out the aims of the parties to the agreement, their obligations and responsibilities, what happens if problems arise, and the criteria for determining whether the agreement has been fulfilled. In practice it is difficult when drafting a contract to foresee every eventuality, and disputes often arise over issues that a contract does not explicitly address. The law of contract provides a legal framework within which contracts can be interpreted; it both limits the kinds of contracts which can be made and supplements incomplete contracts with what are effectively default conditions.

We look at how contracts are made and interpreted before considering the kind of contract which may be used when a software house undertakes to develop software for a client. In particular we look at the ways in which intellectual property rights and disputes over breach of contract are handled. Finally we briefly review some issues which arise in contracts for freelance computer personnel and off-the-shelf software licences. Issues relating to liability for faulty software are discussed in the next section.

Overview of contract law

Contracts are agreements made orally or in writing between two parties, which can be enforced by law. Not every agreement gives rise to a contract, however; if John, say, agrees to meet his friend Bill in the pub after work, then John and Bill have not entered into a contract. On the other hand, if John offers to sell his old Ford Escort to Bill for £500, and Bill agrees, then they have. The fundamental criteria for an agreement to constitute a valid legal contract are as follows:

- There must be an agreement between two parties; more precisely this means that there must have been an offer (e.g. *'I'll let you have the Escort for £500'*). and an acceptance (e.g. *'OK, done'*).
- There must be **valuable consideration**, in other words some benefit, right or profit for one party or some action or loss of benefit or money for the other party. Most commonly the consideration will comprise payment by one party (e.g. £500 from Bill) for goods, rights, or services from the other party (e.g. a Ford Escort from John).

- There must be an intention to create legal relations. Thus when John and Bill agree to meet at the pub, even if John agrees to give Bill a lift home in return for a pint (consideration), they have not made a contract since there is no intention to create legal relations. But with the sale of a car there is (both parties might have recourse to the law if the other did not fulfil its part of the bargain, if John never gets paid or the engine falls out of the car the first time Bill drives it, for example).

However, not every contract is valid even if it does meet these criteria. Some contracts, such as a contract to commit a crime, are illegal. Others may be invalid because one of the parties did not have the capacity to enter into the contract: minors, for instance, cannot enter into trading contracts.

Even where contracts are legal and valid the law extends and constrains them in two main ways: first it provides a framework for inferring contractual responsibilities where the contract is incomplete or unclear and, second, it restricts the clauses and terms that can appear in the contract. Some of these constraints are general but others vary according to the substance of the contract and the parties involved. Thus contracts for selling goods are governed by the Sale of Goods Act 1979 (as amended by the Sale and Supply of Goods Act 1994), contracts for a service of some kind by the Supply of Goods and Services Act 1982, and employment contracts by a range of separate Acts. Consequently the nature of a contract is important since it affects the rights of its parties. But it is not always clear what kind of contract has been entered into. For example, when a computer manufacturer agrees to implement an accounting system, say, in which it undertakes to supply hardware and to develop software, it may not be clear whether the contract is one for the sale of goods or the provision of services.

In principle a contract should give as precise a definition as possible of the obligations and undertakings of the parties. Thus a contract for the development of software will specify the system to be developed, the deliverables, the timescale, the payments to be made and so forth. But it is difficult to foresee every eventuality. For example, what happens if the computer resources provided by the client are insufficient to support the development work? The software house may feel it is the client's responsibility to provide additional computer resources but the client might be unwilling to do this. Such unforeseen circumstances, which are not covered in the contractual agreement, can easily lead to a dispute. When this happens the court will rely on the following sources to interpret the contract:

1 **The contract itself** The first reference point will be the terms in the agreement made between the parties (in so far as these do not conflict with any legal restrictions on contracts).
2 **Inducements** The statements made by the parties to the contract when they were negotiating (known as inducements or representations) provide a further source of guidance. If one or other of the contract parties has

made false statements during the negotiations the other party may be able to sue for damages under the Misrepresentation Act 1967.

3 **Implied terms** Where a particular issue, such as what to do in the event of late delivery, has not been considered by the parties then the court will 'imply terms' – this means that the court will determine what the contract should have specified on the issue. There are two sources which a court may use to imply such contractual obligations, these are:

- the normal practice in the trade or area concerned, and
- specific contract law. The particular legislation used will depend both on the object of the contract and the parties involved. Thus if the contract involves selling goods, the relevant legislation will be the Sale of Goods Act 1979 (as amended by Sale and Supply of Goods Act 1994) and this in turn will be interpreted in different ways according to whether the sale was from a retailer to a member of the public or a sale between two businesses.

Consequently contracts do not exist in isolation but must be understood and interpreted within the framework of contract law. Furthermore many transactions which people do not normally think of as being contractual, such as bidding at an auction or having a haircut, are in fact governed by contract law, and should any dispute arise the law defines what are effectively standard terms and conditions for such transactions.

Besides supplying terms to a contract which is incomplete, the law may also invalidate terms or clauses. This is particularly the case for so-called **exclusion clauses** where a party limits its liability should it be unable to fully discharge its obligations under the contract. We discuss this issue in the next section; in the rest of this section we look at the kind of contracts which are relevant for software development and briefly look at some issues relating to freelance programmers and package licences.

Contracts for software development

It is common for large organizations to sub-contract the design and implementation of software to external developers, such as software houses. The contracts for such projects will be long and complex, making explicit the obligations of both parties. The general structure of such a contract is shown in Figure 7.1. We will not discuss such contracts in detail but will look at just two aspects: the copyright issues, and what happens if a dispute arises because one or other party fails to meet its obligations under the contract.

Copyright issues

There are two main copyright issues which must be dealt with in the contract: first who owns the copyright in the completed software and, second, what happens if the software written actually infringes someone else's copyright.

The contract will probably have three main parts. The first will be a short introduction which names the parties to the contract, possibly defines certain expressions used (e.g. 'the client', 'the project', and so on) and specifies the contents of the rest of the contract. The second part will comprise a set of standard terms and conditions which would probably be used by the software house in all its projects. Structuring contracts in this way obviates the need to write a completely new contract (a lengthy undertaking) for each project. Among the standard terms might be clauses relating to:

Scope of work. Description of the work to be carried out (e.g. develop software).

Client's responsibilities. Definition of what the client needs to do or provide.

Project control. Specification of regular progress meetings and the appointment of project managers by both parties.

Warranty and maintenance. Description of service to be provided after delivery of the software.

Change procedures. Procedures to be followed if the client wishes to alter the requirements for the software to be developed.

Ownership of copyright. Assignment or licensing arrangements for the software produced.

Confidentiality. Description of responsibilities of each party not to disclose any confidential information about the other party.

Indemnity. Protection for the client against copyright infringements by the software house.

Termination criteria. Criteria which enable either party to bring the contract to an end.

Arbitration procedures. Procedures to be followed in the event of a dispute.

This list is not exhaustive. There will be further terms specifying such matters as the legal jurisdiction in which the contract is made, and what will happen in the event of either side going bankrupt or being taken over.

The third part of the contract will be a set of annexes or appendices which define the specific project to be carried out and which are referred to in the second part. For example, the requirements specification will appear as a separate appendix which will be referred to in the scope of work. Among the other appendices will be:

- the definition of deliverables
- acceptance criteria for the deliverables
- the delivery schedule
- the price and payment schedule, possibly also specifying extra payments for delays caused by the client
- names of the nominated project managers

and so forth. This part of the contract is likely to be by far the largest since it contains the specific details of the work to be carried out.

Figure 7.1. *Structure of contract for a bespoke development by a software house*

Where ownership of the copyright is concerned, there are two possibilities. First the contract could specify that the copyright in the software will be assigned to the commissioning organization once the software is completed.[1] The alternative is for the software house to agree to licence the software, retaining the copyright itself.

Assignment is probably the more common approach when a system is developed specifically to meet the requirements of a single commissioning organization. But there are problems with assignment:

- The supplier will probably charge more for the development since it cannot reuse the software in later projects or as the basis for a product.
- The client may wish to retain the services of the software house to maintain and enhance the software after it has been put into service. For this to be possible it will have to licence the software back to the software house so that it can be modified and enhanced without infringing copyright.

Assignment is thus most likely to be adopted when the commissioning organization intends to take over the maintenance of the software once it has been developed.

The other possibility is that the software is licensed to the client once it has been completed. This option is most likely when the software is based on a package which the software company markets and which it is customizing for the client. There is a risk for the software purchaser in this scenario: what if the software supplier goes out of business?

Failure of the software house would leave the purchaser in a very awkward position since it would almost certainly not have the source code of the customized package. The normal way of guarding against this danger is to insist that once the software is completed it be put into **escrow**. This means that a third party will keep a copy of all the code and documentation and release these to the client in certain, clearly defined circumstances. One such circumstance would be if the software house goes bankrupt and ceases to trade; another might be if the software house is taken over by a competitor. Of course, there also have to be provisions to ensure that all subsequent modifications made to the package are likewise put into escrow.

The other issue to be dealt with is the possibility of the software supplier or one of its staff infringing the copyright of a third party. For example, what happens if one of the programmers working for the software house incorporates code into the system which was illegally copied from a former employer? This could be disastrous for the client since the original copyright owner might not agree to the client continuing to use the software, or might demand an unreasonable fee for a licence.

---

1 It is quite possible to agree to assign the copyright in a work which has not yet been completed.

The normal way for the client to guard against such problems is to insist that the contract include an **indemnity clause**. Such a clause protects one party in a contract from the faults of the other. In this case it would state that if the client does incur extra expense due to a copyright infringement, then this cost will be borne by the software house.

Disputes

It is quite common for disputes to arise during software development projects. These may result from relatively small problems, like a deliverable being handed over a few days late, to major disasters, such as the delivered software being completely unusable. What options are available to either side if the other fails to meet its contractual obligations?

If one party fails in its contractual obligations the other may either wish to terminate the contract altogether or simply to obtain some compensation for the resulting expense or inconvenience. Contract law makes a distinction between two kinds of term in a contract which are known as **conditions** and **warranties**.[2] Conditions are contractual terms whose breach by one party gives the other party the right to cancel the contract and sue for damages. Conditions therefore represent the most important aspects of an agreement; completion of the work and delivery dates often have the status of conditions. Thus in *The Salvage Association* v. *CAP Financial Services* (Figure 7.2) the judge ruled that

---

The Salvage Association wanted to computerize its accounting system and awarded a contract to the software house CAP to do this. The software was developed in ORACLE but when user-training began it became clear that it contained many errors. A revised completion date was agreed but CAP failed to meet this. Consequently the Salvage Association rejected all the software and sued for the return of the money it had paid as well as for damages for wasted time. In defence, CAP cited an exclusion clause in the contract which limited its liability.

The judge ruled that the Salvage Association was justified in completely rejecting the software and ending the contract. The Salvage Association recovered the money it had paid out and was further awarded damages to cover the extra expenditure that it had incurred due to time wasted.

This case is important since the judge ruled that the contract was one for the Supply of Goods and Services and that the exclusion clause was unreasonable according to the Unfair Contract Terms Act 1977.

Figure 7.2. *The Salvage Association* v. *CAP Financial Services Ltd* (1995)

---

2 The word warranty has a technical meaning in this context which is distinct from the everyday use of the word.

the client was justified in ending the contract when the supplier twice failed to meet a completion date.

Warranties, on the other hand, are contractual terms whose breach by one party does not justify the termination of a contract by the other party, but is a sufficient reason for the other party to claim damages.

One important point about damages is that the party claiming damages must have taken measures to minimize the loss consequent from the other party's breach of contract. For example, if someone hires a plumber to come and install a radiator and the radiator starts leaking several days later, it is not acceptable for the householder to let the house become completely flooded before claiming damages. But it would be reasonable to claim damages for the cost of getting another plumber to come and repair the leak.

Often it is not clear whether contractual terms have the status of conditions or warranties. For example, a contractual term for a database system may specify that the time taken to process a query should never exceed 2 seconds. Is this a condition or a warranty? If the supplier implements a database in which the response time for queries is frequently more than 5 seconds even when the system is not heavily loaded, then the term can be treated as a condition and it would be reasonable for the client to cancel the contract. If, on the other hand, the occasional query takes slightly more than 2 seconds to process when the system is very heavily loaded, then the term appears more like a warranty. Such terms, whose exact status depends on circumstances, are known legally as **innominate terms**.

Obviously disputes can easily arise over the significance of particular innominate terms or issues where the contract is not clear. If the contracting parties are not able to reach an agreement one obvious course is to resort to legal proceedings. In practice, though, many companies are reluctant to use the courts to resolve disputes unless relations have broken down completely. There are several reasons for this: the outcome of court proceedings is uncertain, the process is lengthy and expensive, and, importantly, companies usually want to maintain a reasonable working relationship, and this is difficult in the wake of a court case.

Consequently many companies prefer to resolve disputes between themselves or, failing that, go to arbitration. This involves the appointment of an independent arbitrator who will listen to both parties' versions of events and make a decision on the basis of this and other evidence. The arbitrator will not normally be a legal expert (though his or her decisions must be consistent with the law) but will have a considerable expertise in the relevant technical field, computing say. Thus an arbitrator is likely to have a better grasp of the practical, if not the legal, issues in the dispute. Arbitration is usually quicker and cheaper than going to the courts and has the further advantage of being private – getting involved in a public dispute rarely does any good to the reputation of either party. Many contracts consequently contain explicit provisions for arbitration in the event of a dispute; an arbitrator may be appointed by agreement or by an independent third party such as the President of the British Computer Society.

Freelance contractors

Freelance contractors, effectively one-person companies who hire themselves out to do programming or other work, are a prominent feature of the modern computer industry. Since contractors are often brought in to help with a project which is behind schedule it is not uncommon for them to start work without a formal contract having been agreed. In such a situation who owns the copyright in any software that the contractor writes? The legal position here is clear; the contractor is not an employee, so he or she will own the copyright. Consequently many organizations who hire contractors insist on a written contract which assigns copyright in the work to be carried out to the organization.

Package licences

When someone buys an off-the-shelf software package, such as a PC spreadsheet, they are actually purchasing two things at once: the physical goods (such as documentation and disks) and a standard non-exclusive licence (see Section 6.3) enabling them to use the software without infringing copyright. Typically such a licence allows the holder to copy the software in order to install and run it, but disclaims any liability for loss consequent from its use. Such conditions would probably not be acceptable for ordinary consumer goods; the software producer is not undertaking to correct errors or to guarantee the functionality of the software.

As outlined earlier, for a contract to exist between two parties there must be an offer and acceptance. Since the buyer does not formally accept the terms at the time of purchase, do such licence agreements have the status of contracts? The answer is that provided the licence terms are available to the buyer at the time of purchase, they have force. If in contrast they are hidden away at the back of the accompanying documentation, then they do not, since such a practice would be tantamount to imposing contractual conditions retro-spectively, which is not allowed in English law. Software suppliers try to get round this problem by including the licence agreement on the box (so called shrinkwrap licences) or printed on a sealed envelope containing the disks with a note promising a refund if the package is returned unopened.

7.2 Liability for faulty software

Liability for faulty software can derive from a contract or from the law of negligence (in particular, negligent misstatement). Where injury or death results from a software error then, depending on the circumstances, other areas of the law such as consumer protection or health and safety may become relevant. We discuss these various sources of liability separately before considering exclusion clauses and the restrictions which the law places on their use. Finally we shall consider what liability software and hardware vendors may have for year 2000-related faults.

Contractual sources of liability

If a company, C, purchases some software from a software house, S, then C's right to a refund or damages should the software contain bugs or be unusable will depend on the kind of contract the two parties are considered to have entered into. Has S supplied C with goods or with a service? This is important since the laws governing contracts for the two kinds of sale are different:

- **The Sale and Supply of Goods Act (1994)** (which amended the 1979 Sale of Goods Act) specifies that goods should be fit for the purpose for which they are sold and must be of satisfactory quality. It is not a defence for the manufacturer to claim that reasonable care was taken in their design or production.
- **The Supply of Goods and Services Act (1982)** specifies that services must be carried out with reasonable skill and care.

The term 'goods' as defined in the Sale of Goods 1979 Act really means physical goods. Consequently the purchase of floppy disks or a computer will be covered by the subsequent 1994 Act; software on its own will not. The development of software on behalf of a client will be covered by the 1982 Act.

This difference is important since the 1982 Act requires only that work be carried out with reasonable skill and care. This criterion is vague and, furthermore, there are few standard practices in software development against which a developer's level of care could be gauged. Since it is generally acknowledged to be extremely difficult to produce error-free software, the criterion of reasonable care gives little protection to a client against errors in delivered software.

Thus it would seem that the client in a software development contract is well advised to include as detailed requirements and acceptance criteria as possible. Express contractual terms will probably give better protection than the 1982 Act. Of course, in *The Salvage Association* v. *CAP* (Figure 7.2) the 1982 Act was held to apply and the client won compensation, but this was awarded for repeated failure to meet a deadline rather than for faulty software as such. In the *St Albans* v. *ICL* case (Figure 7.4) the contract was classified as being a sale of goods and the client received damages for faulty software but in this case the software was supplied in conjunction with hardware.

As far as off-the-shelf packages are concerned the situation is not absolutely clear. The disks and manuals would certainly be treated as goods and the purchaser could get his or her money back if there were missing pages in the manuals or the disks were faulty. What would happen if there was an error in the software would depend on what claims the developer had made for the software and how the courts construed the sale. The *St Albans* v. *ICL* case (Figure 7.4) gives reason to think that it might be treated as a sale of goods and so the software would need to be of 'satisfactory quality'. Until there have been more test cases it is not possible to be sure how the courts will treat various software development or licence contracts.

Negligence

In English law only the parties to a contract can sue for breach of contract. This principle (known as **privity of contract**) means that if A and B have a contract yet another party, C, is harmed by A's breach of one of the contractual terms that C cannot bring an action for breach of contract against A.

The law of negligence gives people a mechanism for obtaining redress from someone whose carelessness has caused damage or injury but with whom they have no contractual relationship. Thus if Sarah, say, is walking along the road and a vase of flowers falls off the window ledge of a flat and injures her, she can use the law of negligence to claim damages from the occupier.

The landmark case in the law of negligence is *Donoghue* v. *Stevenson* (Figure 7.3) where manufacturers were successfully sued for negligently producing a contaminated bottle of ginger beer.[3] An important point in this case is that Donoghue could not have sued the manufacturers for breach of contract since she had no contract with them, the beer having been bought by her friend.

The criteria which must be met for it to be possible to sue for damages due to negligence are as follows:

- A **duty of care** must exist. Such a duty exists when an individual can reasonably foresee that his or her acts may injure someone.

Donoghue's friend bought a bottle of ginger beer and gave it to her. Donoghue poured some out and drank it but when she refilled her glass the remains of a decomposed snail came out. The bottle was of dark glass so the snail had not been visible till then. Donoghue suffered illness as a result and sued the manufacturers for damages.

The case eventually came before the House of Lords who ruled in favour of Donoghue. The manufacturers were held to have a 'duty of care' to anyone whom they could reasonably foresee might be hurt by their negligence.

Figure 7.3. *Donoghue* v. *Stevenson* (1932)

---

3 This would nowadays be covered by the Consumer Protection Act.

This case was brought by a local council responsible for collecting the community charge, a local tax. The council awarded a contract to International Computers Ltd (ICL) to supply hardware and software to maintain a register of eligible charge payers, calculate charges, produce bills and so forth.

The software delivered contained an error which resulted in the chargeable population being incorrectly calculated and as a consequence the charge was set too low. The resulting loss of revenue was over £1 million.

The council sued for damages but ICL claimed it was not liable due to a clause in the contract which limited its liability for defects to £100 000. The judge ruled that this exclusion of liability was not reasonable according to the Unfair Contract Terms Act 1977 and awarded the council the full damages which it claimed.

This decision was upheld later on appeal (though the damages awarded were reduced) at which it was also ruled that the contract was one for goods under the Sale of Goods Act 1979.

Figure 7.4. *St Albans City and District Council v. International Computers Limited* (1995)

- There must have been a breach of that duty; normally the onus is on the person bringing the action to prove that the defendant was negligent.
- There must be resulting damage or injury to the person who brings the action.

These criteria might well be satisfied, for instance, if a patient was injured by a radiation-therapy machine which administered an incorrect dose because of an error in the controlling software. The patient would probably be able to sue the manufacturers of the machine for negligence, but would need to show that the software was written without due care.[4] This would raise the issue of how to assess the care with which software has been developed. The precedent which comes from other professions is that the developers should have exercised a level of care and expertise that could reasonably be expected from a professional in their area. Of course, what is reasonable is hard to determine in the area of software engineering. It seems likely that the adherence (or not) to appropriate standards and the codes of practice of a relevant professional body (such as the British Computer Society) are factors which would be taken into account.

---

4 The patient would be more likely to sue the hospital; an action against the manufacturer would be better carried out by the hospital through its contract for the purchase of the equipment.

English law has been more reluctant to provide redress for negligence where the loss has been purely financial. The reason often given for this is that it would result in excessive litigation. So, while the criteria outlined above are sufficient if there has been injury or physical damage, they are insufficient where the loss is purely financial (as would most often be the case with faulty software). Here the litigant must rely on proving a particular form of negligence known as **negligent misstatement** – this is effectively a special area of negligence law concerned with cases where professional advice or work has been wrong or badly performed. The particular feature of negligent misstatement is that more stringent criteria are applied to establish the duty of care, as follows:

- the resulting loss or damages must be foreseeable
- there must be a relationship between the parties (for example, one is the client of the other), and
- it must be reasonable to impose such a duty of care.

The effect of these criteria is to make the likelihood of a successful action for negligence where someone had suffered loss due to faulty software quite remote. Where the error causing loss occurred in an off-the-shelf package there would not be a sufficiently strong relationship between the user and the software developer. Such a relationship would exist where a one-off development or customization was involved, but such a project would almost certainly be covered by a contract and liability would be determined through the express and implied terms of that contract.

Consumer Protection Act

The Consumer Protection Act 1987 gives a consumer the right to claim compensation for injury or damage caused by a faulty product. This is regardless of whether they have a contractual relationship with the producer and without the need to satisfy the criteria for an action in negligence. So if, for example, someone receives a laser printer as a present and gets an electric shock when changing the ink cartridge, they will probably be able to use the Act to obtain compensation from the manufacturer.

Such protection will probably extend to software errors where the software is embedded in products which are computer-controlled. Thus someone who bought a new car with a computer-controlled brake system and had an accident resulting from an error in the brake-control software would probably be able to obtain compensation. But the Act does allow manufacturers to use the defence that they cannot be held liable for designs or products which reflect the 'state of the art'. Given that ordinary servo-assisted brakes work reliably, it might be hard to apply such a defence to brake faults caused by a software-control system.

At present, under English law, it seems unlikely that the Consumer Protection Act could be used where someone had incurred injury or loss from the use of purchased software alone. Nevertheless, software engineers need to be aware of the possibility that such a claim might be brought.

Health and safety

The Health and Safety at Work Act 1974 places a general responsibility on both employers and employees for health and safety precautions in the workplace. Most of the specific responsibilities, however, such as the provision and maintenance of safe plant and safe systems of work, fall to the employers. Nevertheless, both employers and individual employees can be prosecuted under the Act. Since the Act forms part of the criminal code the infringement of its provisions is a criminal offence. Individuals who have suffered loss or injury due to unsafe working environments or practices can also use the law to bring a civil action for damages.

One important provision of the Act is that it places a duty on designers and manufacturers to ensure that equipment and other items which they design or supply are safe. In particular, this applies to the design and construction of the equipment to be used in a place of work, whose users must be supplied with sufficient information to ensure that the equipment is properly used and maintained.

These provisions have obvious implications for software engineers, especially those involved in developing safety-critical control software for machinery or industrial processes. Thus if a worker or member of the public is injured as a result of an error in the software of a computer-controlled machine, the software developers may be liable for prosecution if they are unable to demonstrate having taken sufficient care in its design and development.

Exclusion clauses

Suppliers often try to limit their liability for losses resulting from their own breaches of contract by including special clauses in the contract. Such exclusion clauses may completely exclude their liability for certain breaches (for delays resulting from strike action, for instance) or limit their liability to a maximum amount.

Contract law restricts the use or applicability of exclusion clauses. For example, no supplier can exclude liability for personal injury or death. Other kinds of exclusion clause may be invalid because of the relevant contract law or because of the Unfair Contract Terms Act 1977. This Act classifies any clause in a contract which reduces a supplier's liability to less than it would have been according to implied terms to be an exclusion clause. It allows such clauses only to the extent that they are considered by the courts to be reasonable.

At first there was some doubt as to whether the Act would apply to software contracts but cases such as *The Salvage Association* v. *CAP* (Figure 7.2) and *St*

Albans v. *ICL* (Figure 7.4) have demonstrated that the courts will apply the legislation to software. In both these cases the defendants had sought to limit their liability with exclusion clauses and in both cases the exclusions were ruled to be unreasonable. A major factor which the courts seem to take into account when determining reasonableness is whether the defendants were insured against liability claims and whether it would be easier for them to obtain such insurance than their clients.

Liability for year 2000 problems

At the time of writing it seems highly probable that there will be at least some problems at the end of the century with software which is not able to process dates properly. If the software was supplied by a software house, who will be liable in law for any resulting losses?

The answer to this question will probably depend on when the software was developed and the contractual terms under which it was purchased. Normally, actions for breach of contract must be brought within 6 years of the breach occurring so for software supplied a long time ago there is unlikely to be any prospect of obtaining damages from the supplier.

For recently supplied software, the year 2000 problem has become so well known and the chances of the software needing to process dates beyond the end of the century are so high that were it not able to do this, the purchaser would almost certainly be able to obtain damages. Much of this software will, in any event, be under warranty at the turn of the century. In this case it will probably fall to the supplier to correct any errors in date processing.

The more complex scenario is where software was supplied a few or more years ago. If the ability to process dates after the end of 1999 was explicitly mentioned in the contract or if this could be implied, the supplier would be liable for any shortcomings. If there were precise requirements specifications and acceptance criteria which did not mention such a facility, then the supplier would probably not be liable. Of course, there is a grey area of development projects which were not carried out so long ago that year 2000 compliance was obviously not a requirement nor so recently that it obviously was. For such borderline cases there is a high chance of litigation.

A separate legal issue arises from the Data Protection Act (to be discussed in the next chapter). Under the terms of this Act, companies who hold and process data relating to individuals are (with some exceptions) responsible for keeping that data up-to-date and accurate. If personal data is corrupted as a result of year 2000 software errors then companies would be in breach of data protection law. In the first instance infringing organizations would receive an enforcement notice asking them to rectify the problem, but if they were not able to do this within a reasonable time, they could become liable to criminal prosecution.

7.3 Summary

In this chapter we have considered some of the contractual and liability issues which arise from software development.

A contract is essentially a formalized legal agreement between two parties. Such agreements are complicated by the terms which the law implicitly adds and the restrictions it imposes on what they may contain. The legal framework which surrounds each contract varies according to its type (e.g. for the sale of goods, or the provision of services) and the parties involved (e.g. sale between businesses or to a consumer). Most contracts for software development will be viewed as service contracts but the status of package software is less certain.

Liability for faulty software is an extremely complex issue and it is an area of the law where there is much uncertainty. Where there is a contract between two parties then the liability of a supplier for faulty software will be determined by the contract and contract law in general. Software suppliers have, in the past, sought to limit their liability for software errors through exclusion clauses but recent cases suggest that this approach does not find favour with the courts.

Where there is no direct contract between parties then a claim for damages to compensate for purely economic loss is unlikely to be successful. Where safety-critical software and personal injury are concerned there are several laws which may apply. For consumer goods the Consumer Protection Act and for injuries at work the Health and Safety at Work Act may both provide a mechanism to claim damages. These laws relate to specific areas and have the advantage, for the plaintiff, that there is no requirement to establish negligence, only to demonstrate that a piece of machinery was faulty and that it caused injury or damage. For circumstances where these laws cannot be used the general law of negligence may still provide a means of obtaining compensation, but here the plaintiff will need to be able to demonstrate that the defendant was negligent in some way.

For software engineers the possibility of being held liable for faulty software, especially where safety-critical software is concerned, underlines the need to adopt and adhere to appropriate professional standards and codes of practice.

Further reading

The introduction to English law by Keenan (1995) contains much general background on contracts and negligence. *Computer Contracts* by Morgan and Stedman is a general introduction which contains many examples which give a good idea of what computer contracts look like. Two books which deal with these issues specifically from a computing perspective are *Introduction to Computer Law* by Bainbridge (1996) and the collection of articles edited by Reed, *Computer Law* (1996).

Points to consider

1 The publishers of a multimedia CD on, for example, a well-known film producer may use material from many sources – film fragments, interviews, background music, copies of articles and reviews, excerpts from biographies and so on.
   Potentially how many different copyrights could be involved? What might happen if, for example, the author of one of the articles included is sued for breach of copyright by another author and the CD has already been distributed?
2 Software engineers who work on the design and development of safety-critical software may ultimately be held liable for its failure, both collectively and individually.
   What working practices and measures are appropriate to avoid such an eventuality? Is the desire to avoid being held legally responsible for faulty software likely to help or hinder the development of safe software?
3 What might be involved in proving that developers of safety-critical software which had faults had been negligent?
4 Some areas of the law, such as the Consumer Protection Act, allow a defendant to argue that a particular product which caused damage or injury represents the state of the art. Is this a reasonable defence? Were this defence applied to software systems, would it be possible to avoid liability for any injury resulting from faulty software on the grounds that current standard practice does not result in error-free software?

CHAPTER 8

Privacy and the Data Protection Act

What happens if your application for a credit card is turned down one day, even though you have never had a debt in your life? Can you find out what credit reference agencies hold information on you? Can you get them to change it? Can you prevent certain kinds of information being kept about you or being passed on?

Overview

This chapter is concerned with the law which regulates the processing of personal information on computers. The main piece of legislation which is relevant here is the Data Protection Act 1984. This Act was passed after a long period during which concerns had been expressed about the processing of personal information on computers. The final impetus for the legislation came from a Council of Europe agreement on data protection.

We first consider the background to the Data Protection Act and the reasons why it was eventually passed. We then look at the Act itself and what safeguards it provides against the misuse of computer-based personal information. Finally we shall consider some of the weaknesses of the legislation which have been commented on by its many critics and look at the ways in which the legislation may be changed in the future.

Relation to other chapters This chapter is largely concerned with the legal response to some of the privacy problems arising from data processing which were identified in Chapter 2.

8.1 Background to the Data Protection Act 1984

In the United Kingdom concern about the way computer databases could compromise the privacy of individuals goes back to the 1960s. Privacy in this context can be taken to mean people's rights to control what information is held or passed on about them. The concern was prompted by the development of computer technology and the potential it provides for compiling and storing personal data. Moreover, since there is no constitutional right to privacy in

Britain, there were few restrictions on how personal information might be processed.

As a consequence a Right to Privacy Bill was proposed in 1967 but it did not pass into law. A few years later, a second proposal led to a Royal Commission being set up, the Younger Commission on Privacy. The terms of reference of this Commission were limited to considering the uses of data by private individuals or organizations. This meant that the storage and use of data by government or public sector agencies, seen by many people then and now as the main threat to privacy, were explicitly excluded. Nevertheless, a survey of the general public carried out by the Commission showed that the possibility of creating a centralized computer databank, holding everything known on individuals, was generally viewed with deep misgivings.[1] The Commission reported in 1972 and highlighted three areas of concern about the potential use of computers, as follows:

● compiling personal profiles
● data matching (that is, combining information from different sources) and
● the dangers of unauthorized access to personal or confidential information.

The Commission concluded that computers did not, at the time, pose a threat to privacy but that their use could do so in the future. It proposed a set of ten principles which should be adhered to when computers were used to process personal information. Among these were that data should be held for particular purposes, only used for those purposes, not be kept longer than necessary, and that people should be able to find out what information was held on them.

The reaction of the Home Office, the government department which would be responsible for proposing any privacy legislation, was to announce that a consultation exercise would be undertaken. However, a change of government led to the publication of a White Paper on the issue and the setting up of a 'Data Protection Committee' (known as the Lindop Committee after its eventual chairman) to study how to set up a 'Data Protection Authority'. This Committee published its report and recommendations for legislation in 1978. In response the Home Office once again embarked on a consultation exercise involving talking to so-called interested parties. By 1980, there were still no specific proposals for legislation and the Home Office was being publicly criticized for its apparent prevarication over the issue.

It was to be pressure from abroad which finally brought about data protection legislation in the United Kingdom. The United States and many European countries had already enacted data protection laws (Sweden had had such a law since 1973) and in 1980 the Council of Europe, comprising 21 non-Soviet bloc European countries, approved a *'Convention for the Protection of Individuals*

---

1 Reported by Campbell and Connor (1986).

with regard to Automatic Processing of Data'. This Convention, which was signed by the United Kingdom the following year, required each country to implement data protection legislation. More importantly, it also barred signatory nations from exchanging data with those countries where there was inadequate data protection legislation. This restriction on **transborder data flows** raised the possibility of the United Kingdom losing trade, since other countries might not exchange data with it if it had no appropriate legislation.

It was this fear of being excluded from international data processing business which appears to have provided the final impetus for legislation. The Data Protection Act was passed in 1984, though it did not take full effect until 1987, more than 20 years after concerns were first expressed about the issue.

8.2 The Data Protection Act 1984

The introductory rubric to the Data Protection Act 1984 presents it as a measure to regulate the computer processing of data held on individuals. Essentially the Act defines what kind of data it applies to, sets up a register of those processing personal data, specifies a set of principles which should be adhered to in the processing of such data, and creates two new bodies: the **Data Protection Registrar** and the **Data Protection Tribunal**. The Registrar is responsible for promoting data protection and enforcing the Act; the Tribunal is a special court to which organizations or individuals can appeal against decisions made by the Registrar. The Act also specifies a number of exemptions relating to uses of data where no threat to privacy is considered to exist, or where other considerations, such as national security, are believed to take precedence.

The Act is specifically concerned with what it terms **personal data**. This is data consisting of facts or opinions relating to an identifiable living individual and which can be automatically processed by a machine. On this definition, a computer file holding names and addresses of customers is considered to be data. If some of those customers are individuals (as opposed to companies or organizations) then the file contains personal data. The same information held on a card file or jotted down in a notebook would not be personal data, according to the Act, since it would not be machine-processable. Note also that information concerning intentions about individuals is not covered by the Act. Thus a file containing names of employees to be promoted or who will receive a bonus at the end of the year is not considered to be personal information since it relates to intentions.

The Act identifies three kinds of individual or organization to which it relates:

1 **Data subjects** who are individuals on whom personal data is held

2 **Data users** who are organizations or individuals who hold (that is control and make use of) personal data
3 **Computer bureaux** which are organizations or individuals who process or maintain data on behalf of others without having control over its content.

Data subjects are accorded limited rights under the Act to find out whether information is held on them and, in certain circumstances, to get it changed or deleted and possibly to obtain compensation from a data user. The Act also imposes a number of duties and obligations on data users and computer bureaux, who must both register with the Data Protection Registrar; data users in particular must give details of the kind of personal data they hold and the purposes for which they process it. Data users and computer bureaux are also obliged to adhere to a set of 'Data Protection Principles' governing the collection, use, and disclosure of personal data.

Data Protection Principles

The Act specifies eight Data Protection Principles which must be respected by data users holding or processing personal data. These principles are largely based on those outlined in the 1972 Younger Report and are as follows:

1 Personal data must be obtained and processed fairly and lawfully.
  This is one of the most important principles in the Act. The need for data to be obtained fairly has been used to prevent companies selling lists of customer details where those customers were not warned in advance that this would be done (Figure 8.1). Similarly, the requirement for fair processing has been used to control the way in which credit reference agencies assess credit risk (Figure 8.2).
2 Personal data must be held only for the purposes which the data user has declared.
  So if customer details are kept for sending invoices it would not be acceptable to sell that information to other companies (unless that had also been declared as a purpose).
3 Personal data must not be used for purposes other than those which have been declared.
  Thus when a company registers that it is keeping records for personnel administration it cannot use that same data for marketing purposes (unless it has registered that use as well).
4 The personal data kept for a declared purpose must be relevant, adequate, and not excessive in relation to that purpose.
  Consequently an organization should not seek to obtain more information than is needed for the purpose it has declared. Many local authorities, when gathering information about local residents in order to levy taxes,

Innovations was a mail order company which also sold lists of its customers' names and addresses to other companies. It obtained a significant proportion of its revenue from this source.

Innovations' advertising did not specify that customer details would be sold on to other companies. Instead, when customers ordered something from Innovations they would receive an acknowledgement slip. On the back of the slip there was a notice that the company sold address lists to other companies and that the customer could prevent their own details being sold on in this way by writing in.

The Data Protection Registrar served an enforcement notice on the company ordering it to change this practice on the grounds that it infringed the first Data Protection Principle.

Innovations appealed against the notice to the Data Protection Tribunal but the Registrar's notice was upheld; the data was not being obtained fairly since customers were only informed retrospectively of how it might be used and this use would not be obvious to most of them.

Figure 8.1. *Innovations (Mail Order) Ltd* v. *Data Protection Registrar* (1993)

have also sought to collect other information (such as date of birth) which they did not need to assess the tax liability. Such practices are in breach of this fourth principle.

5 Personal data should be accurate and kept up to date (where appropriate). The exception relates to historical data which a user would not be obliged to keep up to date.

6 Personal data must not be kept longer than is necessary for the purpose for which it is held.

Hence data which is no longer needed should be erased.

7 An individual is entitled to find out whether and what data is held on him or her and, where appropriate, to have such data corrected or erased. Organizations can charge a fee of up to £10 for disclosing whether they hold information on an individual. The right to have data erased only applies where the data is being held in contravention of one of the other principles.

8 Appropriate measures must be taken to prevent unauthorized access, or modification of personal data.

This last provision applies to both data users and computer bureaux.

Ensuring that data users and (where appropriate) computer bureaux abide by these principles is the duty of the Data Protection Registrar.

Equifax was a credit reference agency which supplied assessments to clients as to whether particular individuals were a good credit risk. To make its assessment Equifax used not just the details it held on the individual for whom the credit reference was sought but also the details of people who were currently or had previously been at the same address. This approach was used since the statistical probability of someone being a bad debtor was higher if they lived at an address where other bad debtors were or had been resident.

The Data Protection Registrar served an enforcement notice preventing the use of data about other or previous occupants on the grounds that it constituted unfair processing. Someone who moved into an address where a bad debtor had lived could find themselves classed as a poor credit risk for no good reason.

Equifax appealed against this decision but the Tribunal upheld the enforcement notice though it reduced its force by permitting the use of information on other people with similar names at the same address to be used in compiling risk assessments.

Figure 8.2. *Equifax Europe Ltd* v. *Data Protection Registrar*

The Data Protection Registrar

The Data Protection Act creates the role of Data Protection Registrar; the Registrar has a number of powers and duties to enforce and promote the Act.

The initial duty of the Registrar, when the Act came into force, was to establish a public register of data users and computer bureaux. All data users and computer bureaux (except those to whom exemptions apply, as outlined below) must register; non-registration or supplying incorrect registration details are criminal offences punishable by fine. For data users, registration involves declaring what personal data will be held, for what purposes, the sources from which it will be obtained, the address to which data subjects may send requests, to whom it may be disclosed, and to what overseas countries it may be transferred. Registration is simpler for computer bureaux, who need only supply their name and address. The Registrar may refuse registration if the details supplied are insufficient to determine whether the applicant would be complying with the Data Protection Principles. At the time of writing the registration fee is £75 for a 3-year period. The register is publicly available (it can now be accessed over the Internet at the Registrar's Web site). By 1997 about 200 000 data users had registered under the Act (Data Protection Registrar, 1997).

The Registrar is also responsible for promoting good practice and a general awareness of the Act. This involves liaising with bodies representing various industries or professions to help them draft codes of practice which are relevant to their sector. Awareness of the Act is promoted by advertising and publicity campaigns as the Registrar considers appropriate.

Finally the Registrar is charged with ensuring that data users adhere to the Data Protection Principles outlined in the Act; in particular it is the Registrar's responsibility to consider complaints made by data subjects and, if appropriate, to take action against the offender. In order to carry out this enforcement role the Registrar is given certain rights and powers. To investigate alleged breaches the Registrar can apply for a warrant to search premises and, where an offence appears to have been committed, can instigate a prosecution.

The Registrar can also ask data users or computer bureaux who are in breach of one or more of the Data Protection Principles to change their practices to rectify the breach. Where organizations do not cooperate there are three kinds of formal notice that the Registrar can serve:

1 **Enforcement notices** which outline the particular breach which has been made and give the data user or computer bureau a fixed period to correct it.
2 **De-registration notices** which remove the data user's or computer bureau's entry from the register. Such a sanction would only be used where the infringement was particularly serious and an enforcement notice had already been served to no effect.
3 **Transfer prohibition notices** which prevent data being transferred to foreign countries.

Failure to comply with any of these notices is a criminal offence punishable by fine. The court can also order material to be destroyed or handed over.

As a check on the Registrar, the Act also creates a special tribunal, the **Data Protection Tribunal**, to which data users or computer bureaux can appeal against the Registrar's decisions. The tribunal deals with appeals against refusal to register and enforcement notices. A data subject has no right of appeal to the tribunal.

Exemptions from the Act

The Act specifies a number of exemptions from its provisions. Some kinds of personal data are exempted because their processing on computer is not seen as giving rise to any threat to privacy and so applying the Act in these cases would be excessively burdensome. The other main exclusions occur where the need to keep data confidential takes precedence. Such exemptions relate to areas such as law enforcement or national security.

The Act itself specifies three categories of exemption:

- exemption from the whole Act
- exemption from subject access, and
- exemption from disclosure

which apply to different kinds of data or groups of data users.

Personal data which is completely exempt from the Act includes data whose confidentiality is necessary for national security, data kept for domestic purposes, data whose disclosure is required by law, and a number of limited categories of data including payroll and accounting data, club membership lists, and simple lists of names and addresses. The national security exemption is perhaps the most significant. For this exemption to apply to a certain category of data it must be authorized by a cabinet minister.

There are several categories of data which must be registered, but with respect to which the data user can refuse to comply with a data subject's request to see what information is held on him or her. Important categories here include data which is held for the detection and prevention of crime, taxation data, and data held for health and social work. Also, more contentiously, information can be exempted from the subject access provisions if its disclosure is already prohibited by other legislation and the Home Secretary believes that this prohibition ought to take precedence.

The final class of exemptions relates to the disclosure provisions. When data users register under the Act they must specify to whom they will disclose the personal data which they hold; disclosure to other individuals or organizations than those specified constitutes a criminal offence with a number of exceptions. These exception include the disclosure of information for the purposes of protecting national security, investigating crimes, assessment of tax liabilities, and for legal purposes.

8.3 Criticisms of the Act and forthcoming changes

Ostensibly the 1984 Data Protection Act is intended to regulate the computer processing of personal data. Given the circumstances in which the Act came to be passed, however, it may seem that it was simply the minimum legislation required for the United Kingdom to honour its Council of Europe treaty obligations. Had these obligations not been honoured, then other nations might have stopped exchanging data with the United Kingdom, which would have had an adverse effect on UK trade.

The Act has indeed been strongly criticized by commentators who argue that its provisions do little to protect individual data subjects. They point to statistics published by the Registrar in the annual reports. For example, in the year 1996/7 there were about 4000 complaints made to the Registrar (up from about 3000 the year before) but only 67 prosecutions were brought (Data Protection Registrar, 1997). Most of these prosecutions were successful but the typical fine imposed by the courts was in the region of £500. To put such figures in perspective, about 400 000 people a year are prosecuted for not having a television licence.[2]

We now look at some of the criticisms and concerns about the current legislation before considering the 1995 European Union Directive which will lead to revised legislation before the end of 1998.

Criticisms of the current Act

One of the main criticisms made of the current Data Protection Act is that it is too weak and too narrow in its scope. For example, the Home Secretary has the power to exempt any information from disclosure which was covered by previous legislation. The Official Secrets Act forbids the unauthorized disclosure of all information handled by the government, so the effect is that individuals have no right of access to any information that the government may hold on them. Yet as Sir Norman Lindop (the chairman of the Data Protection Committee which reported in 1978) has said: 'The greatest threat, if threat there be, does not come from the private sector, from the entrepreneurial sector, it comes from the public sector.'[3] Furthermore those exemptions which are made do not have to be justified; there is no provision for a court or tribunal hearing to assess the validity of the exemption.

A further criticism that has been made of the Act is that it does not effectively control the use of personal data. The Act places no restrictions on the ways in which personal data is used, data users are free to process data largely as they wish provided they register appropriately. Nor does it give data subjects any rights to restrict what information is held on them, how it is used, or to whom it is passed on.

There are also a number of specific issues and abuses which currently cause concern. **Enforced subject access** is a way round the data protection law which is used by some employers to find out information on potential employees. Employers are not able under the terms of law to access personal information on potential employees such as details of any criminal record or information held by the Department of Social Security. What some employers do therefore is to insist that the job applicant make a request to the appropriate data users for such information. Many job applicants comply out of fear that they will lose the chance of being employed should they refuse.

Another area of concern is that the development of the Internet and the ease of transferring data over the telephone network has made it impossible to police the data protection laws. Moreover, the current legislation does not address paper-based data. This is an important omission since paper-based information is sometimes sent abroad to be entered on computer by cheap labour. At one

---

2 Figures quoted in Davies (1996).
3 Quoted in Campbell and Connor (1986).

stage the Home Office was in negotiations with a Philippine company to have paper-based criminal records typed onto computers though the idea was later abandoned (Davies 1996).

The European Union Data Protection Directive

The Data Protection Act is due to be amended. As before, the legislation is being driven not by domestic concerns about privacy or the adequacy of protection, but by events abroad. In October 1995 the European Commission published a Directive on data protection, and member states of the European Union must pass laws to bring their own legislation into line with the Directive by November 1998.

The impetus for the European Directive came from the establishment of the Single European Market in 1992, when all restrictions to the free flow of goods and services within the European Community were removed. However, barriers to the free flow of data still remained, since not all EU countries had signed the Council of Europe Convention on Data Protection. This meant that, potentially, some EU countries would not be able to exchange data freely. In order to remove this problem, the European Commission published a Directive on data protection, so that all EU countries would have consistent legislation in this area.

Much of the current UK data protection law is consistent, but there are areas where the law will need to be changed to bring it into line with the directive. Among the changes that will be required are:

- the extension of the law to cover some manual files as well as machine-processable ones,
- further controls on the processing of sensitive data (such as data on political beliefs, health, sex life and so on)
- the requirement that data subjects must be informed about how their personal data will be used, either when it is collected or at a later stage if it is obtained from a third party.

Just how these and other components of the Directive will be translated into UK law is, at the time of writing, uncertain. There is some debate as to what extent the current law covers certain provisions of the Directive.

8.4 Summary

The Data Protection Act was passed in 1984 after a long period during which legislation had been discussed. The final impetus was the need to ratify a Council of Europe convention concerning data protection. Had the Act not been passed, there would have been a danger that those countries which had passed data protection legislation would be unwilling to exchange data with the UK.

The Act creates a register of those individuals or organizations which hold and process personal data. It also sets out eight principles which must be adhered to by those processing personal data. Essentially these principles ensure that data held has been fairly obtained, is accurate and not excessive, can be seen by the data subject, and is held in reasonable security. To enforce the Act, the office of Data Protection Registrar has been created. It is the responsibility of the Registrar to compile the register, promote the Act, and enforce it through a mechanism of enforcement notices and possibly criminal prosecutions. The Act also creates the Data Protection Tribunal, a special court to which appeals against decisions of the Registrar can be made.

The Act has received much criticism. The main complaints are that processing by government authorities is effectively exempted, and that it gives few effective rights to individuals. The law in this area is, at the time of writing, due to be amended to reflect an EU Directive on data processing. The extent and importance of the changes that will be made as a consequence remain to be seen.

Further reading

The first chapter of *On the Record* by Duncan Campbell and Steve Connor (1986) contains a detailed account of the political prevarication which took place before the Data Protection Act was finally passed.

Thorough accounts of the Data Protection Act are contained in *Introduction to Computer Law* by David Bainbridge (1996) and in the chapter by Ian Walden in the collection *Computer Law* edited by Chris Reed (1996).

The Data Protection Registrar maintains a very thorough Web site at

http://www.open.gov.uk/dpr/dprhome.htm

where the Registrar's annual reports as well as the Act itself can be viewed.

Big Brother by Simon Davies (1996) contains some trenchant criticism of the Data Protection Act.

Points to consider

1 In the United Kingdom the Data Protection Act obliges data users to register centrally that they process personal information and, on request, to reveal to individuals what information is held on them. In some countries a different approach has been adopted whereby data users must inform data subjects when they create a computer record about them. What are the relative merits of each approach? Which is more likely to be effective in protecting individuals' rights?

2 In Chapter 2 we discussed the case of Penn Kimball, who was able to look at the way he had been classified in government files and find out the effects on his career. This was possible as a result of the American

Freedom of Information and Privacy Act. Equivalent rights do not exist under UK law. In some Continental countries (notably France) the data protection legislation makes provision for a government official to vet the processing of personal data by government agencies. Should such a provision be added to the UK law? Would it be effective in ensuring proper processing of information by government authorities? If not, what other measures might be appropriate?

3 Is it reasonable to allow companies to charge a fee for disclosing the information they hold on an individual? How much money might an individual have to spend to find out all the information held on him or her?

4 What does the Data Protection Act do for individuals? Does it provide any effective rights? Does it need to be changed to make it more or less stringent?

5 Individuals have no right of appeal to the Data Protection Tribunal whereas companies do. What justifications are there for this apparent inbalance?

CHAPTER 9

Computer misuse

Have people been sent to jail for hacking or writing virus programs? What kinds of computer-based activities can put an individual on the wrong side of the law?

Overview

This chapter is primarily concerned with the main criminal offences which can be committed using a computer. Some of these, such as fraud, are old crimes appearing in new surroundings whereas others, like hacking or virus writing, are new forms of crime altogether.

We first look at computer fraud and the law which relates to it. Next we consider some of the new kinds of offence such as hacking which have appeared in the wake of the computer. The very novelty of such activities meant that, initially, there were difficulties in bringing prosecutions. We shall consider some of these problems and how they led to the passing of the Computer Misuse Act in 1990. This Act created new offences, such as unauthorized access to a computer and unauthorized modification of programs or data, which are outlined before considering the effectiveness of the legislation.

Lastly we shall briefly look at the legal situation with respect to the Internet; in particular the issues concerning publication of obscene material or libellous statements.

Relation to other chapters Computer crime was discussed in Chapter 4 and this chapter presents the legal reaction to such crime. In particular we shall see how the Computer Misuse Act addresses some of the weaknesses in the law which were highlighted at the end of Chapter 5.

9.1 Computers and fraud

The term fraud traditionally covers a range of crimes in which some kind of advantage has been obtained by deception. One example of fraud would be where directors or accountants falsify a company's accounts in order to obtain a loan which would not otherwise be available. Another common form of fraud involves making false statements to the revenue authorities to avoid paying tax. There is no offence of fraud as such; people committing fraud may be prosecuted under the Theft Acts of 1968 and 1978 or, where tax evasion is concerned, under the Finance Act of 1972.

Computer fraud generally involves interfering with the operation of a computer in some way to obtain financial advantage. The simplest way is to tamper with the data entered or the results produced. Entering incorrect data is by far the most common method; this may be done either directly or by modifying paper-based information which someone else then unwittingly enters into a computer. One survey suggests that such techniques account for about 90% of computer frauds. A more sophisticated, and potentially more damaging, approach involves altering programs or writing programs which have hidden 'functionality', for example to channel money into a particular account.

The current scale of computer fraud is largely unknown. Some surveys suggest that it is relatively uncommon and small scale compared to other forms of embezzlement. But there are reasons to believe that much computer fraud goes undetected or that, where it is detected, organizations are reluctant to reveal what has happened. This, along with fears about the potential for major fraud in electronic funds transfer, has led to its being viewed as a serious offence and, as discussed in the next section, the law has been strengthened through the Computer Misuse Act to make it easier to prosecute attempts at computer fraud.

Those committing 'conventional fraud' are normally prosecuted under the 1968 Theft Act for the crime of 'obtaining property by deception'. There is a problem in using the same approach to prosecute computer fraudsters; the legal position is that for a deception to take place another individual (or individuals) must be deceived. Someone who directly enters incorrect data into a computer, or writes a program which carries out transfers into his or her own account, may well be able to carry out a fraud without the need to actually mislead or deceive any person. In such circumstances a prosecution which depends on showing *deception* will fail.

Consequently, those carrying out computer fraud are more likely to be simply prosecuted for theft. Under the 1968 Theft Act an individual commits theft if he or she *dishonestly appropriates property belonging to another with the intention of permanently depriving the other of it*. In some circumstances fraudsters may also be prosecuted for other offences such as, if more than one person was involved in perpetrating the fraud, conspiracy to defraud.

9.2 The Computer Misuse Act

In the late 1980s there was growing concern about hacking and the damage which could be done by hackers, particularly if they gained access to computers running safety-critical applications. This concern was increased by the appearance at this time of the first computer viruses.

There were a number of attempts to prosecute hackers under the then-existing legislation but with varying degrees of success. For example, the abstraction of electricity is an offence under the Theft Act of 1968 but an attempt in Hong Kong (see Chapter 5) to prosecute a hacker for theft of electricity failed. Likewise an attempt in the United Kingdom to convict two hackers of forgery (see *R* v. *Gold*, discussed in Chapter 5) also failed. However, the prosecution of a hacker for criminal damage (Figure 9.1) was successful but the result rested on a somewhat counter-intuitive interpretation of 'damage'. In any event a criminal damage prosecution would only be appropriate where the alterations made by a hacker had actually caused loss. Were a hacker to make no modifications at all but only inspect the contents of confidential files then it is not clear that any charge could be brought. The case which is often cited here is that of *Oxford* v. *Moss* (Figure 9.2) which indicates that information is not property and so there is no 'theft of information' offence.

It became clear that the law, as it was at the time, was poorly equipped to address the activities of hackers and virus-writers. The result of the *R.* v. *Gold* case in particular caused concern since it was seen as indicating that hacking was not against the law. Two studies were carried out into the issue: one by the Scottish Law Commission which reported in 1987 and a later one by the English Law Commission which reported in 1989. The approach taken by these commissions was to look at the various forms of computer misuse (fraud, hacking and so on) and to see whether they were addressed by the law.

Whiteley was a hacker who managed to gain unauthorized access to JANET (the UK joint academic network). He deleted files, added new users, changed the passwords of some existing users and so on. He even deleted the log files which recorded his activities. As a result a number of computers on the network would not operate correctly and had to be shut down temporarily.

Whiteley was prosecuted for two instances of criminal damage under the Criminal Damage Act 1979: first, for impairing the operation of computers and, second, for damaging disks containing password and other files. He was convicted for damage to the disks but not to the computers.

Whiteley appealed on the grounds that altering the information magnetically stored on the disks did not constitute damage. This appeal was rejected. The judge ruled that the usefulness of the disks had been impaired by the alteration of the data recorded on them and that this constituted damage.

Figure 9.1. *R* v. *Whiteley* (1991)

Moss, a university student, managed to get hold of a proof of an examination paper before the examination was held. He read the paper but then returned it.

He could not be prosecuted for theft since he had returned the original item. He was, however, prosecuted for theft of the confidential information in the paper. He was acquitted on the grounds that information itself cannot be regarded as property and so cannot be stolen.

Figure 9.2. *Oxford* v. *Moss* (1978)

The report of the English Commission made specific proposals for new criminal offences relating to hacking. In this it was influenced by the consideration that any unauthorized access to a computer system caused considerable disruption since it meant that the system's operators would be obliged to check the integrity of the system whether any alterations had been made or not. The recommendations of the Commission's report formed the basis of the Computer Misuse Act which was passed in 1990.

Offences created by the Computer Misuse Act

The Computer Misuse Act 1990 was designed to protect the integrity of computer systems by deterring the activities of hackers. It created three new offences:

● unauthorized access to computer programs or data
● unauthorized access with a further criminal intent (known as the 'ulterior intent' offence), and
● unauthorized modification of computer material.

Besides addressing computer misuse the Act also contains special provisions in recognition of the fact that computer hackers may operate from other countries or gain access to computers abroad. In order to ensure that perpetrators are still liable to prosecution even if their activities span more than one country, the Act contains special provisions relating to jurisdiction and extradition of suspected offenders. Where the offence involves a country other than the United Kingdom the perpetrator can be prosecuted provided that:

● the offence either affected a computer based in the United Kingdom or the perpetrator was in the United Kingdom when the offence was committed, and
● the activity engaged in is also an offence in the other country.

We consider the offences the Act creates in greater detail below.

Unauthorized access offence

According to the Act someone is guilty of unauthorized access if he or she:

- causes a computer to perform any function with intent to gain access to any computer
- the access gained would be unauthorized and
- he or she is aware that the access would be unauthorized.

Note that attempts at access do not need to be successful; merely getting a computer to check a password is causing it to perform a function. Thus a hacker who knew a user's logon but not the password and tried out different guesses in turn would be guilty of the offence even if he or she never actually gained access.

As the offence is defined it clearly covers attempted access over a network but there is no need for more than one machine to be involved. An attempt to gain unauthorized access to a computer directly, by trying out logons at a terminal for instance, is similarly an offence. The offence can also be committed by someone who is a legitimate user of a computer but who tries to access information which they are not authorized to see. Thus an employee of a company who tries to query a personnel database to find out the salaries of other employees would be guilty of an offence provided it could be shown that he or she was not authorized to access the information and was aware of the fact.

The need to show intent is an important feature of unauthorized access. It means that someone who unwittingly gained access to information, by making a typing mistake when entering their own logon, for example, or by looking at data which they thought they were authorized to see, could not be prosecuted.

The offence of unauthorized access is triable in a magistrates' court. If convicted, the offender faces up to 6 months' imprisonment or a fine of up to £5000.

Ulterior intent offence

A person is guilty of the ulterior intent offence if he or she:

- is guilty of unauthorized access and
- the unauthorized access was made with the intention of committing (or facilitating the commission of) a further offence.

Ulterior intent only applies where the further offence which was to be committed is itself serious and punishable by a maximum penalty of not less than 5 years' imprisonment. Thus someone gaining unauthorized access to a computer in order to commit fraud, blackmail, theft or other major offences could be prosecuted for ulterior intent. If unauthorized access had been obtained to perpetrate a less serious offence, a breach of the disclosure provisions of the Data Protection Act for instance, then it would not be possible to prosecute for ulterior intent.

The ulterior intent offence was introduced to make it easier to prosecute attempts at fraud (or other crimes) which involved the use of a computer. Before the introduction of this offence it had been difficult to secure convictions in such circumstances.

The ulterior intent offence is triable in either a magistrates' or a Crown court. It attracts a maximum penalty of 5 years' imprisonment or an unlimited fine or both.

Unauthorized modification offence

Someone is guilty of unauthorized modification of computer material if he or she:

- carries out any act which results in unauthorized modification of material on any computer, and
- he or she does so with 'requisite intent' and 'requisite knowledge'.

The Act defines the phrase 'requisite intent' as meaning the intention to modify the contents of a computer in such a way as to impair its operation, hinder access to any stored item, or change any program or compromise the reliability of any data. The phrase 'requisite knowledge' means that the perpetrator must be aware that he or she was not authorized to make the changes.

Hence someone who hacks into a computer and modifies any files or programs (for example, by adding a new user logon so that they can gain access more easily at a later stage) will have committed an unauthorized modification offence. Moreover, the intent to make a modification need not be directed at any particular machine. Thus someone who writes and distributes a computer virus which alters the contents of machines on which it is loaded will be guilty of unauthorized modification; this offence was used to secure one of the first convictions for virus writing (Figure 9.3). But an individual who loads some software onto a machine at work and unwittingly infects it with a virus would not be guilty of the offence since he or she does not have the 'requisite intent' to make unauthorized modifications.

A disgruntled programmer who inserts a 'logic bomb' (a piece of code which will result in an error or deletion of data when a certain condition occurs) into

---

In 1995 the so-called Black Baron, Christopher Pile, admitted 11 charges under the Computer Misuse Act and a further charge of inciting others to spread viruses by making instructions on virus creation available. It was alleged that the disruption caused by the viruses which Pile had written and distributed cost companies over £1 million. Pile was the world's first convicted virus writer and received a jail sentence of 18 months (*The Independent*, 27 May 1995, Victor).

Figure 9.3. *R* v. *Pile (The Black Baron)*

a program he or she writes will also be guilty of unauthorized modification. Consultants or freelance programmers who use logic bombs as a threat to try to obtain payment for their services may be further guilty of blackmail; that is, making unwarranted demands with menaces.

As a result of the Computer Misuse Act coming into force, the 1971 Criminal Damage Act is no longer taken as applying to changes to stored data. Thus in *the R* v. *Whiteley* case (Figure 9.1) discussed above a prosecution would now be brought for unauthorized modification under the Computer Misuse Act rather than for criminal damage.

Unauthorized modification is an offence which is triable in both magistrates' and Crown courts. It is punishable by up to 5 years in prison or an unlimited fine or both.

Impact of the Computer Misuse Act

One result of the Computer Misuse Act coming into operation is that activities such as hacking and virus-writing are now clearly illegal. There is no longer the need to try to interpret previous legislation to cover activities which did not exist when it was passed and which it was clearly never intended to address.

On the other hand, it is not clear how effective the legislation is in reducing computer crime. There are still many hackers and virus-writers active, so the Act does nothing to reduce the need for security for computer systems, especially those connected to networks. Moreover, there have been relatively few successful prosecutions under the Act. This may be because it is a difficult and long process to track a hacker down and assemble the necessary evidence for prosecution (as borne out by various accounts, see Stoll 1989 and Shimomura 1996). Another reason may be that the authorities feel it is difficult to secure criminal convictions for activities carried out several years in the past (by the time a prosecution is brought) often by relatively young teenagers. One of the earliest prosecutions failed when a jury apparently accepted the defence's argument that the accused teenager had a compulsive obsession to hack and so could not form the necessary guilty intent (Watts and Pithers 1993).

9.3 The Internet and the law

Much discussion and reporting concerning the Internet presents it as a kind of 'virtual frontier' where national laws do not apply. This view is misleading. In a way the Internet does not provide anything new: e-mail, Web sites, and so on have close parallels to traditional postal services and publishing activities which have long been regulated by national laws. There is little reason to suppose that older legislation will not be applied to activities on the Internet (this is already happening) though there are as yet few reported cases which can be used as reliable precedents.

It is true that from a purely practical viewpoint the Internet does present problems for law enforcers. For one thing the Internet is effectively global but laws and law enforcement agencies are limited by national boundaries. Consequently differences in national laws or the simple administrative problems of pursuing hackers, say, through different jurisdictions makes law enforcement more difficult.

Another factor to take into account is the Internet community itself. In the early days this was composed overwhelmingly of university researchers and students. Many of these people made information freely available on their research and assumed that other Internet publishers also provided information without being concerned whether it was copied. However, as discussed in Chapter 6, the fact that many Internet users disregard intellectual property laws does not mean that they do not apply. It is undoubtedly the case that many users are unaware of much of the law which applies to their activities. Journalists and editors will have a good idea of the laws of libel and the kinds of statements they can and cannot make in print without the risk of legal action. A new Internet user, on the other hand, may set up Web pages containing libellous information unaware that he or she runs the risk of being taken to court.

Below we briefly consider two areas where the law impacts on the use of the Internet. First, we look at how the laws of libel affect the use of e-mail and second, we consider the legal position of Internet service providers.

Libel

Any statement of fact made about a company or an individual which is untrue and which damages the reputation of that company or individual or holds them up to ridicule, contempt, or hatred is a libel if it is published in some permanent form. In this context, it is sufficient for the statement to be communicated to one person (other than the person libelled) for it to be considered as published. Statements made in a Web page or e-mail message qualify as being published.

Note that true statements are not libellous. Consequently a report that company X is in financial trouble, for example, is not libellous if it is an objective statement of fact. It is libellous, however, if it is merely an opinion or an unsubstantiated rumour.

Recently there have been a number of cases of e-mail libel. In one case a policeman had sought compensation from a supermarket chain for some unsatisfactory meat. The policeman later learned that an internal company e-mail had accused him of fraud. He sued for libel and won (Dadak 1997). A large insurance company also had to pay out £450 000 in damages to a rival insurer for libellous e-mail messages claiming that the rival was in financial trouble.

The legal position with respect to libel is not new and has not substantially been altered by the advent of the Internet (though there are some issues for so-called Internet service providers, as discussed below). Recent libel cases concerning e-mail have probably had more of an impact because many computer users have occasionally included comments in e-mails of a kind which they would never put in a letter. In effect some users have fallen into thinking of e-mail as being like informal conversation whereas, from a legal standpoint, it is considered in the same way as ordinary letters or published material would be.

Internet service providers

Internet service providers are companies or other organizations who provide Internet users with both a gateway to the Internet as well as a number of supplementary services (such as the facility to set up Web pages or supporting newsgroups). Service providers are, according to the Defamation Act 1996, not held responsible for libellous statements posted at sites they maintain provided they can show that they do not edit or vet the material that their users post. But the legal position of service providers is confused by the fact that they are supposed to take reasonable care in preventing libellous material from appearing. This situation leaves service providers in something of a dilemma. They must strike a balance between the extremes of allowing any material to appear on their site (thus failing to take reasonable care) and vetting material excessively, so putting themselves into an editorial role and becoming liable as editors.

Service providers can also find themselves legally exposed in other areas, such as when obscene material is posted to a site they maintain. The Obscene Publications Act 1959 as later amended by the Criminal Justice and Public Order Act 1994 makes it an offence to publish an obscene article or to possess such an article for gain (for example, with the intention to sell or later publish it). Recent amendments to the law make it clear that publication includes electronic transmission of data which is obscene when viewed. This means that sending e-mails containing obscene material is an offence (even if the contents of the e-mail are encrypted). More stringent controls are applied to certain kinds of obscene material; for instance, possession of indecent photographs of minors with intent to show them is a separate, more serious, offence.

The particular problem posed for service providers by obscene material is that should they unwittingly provide such material (for example, by maintaining a bulletin board or FTP site where someone has uploaded obscene material) they may be held legally responsible as the publishers of the material.

The only defence available to such providers is to show that they both did not look at obscene material which they unwittingly published and that they had no cause to inspect it. Recently the police in the United Kingdom have adopted a policy of warning service providers of newsgroups which they believe may sometimes contain obscene material. This means that a service provider would certainly be held responsible for publishing any material posted to those groups.

9.4 Summary

In this chapter we have looked at some of the criminal offences which can be committed through computer misuse and briefly considered some implications of the law for Internet use.

Computer fraud has attracted widespread media interest but this is not an area which presents any particular legal difficulties. Someone who has dishonestly obtained money by tampering with computer data or programs will certainly be liable to prosecution for theft.

Where the law has had problems is in addressing some of the novel crimes, such as hacking and virus writing, which can be committed using computers. Initial attempts to prosecute hackers using existing offences, such as theft of electricity or forgery, had very variable results and it became clear that the law needed to be reformed. This was done with the passing of the Computer Misuse Act in 1990.

The Computer Misuse Act created three new offences. The basic unauthorized access offence is intended to deter hackers trying to gain access to computers. Two more serious offences, ulterior intent and unauthorized modification, are designed to make it easier to prosecute those who are hacking in the course of committing other offences and to criminalize the activities of hackers and virus writers.

Lastly we looked briefly at some implications of the law for Internet use. The main areas of law which are relevant here relate to publication, in particular publication of libellous or obscene material.

Further reading

There are general surveys of the law as it relates to computer crime in the chapter by Ian Lloyd and Moira Simpson which appears in the collection *Computer Law* edited by Chris Reed (1996) and in *Introduction to Computer Law* by David Bainbridge (1996). There is a useful short guide to the Computer Misuse Act written by Tony Elbra (1990).

A comprehensive source of information on the law affecting the Internet, though it assumes some legal knowledge, is *The Laws of the Internet* by Clive Gringras (1997).

Points to consider

1 One result of the Computer Misuse Act is that it gives special status to crimes related to computers. For example, a student who manages to see

a copy of an examination paper by gaining unauthorized access to a computer system faces up to 6 months in prison; a fellow student who manages to 'borrow' a paper draft of the examination has probably not committed any offence. Are such disparities defensible? If not how could they be resolved? Is there any justification for treating behaviour involving computers differently from similar behaviour which does not involve a computer?

2 It seems from various accounts that many computer hackers are adolescent computer enthusiasts motivated by curiosity rather than personal gain or the desire to do damage. On the other hand, their activities can cause enormous disruption and it is also the case that many hackers do commit fraud and other offences. Is it therefore appropriate that hacking be criminalized? Are there other options available to deter hacking?

3 Through the Computer Misuse Act, the law now provides greater protection for information held on computers than it does for the privacy of individuals. On the other hand, the Act was not primarily intended to protect information so much as to avoid the disruption caused by hackers and others. Should the current situation be changed? Are there instances where hacking can be seen as beneficial – in bringing to light information of general public interest, for example?

4 Should Internet service providers be liable for material on bulletin boards? Can providers reasonably be expected to check all the material that appears? Will they simply move to countries with less stringent laws if they are prosecuted?

CHAPTER 10

Software development and engineering

What is it that distinguishes engineering from other disciplines such as medicine or science? Is it reasonable to use the term 'software engineering'?

Overview

This chapter is concerned with the nature of software development and whether it can (or could) be regarded as a branch of engineering. In the first section we review the development of professional engineering from craft practices, and the characteristics which distinguish modern engineering approaches.

Next we consider whether it is reasonable to regard software development in its current state as an engineering discipline. The way in which software development practices have evolved are reviewed in order to see whether a similar progression is occurring here as has taken place in the more established branches of engineering.

One of the most important aspects of engineering is the use of careful measurement and analysis; this is crucial in enabling engineers to learn from their mistakes. A similar concern with quantification and analysis appears in modern approaches to quality management. These have been so successful that so-called Total Quality Management is now a widely used approach for improving performance. Because careful monitoring and measuring along with considered attempts to improve are an important aspect of the transition from an *ad hoc* approach to one that is consistent with engineering, we look at quality management in some detail. We first review how the idea of quality has developed and then consider its application to software and, in particular, to managing software development. We also look at the ISO 9000 quality standard, and at a model of the software development process, the Capability Maturity Model. This model is significant in that it sets out a blueprint to help software developers improve the predictability of their projects and the reliability of what they produce.

Relation to other chapters The drive to make software development a more rigorous and 'engineering-like' activity is motivated by the poor performance of the software industry in general, as reviewed in Chapter 1. The potential liability of software developers for the software they develop, discussed in Chapter 7, also means that it is very much in their interests to achieve the same degree of rigour and predictability of performance as other branches of engineering.

Following on, the next chapter looks at the training and professional context which are appropriate for a software engineer and Chapter 12 considers some of the ethical and professional responsibilities of a software engineer.

10.1 What is an engineering discipline?

What distinguishes the way that modern engineers approach problems? How does it differ from the approach of other professional groups such as doctors or scientists? Engineering is now a very broad field which encompasses a wide range of activities and concerns: from mass production of cars to the one-off development of satellites, and from the design of electronic chips to the construction of tunnels and bridges. There are two features which all these activities have in common, and which appear in some form in most definitions of engineering. These are:

- the solution of practical problems for the benefit of humankind and
- the use of scientific and other formalized knowledge to design and build artefacts within economic constraints.

Of course, engineering activities go back as far as civilization: Roman engineers were responsible for an enormous network of roads and viaducts, for example. The activities of such early engineers can be distinguished from modern engineering in that they relied on accumulated experience rather than a formalized body of knowledge. It is the exploitation of scientific and mathematical results and techniques that has enabled modern engineers to make such tremendous technological advances.

Although modern engineers make considerable use of scientific results, engineering is a quite different activity from science. Scientists are primarily concerned with describing and understanding the natural world. This involves a process of formulating theories or laws and using experiments to test their validity. Theories which are not contradicted by experimental results are taken as sound (at least until they are contradicted in some way). Those which are contradicted are rejected or modified and the new theories then tested out. On this basis, scientific reasoning and research is essentially *inductive*: scientists try to infer general rules or laws from the results of a limited number of observations or experimental results.

The activities of engineers are quite distinct: rather than explaining or modelling the natural world, their objective is to change it for human benefit. Engineers make use of scientific results but only to the extent that they are of help in solving practical problems, and they use such results in a *deductive* way; that is, to verify whether designs and ideas are feasible and safe.

The exploitation of scientific and mathematical results, along with the systematized use of experience, are so central in engineering that we consider next the way in which this has come about. We then look in greater detail at the characteristics of modern engineering.

Development of engineering disciplines

The discussion above identified two features of engineering: the development of solutions to practical problems, and the use of scientific and formalized knowledge in this process. The first aspect, solving practical problems, has always been present from the earliest times. The question is, how does engineering come to make use of scientific and formalized knowledge? Consideration of various branches of engineering suggests that this development can be seen as a three stage process.

Initially, the discipline starts in a state of **craft practice**. At this stage engineering is carried out by practitioners with little or no formal training. Knowledge is acquired during apprenticeship or by word of mouth and practitioners reuse approaches which are well proven. Progress is slow and *ad hoc;* when engineers are confronted with novel problems they are unable to assess whether given designs will work without trying them out. Roman engineers and the mediaeval master masons who built castles and cathedrals were working at this level. They relied on their own experience along with pragmatic rules as to what was possible, and learnt from each others' mistakes. There was no understanding of the structural theory underpinning what they did and designs were often altered during construction when it became clear that a building as planned would be unstable.

The second stage of development is that of **commercial exploitation** when pressures arise to make economic use of resources or to increase output. The characteristics of this stage are that practice becomes more organized and standard procedures are established. Such procedures enshrine current knowledge about the best way to proceed and pave the way for pragmatic improvements to be made on the basis of experience. Civil engineering went through this stage around the eighteenth and early nineteenth centuries. The widespread construction of roads and canals in the eighteenth century and the rapid development of railways in the nineteenth meant there was a continual stream of large construction projects. Such pressures led to some systematization and, in particular, to a consulting system where experienced engineers would advise on large projects but leave the details to others.

The final stage in development sees the emergence of **professional engineering**. At this stage engineering is carried out by educated professionals who make use of formal analysis and scientific theory to understand and verify their designs. This understanding makes it possible to undertake novel projects with much greater certainty: the scientific underpinning helps in determining the limits of particular designs or techniques. Engineering problems also stimulate research into phenomena which are poorly understood. Another characteristic of this stage (discussed in greater detail in the next chapter) is the emergence of professional engineering societies and institutions. The underpinning of civil engineering with firmly understood scientific principles began in the early seventeenth century when Galileo began the scientific investigation into the strength of materials and the properties of beams. This period also saw the development of much of the mathematics required to enable the forces in structures to be analysed. The underlying science continued to be investigated during the seventeenth and eighteenth centuries with the development of structural theory, and investigations of properties such as elasticity. The late eighteenth century saw the development of engineering drawing by the French engineer Monge, which was to become the main way of representing and communicating engineering designs. There was a long period before all these techniques were mature enough to be used by practising engineers but by the middle of the nineteenth century it was possible for engineers to undertake detailed structural analyses of bridges and buildings.

Of course, this evolution from craft practice to commercial exploitation to professional engineering is not uniform or clear cut. There will be long periods of overlap and transition but the main stages do appear in the development of many engineering disciplines.

Characteristics of engineering

What are the characteristics of the approaches adopted in established engineering professions which enable engineers to achieve high levels of reliability and safety in the artefacts they produce?

Although by the middle of the nineteenth century many traditional areas of engineering had evolved into modern professional disciplines, that is not to say that there were no longer any mistakes or even major disasters. In the eighteenth century, for example, many iron railway bridges collapsed due to problems of fatigue, a property exhibited by all materials: repeated stress gradually weakens a material leading to eventual failure. The vibrations of ever heavier and faster railway trains were causing such fatigue failures in iron bridges. This problem was not properly understood when the bridges were built but, with the benefit of experience and greater understanding, engineers came to change their designs to be more resilient.

In an earlier stage of engineering development, at the craft stage for instance, engineers would probably have retreated from the use of iron in bridge-building and fallen back on the use of brick or wood. Professional engineers were able to learn from and overcome such problems. Among the factors which enable them to do this are the reliance on precise definitions and quantification, the careful analysis of failures, and the refinement of techniques in the light of experience.

Engineering projects tackle clearly defined and quantified problems. For instance, an engineer designing a bridge will know what loads it must be capable of carrying, what distance it must span, what stresses it is likely to be subject to from the wind or vibration, what safety factor should be built in, and how long it should last. Using this information it is possible to produce designs for bridges, and estimate the cost and time needed to build them. Once a design has been selected it is further possible to precisely estimate the quantity of materials required along with the requisite strength of components and the time taken to complete various stages of the construction. These estimates can be used as a basis for controlling the progress of the project and recognizing problems or difficulties as they arise.

Another important aspect of modern engineering is the use of systematized knowledge. Much of this will come from a relevant area of science (such as mechanics or metallurgy) and be supplemented with a range of mathematical techniques. This knowledge gives the engineer a good understanding both of the problems that he or she is addressing and the materials available for their solution. This theoretical knowledge can be used to build up mathematical models of designs and verify their feasibility and characteristics. A further point about this knowledge is that an engineer will know its limitations. Designs which cannot be verified theoretically may be tested by building scale models or carrying out relevant experiments. Even in the mid nineteenth century engineers were testing out scale models of designs when they were unsure of the strength of a bridge. In addition to science-based knowledge engineers will have considerable knowledge of proven procedures and designs which they can reuse where appropriate. An important aspect of this codified knowledge is the ability to learn from failures. Where novel designs are tried out and prove to be faulty, investigation can pinpoint the problems, allowing the technique to be refined and made safer. Professional institutions (discussed in the next chapter) have an important role in disseminating this systematized knowledge and results of experience.

10.2 Software development as engineering?

How far has software development progressed as an engineering discipline? Has it reached the stage of professional engineering or is it at an earlier stage of development? Moreover, given some of the problems which are peculiar to systems development, is it right to think of software development in terms of engineering at all?

We look at two areas, compiler writing and large-scale systems, to assess how much progress has been made before discussing whether software development is properly viewed as an engineering discipline.

Development of compiler technology

In the 1950s when high-level programming languages were first being designed and implemented, compiler writing was regarded as notoriously difficult. The development of the first compiler for FORTRAN, completed in early 1957, required about 18 person-years of effort. There were even people at the time who doubted whether the use of high-level programming languages, as opposed to computer-specific Assembler codes, was viable. They believed that compilers would invariably translate high-level programs into slow and inefficient machine-code.

Compiler technology has progressed so dramatically, however, that a compiler can now be implemented in anything from 6 person-weeks to a person-year. Modern compilers generally produce executable code that is very efficient and it is rare for programmers to need to resort to lower-level languages. Moreover, compilers are usually extremely reliable being at least as free from errors as most other software on a typical computer.

How has such an enormous improvement come about? Certainly the general programming environment in which modern developers work makes things much easier. Compilers are now usually developed in high-level languages themselves and the modern programmer, working on time-shared computers, can edit, test, and debug programs much more easily than was the case 40 years ago. Nevertheless, these general improvements cannot account for the dramatic improvements in compiler development.

Perhaps the single most important development since the first compilers were written has been the advent of formal language theory. This theory underpins the description of program syntax through formal grammars whose properties can be analysed. Using the theory it is possible to devise algorithms which, taking a grammar as input, will produce a parser (a program to analyze a piece of code and check that it conforms to a particular grammar) for the corresponding language. This understanding of syntax and grammars makes it easy to develop the front-end of a compiler which analyzes a program and reports any errors. Other areas where a theoretical understanding of issues has contributed to compiler development are in type-checking and optimization.

Not only have the theoretical underpinnings of program languages and how to parse them become better understood but this has also been used to develop a number of tools to aid the compiler writer. Among the best known of these are LEX, which splits a source program into its individual words, and YACC, which parses a sequence of words to determine whether they represent a legal sequence of statements in a language. LEX and YACC are both program generators; given an appropriate grammar for a language or its words YACC and LEX can generate a corresponding analyzer to read in a program written in the language. Such tools have had an enormous impact because they make compiler writing both quicker and less error-prone.

Finally, experience and knowledge of compiler writing has been widely disseminated through university courses and books. This shared knowledge makes the implementation of individual compilers much easier; compiler writers know that compilation is most naturally carried out in a number of phases such as syntax analysis, semantic analysis, intermediate code generation and so on. Such well-known design decisions facilitate compiler writing since they allow the writer to concentrate on any novel or specific problems which may arise.

Of course, there are still many difficulties. Optimization is not a simple problem and the advent of RISC machine architectures means that new approaches to register allocation must be developed. Nevertheless, the development of appropriate theoretical knowledge has made tremendous improvements in compiler writing techniques possible.

Large-scale development projects

Large-scale projects have always been much more prone to problems or failure than smaller developments, such as compiler implementations, due to difficulties of organizing and coordinating teams, and dealing with clients. Although a high proportion of such projects do encounter problems or even fail altogether, this is by no means always the case, and we shall consider two examples of large and highly successful projects.

One of the earliest major developments of software to support a business was SABRE, an Airline Reservation System developed for American Airlines. From start to finish the project took some 10 years; an extensive 5-year study was begun in 1954 and program design did not start until 1960. The system was designed to support reservation terminals in over 30 cities and to hold over 3 million customer records. It was first implemented in the course of 1963 and then extended to other cities over the period of a year. The SABRE system was a signal success; it enabled American Airlines to achieve a significantly higher rate of occupancy of seats on its flights. The project itself delivered about 1 million lines of code and involved around 400 person-years of effort. This success is all the more striking because of the lack of supporting software – there were no database systems available at that time, for instance.

Another highly successful large-scale development has involved the production of software for the NASA Space Shuttle. This project has some 270 people working on it to develop and maintain the safety-critical flight-control and navigation systems. This software is complex; during critical periods in the flight it runs on four onboard computers simultaneously, thus giving rise to difficult synchronization problems. There is even a backup system, supplied by a different contractor, to which control can be switched in the event of a serious software error occurring. The software comprises some 420 000 lines of code which run on the Shuttle's on-board computers as well as a further 1.7 million lines of software tools and testing aids used by the developers.

The Shuttle project has achieved remarkable levels of reliability. NASA itself requires near-zero-defect software, and the last safety-related fault found in the on-board software was eliminated in 1986. Only one software error (which was benign) has occurred in flight since 1985. Since the project started improving its development methods in the early 1970s there has been a 300% increase in productivity and the number of defects per thousand lines of code delivered has been reduced to a figure in the region of 1% of the initial error-rates. Moreover, managers are able to estimate costs to within 10%.

These improvements have been achieved by introducing rigorous control of software development, tracking all changes and errors, and constantly refining the development process to ensure that errors are eliminated at the earliest possible stage. Only about 18% of the staff are involved in actually writing software for the Shuttle; 26% work on its verification, and every line of code delivered will have been inspected by at least six people. The project has detailed statistics on errors found in releases and so is able to predict quite reliably the likely number of residual errors and how much effort is required to reduce them. These precise statistics mean that the costs of error elimination are quantified and the savings or additional costs of producing less or more reliable software are known.

Discussion

In discussing the characteristics of software in Chapter 1, a number of problematic areas for the developer were identified. These include the difficulty of reasoning about software, its complexity (which limits the effectiveness of testing as a way of finding errors), and its malleability. Notwithstanding these difficulties there are areas, such as compiler development, which have undergone dramatic improvements in productivity and reliability. In the case of compilers these improvements have been brought about by the development of theoretical underpinnings such as formal language theory. This in turn has allowed appropriate software tools to be developed to support the development process; these are particularly valuable since they produce predictable and reliable results. The malleability of software and the consequent danger that errors are introduced by quick changes can be overcome by proper management and control of the development process.

Compiler writing appears to be a domain where the development of relevant theory and tools, and the dissemination of experience and proven techniques, has transformed practice from craft to professional engineering level (in terms of the model of engineering development introduced above).

Consequently, although software does present novel problems, it appears that its development can be greatly improved by the adoption of an engineering approach. The distinction between the complex and non-continuous behaviour of software and that of other engineering artefacts may not be as great as it appears at first sight. It is true that software development differs from much engineering in that there is no underlying physical science which can be used, like physics for construction engineering for instance. But this is also true for much of digital electronics which behaves according to Boolean logic, allowing the underlying physical properties of components to be largely ignored. Moreover, although the behaviour of conventional engineering products, such as bridges, is amenable to mathematical analysis and description, there are still many aspects of such structures which are not so easily analyzed. Bridges, for instance, do not generally fail in obvious ways: the ways components are joined, the gradual effects of corrosion or metal fatigue, and shoddy or negligent construction techniques all make the behaviour of a real bridge extremely complex and hard to analyze. Producing a safe design for a bridge (or other building) involves foreseeing all the ways in which it could fail and ensuring that none of these ways could be triggered. Of course, this gives rise to the kinds of difficulties software engineers face in verifying or testing software. How can one be sure of having thought of all the modes of failure, and of having properly estimated the chances of these being triggered?

Nor have other branches of engineering been free of major disasters. A few of the more dramatic failures in this century have included:

● The failure of the Tacoma Narrows suspension bridge in America. Opened to traffic in 1940 it was known to locals as 'Galloping Gertie' because of its tendency to oscillate in even moderate winds. Finally the bridge collapsed when a 40 mph wind set the roadway oscillating and twisting so violently that it broke up altogether.

● In the early 1950s the first operational passenger jet airliner, the de Havilland Comet, was involved in a series of tragic disasters in which the plane appeared to explode in mid-air. Eventually the planes were grounded and an extensive investigation launched, which tracked the cause down to metal fatigue. The repeated pressurization and depressurization of the cabin weakened the area around a window, which would eventually blow out in flight.

● The collapse in 1968 of Ronan Point, a high-rise block of flats in London, after a (minor) gas explosion in a top flat. The block was constructed using prefabricated components, the explosion blew away two outer walls of the top flat. This left the roof unsupported and it fell, setting off a chain reaction in which, floor by floor, one whole corner of the 22-storey building collapsed.

● In 1980, in the Hyatt Regency Hotel in Kansas City, Missouri, a suspended walkway which connected hotel floors on separate sides of the building collapsed causing the deaths of 114 people. The failure was due to the combination of design and construction flaws which meant that the walkway was barely able to support its own weight.

All these incidents involved design faults, and the first three occurred in structures which were novel in some way. The Tacoma bridge was extremely slender and more susceptible to the wind than previous bridges; the Comet was the first passenger jet plane; and Ronan Point used a novel construction method.

It is interesting that, in the case of the Comet, some 60 hypotheses for the causes of the problem had to be investigated and that, before the fault was located, about 50 design changes were made as a result of other less-critical problems which were found in the aircraft's design. This experience of a rigorous search for a fault revealing other errors is only too familiar to software developers.

The development of a compiler is usually a relatively small-scale project and, as we saw in Chapter 1, most problems seem to arise in larger developments where there are the additional problems of coordinating work and dealing with organizational issues. However, as demonstrated by projects such as SABRE or the Space Shuttle development, even large projects can succeed and, as in the Shuttle case, develop systems with very low error rates. They do this by carefully managing and monitoring the development process; it is the aspect of monitoring and compiling statistics on past performance which is perhaps key. With detailed historical data it is feasible to estimate timescales for future projects and to refine and improve techniques.

Careful monitoring and control of processes, such as software development, are part of the 'Commercial Exploitation' phase of the development of an engineering discipline (according to the model presented earlier). This phase is critical to the introduction of more sophisticated techniques since without a clear picture of the problems presented by software development it is impossible to successfully introduce new techniques.

Consequently, although much practice is still at a craft level, there appears to be no reason in principle why software development cannot develop into a proper engineering discipline. Already some areas of development and some projects can be carried out using approaches which are more akin to the commercial development or even professional stages of engineering development. Moreover, as a consideration of other areas of engineering shows, the problems of complexity are not peculiar to software; more established forms of engineering also have to tackle complex projects where absolute certainty of success is hard to guarantee.

One of the most important aspects of a transition from craft practice is the proper control and monitoring of processes. Such efforts are usually seen as being part of Quality Assurance or Quality Management. Since such practices lay the foundations for the introduction of more sophisticated techniques we look at quality issues in detail in the next section.

10.3 Quality and software development

In modern industry and business there is enormous concern to try to produce goods and services of high quality. The origin for this concern lies in the tremendous success of the Japanese economy over the 30-year period from 1960. This was achieved, at least in part, by a preoccupation with producing high-quality goods and continually striving to improve manufacturing processes. The impact of this approach has led to quality becoming a central concern in many Western businesses as well.

In this context the term 'quality' can be taken as being defined as:

The set of characteristics of a product or service which satisfy a customer's requirements and expectations.

A more succinct definition attributed to the American Joseph Juran, one of the early advocates of quality management, is **fitness for use**. The current concern with achieving quality, as defined in this way, stems from the central importance for businesses of satisfying customer expectations.

The techniques which have been developed to help organizations produce high-quality goods are very similar to the kinds of techniques which represent the transition from craft to engineering practice, as discussed above. The approach to quality which is now generally advocated focuses on defining processes and monitoring them closely to derive insights into how they can be improved. This approach, as it has been applied in areas such as manufacturing, has made extensive use of measurement and statistical analysis to locate the source of errors or faults as a precursor to their elimination. It is striking that the Shuttle project, discussed above, makes use of detailed statistics to monitor the development process and to predict reliability of error rates. Detailed tracking of error statistics during development has been found by other developers, such as Microsoft, to be extremely useful even though they may adopt a more informal approach to managing software development (Cusumano and Selby 1997).

Such an approach, we suggest, forms a foundation for the introduction of techniques derived from research and so makes the move towards a fully fledged engineering discipline feasible. Certainly, if current practice is not clearly defined and sources of problems not identified it is hard to see how new techniques can be exploited – no one would know if they helped to improve a process or not.

In the rest of this section we first look at the development of modern thinking about quality management before considering how such ideas can be applied to software projects.

Development of ideas about quality

Until relatively recently quality was primarily seen as being a concern of manufacturing industries. The approach that was adopted involved inspecting items which came off a production line and rejecting or reworking those that were unsatisfactory. This approach – inspection and rejection – had several weaknesses: some faulty items would inevitably escape detection, it led to the additional costs of reworking and wasted materials, and it meant that productivity and quality were unlikely to improve. The received wisdom at the time was that it was more expensive to produce high-quality goods because of the additional resources needed to detect a higher proportion of faulty products. Hence manufacturers were content to run factories which produced a high proportion of defective items – 5% of their output might be returned after delivery.

During the Second World War some American statisticians became involved in quality control of the products delivered by defence contractors. They used statistics to devise and implement sampling techniques to determine whether a delivery should be accepted or not. Some statisticians went further and advocated that statistical techniques could be used not just to estimate fault rates but also to detect the sources of faults. They advocated an approach whereby high quality would be achieved not by inspection but by tracking down and eliminating the sources of faults in the production process. They pointed out that the costs incurred by faulty items far outweighed the cost of eliminating the causes of faults from the production process itself (this idea was later to give rise to the saying 'Quality is Free').

Two of these experts, W. Edwards Deming and Joseph M. Juran, became involved in advising Japanese companies as part of the American effort to help Japan recover after the war. In the 1950s, Japan had a reputation for producing cheap but low-quality goods. The techniques advocated by Deming and Juran were widely adopted and led to enormous improvements in quality; these improvements were one of the key factors behind the unprecedented success of the post-war Japanese economy.

The experience of many manufacturers in losing market share to higher-quality Japanese goods sparked interest in the West in quality management and the ideas of Deming, Juran and others. This new approach became known as **Total Quality Management** (TQM); the distinguishing characteristics of the TQM approach to quality are:

- clearly defining quality in terms of customers' or consumers' requirements
- concentrating on achieving quality by improving production processes rather than by inspection of end products
- the clear specification of processes and the use of statistical analyses and other techniques to track down the sources of faults so that the process can be improved
- the involvement of everyone in quality improvement and
- constantly trying to improve quality by learning from faults and improving processes and designs.

The high level of interest in quality management has led to standards for quality management being defined. These include the British standard BS 5750 and the international standard ISO 9000. These standards require the setting up of strategies for documenting processes and achieving predictable levels of quality.

The application of quality management to software development

The current ideas on TQM developed in manufacturing, where it is possible to define production processes precisely and apply statistical analysis to track down sources of faults. One of the key insights of this approach was that the quality of a process determines the quality of its output.

How applicable are these ideas to software development? On the face of it each development of a system is a one-off project so it is not obvious that insights derived from improving manufacturing processes are applicable. On the other hand, the argument of Deming and others that quality cannot be achieved by testing alone is borne out by the experience of many software developers, who have seen that systems which start out with high rates of errors often seem to carry on being error-prone however much effort is put into testing and error correction.

There is now a trend among a small proportion of software developers to try to apply the lessons of TQM to software development. Often this means adopting a quality standard, such as ISO 9000, but research has also been carried out to see how quality management ideas can be adapted and made appropriate to software. We shall look at the applicability of the ISO 9000 quality standard to software projects and then discuss the Capability Maturity Model, an attempt to use quality management ideas in characterizing software development.

Quality standards – ISO 9000

High quality of manufacturing and service is now seen as critical in so many areas of business and government that quality management and improvement has become the object of official standards. In the United Kingdom, the British Standards Institution introduced the quality management standard BS 5750 in 1979, and many other countries have introduced similar standards. In 1987 the International Standards Organization, to which the standards-setting authorities of more than 90 countries are affiliated, also published a quality standard, ISO 9000, which was strongly influenced by BS 5750.

ISO 9000 is really a range of standards which can be applied to different kinds of business or product. Independent bodies are accredited to carry out ISO 9000 audits and these bodies can award ISO 9000 certification to a company if its quality procedures are consistent with the standard. In order to achieve certification a software company must be able to show that:

- it has standards against which to measure all aspects of its development practices (e.g. requirements analysis and specification, document production, and so on),
- it has procedures in place to assess performance against these standards and
- both the standards and the assessment methods used are recognized in the industry.

The standard ISO 9000–3 sets out how these particular criteria are to be interpreted in the context of software development.

The aim of ISO 9000 is to ensure that companies which are certified are capable of producing quality products and services. However, this only means that the company would be able to produce a consistent level of quality, not that the level would be particularly high. Indeed ISO 9000 has been criticized for introducing too much paperwork and ignoring the importance of continuous improvement.

Capability Maturity Model

In the United States, the Software Engineering Institute based at Carnegie Mellon University has applied the quality ideas of Deming and others to software and proposed a model of the development process. This model, the Capability Maturity Model (CMM), is primarily concerned with the way in which projects are managed and organized and proposes five levels of maturity in development practices (Figure 10.1). At the lowest level, 1, software projects are essentially chaotic and at the highest level, 5, a process of continuous improvement has been achieved very much along the lines advocated by TQM practitioners.

The Software Engineering Institute has also proposed two ways in which the CMM may be used: Software Process Assessment, where an organization audits its own practices to determine their maturity level; and Capability Evaluation where software buyers can assess the level of the organization from which they are buying.

The CMM focuses very much on managerial and organizational issues because research suggested that these were the main source of problems in software projects (Carnegie Mellon University Software Engineering Institute, 1995). Furthermore, organizations whose development practices are at a low level of maturity are unlikely to be able to benefit from the introduction of new techniques or software tools. Their practices are not sufficiently disciplined for them to be able to identify appropriate technologies or tools. As was discussed in Chapter 1, research suggests that the overwhelming majority of software developers are currently at the lowest levels of the CMM and so would be unlikely to be able to make good use of new technology or techniques.

The CMM was originally developed in order to help the US Department of Defense to assess the capability of software contractors bidding for projects. Consequently the model has been criticized for focusing on the managerial

1 **Initial Level** There is not a stable environment in which to develop software. Projects are essentially chaotic with success heavily dependent on the contributions of key project staff.
2 **Repeatable Level** Policies and procedures for managing software projects, based on previous experience, are established. Project progress is tracked and under control.
3 **Defined Level** A standard process of software development (which may be based on any well-known model or even be specific to the organization) is documented and is used across the organization. This standard process is adapted and tailored as appropriate for individual projects.
4 **Managed Level** Measurable quality targets (such as acceptable error rates in programs) are set for projects and the results achieved by all projects are monitored.
5 **Optimizing Level** Measurements obtained from the monitoring of software development are used as a basis for refining and improving the processes used. The statistics on software development may also be used in deciding whether and how to introduce new technology and in assessing its impact. This level is one of continuous improvement.

Figure 10.1. The five levels of process maturity defined by the Software Engineering Institute's Capability Maturity Model

issues of large software projects and ignoring other factors such as the use of formal methods, software tools and so on.

Discussion

One of the central ideas of modern quality management is that quality cannot be added to a product retrospectively by inspection or testing. The way to improve quality is to concentrate on improving the processes involved in producing a product or service and to use information on faults or problems to guide these improvements. The rationale behind this approach is simple: correction of one error can never be as efficient as improving a process and so preventing dozens or hundreds of similar errors occurring in the future. As such, the approach should appeal to software developers who know how difficult it is to correct software which is badly designed or implemented.

Although the TQM approach to quality has now found widespread acceptance in manufacturing, it is still relatively novel in software development. As yet only a small proportion of companies have experimented with quality programs, though some report considerable increases in both productivity and quality of software (Fox and Fakes 1997). This is not to say that implementation of quality management is simple or easy. One of the main problems is that the benefits of such an approach cannot be quantified in advance, and significant improvements in quality are likely to require a considerable investment of time and may not become apparent for several years.

It is clear that quality approaches to software result in a development approach which is defined and monitored. Once this has been done there is then the potential for improvement and for experimentation with more sophisticated methods of specification, configuration management, testing and so on. It is when new techniques, possibly derived from research results, can be put in place and assessed that software development becomes a professional engineering discipline.

10.4 Summary

In this chapter we have discussed whether software development is, or could become, an engineering discipline. Engineering is not simple to define but generally appears to have as its objective the construction of artefacts for the benefit of people and to rely on a systematized body of knowledge, much of which is derived from scientific research. One view of how engineering disciplines such as civil engineering have developed postulates three main stages: an initial craft stage which relies on a trial-and-error approach, a more intensive stage when commercial pressures result in standardized practices, and a final professional stage. In this final stage engineers will undergo lengthy training and the discipline makes use of scientific and codified knowledge and approaches.

We next considered software engineering and looked, in particular, at compiler writing which appears to have advanced from a stage of craft-practice to a state of professional engineering. Compiler technology is somewhat exceptional in the degree of formalized knowledge that exists; however larger-scale projects, such as the Space Shuttle software, have achieved high levels of reliability in the software they deliver and can also be regarded as having advanced far beyond a stage of craft practice. From considering some of the difficulties and failures which have been encountered in other engineering areas it also appears that the differences between software development and traditional engineering practice may not be as great as are often supposed: other engineers often have to deal with enormous complexity and can also run into problems due to design faults or lack of experience.

Finally we looked at modern ideas on quality since these ideas, in particular the emphasis on defining and continually improving processes, appear to have produced considerable improvements where they have been deployed on software projects. More importantly still, an approach along these lines is an important part of progressing from *ad hoc*, craft-style techniques to a proper engineering discipline of software development. We also briefly considered the ISO 9000 standards for quality and the Software Engineering Institute's

Capability Maturity Model. The latter is particularly important because it represents a considered attempt to apply quality management ideas to software.

Further reading

The distinction between engineering and craft or other disciplines is discussed in *The Engineer and his Profession* by John Kemper (1975) and in the articles by Hoare (1989) and Shaw (1990). *To Engineer is Human* by Henry Petroski (1985) gives a good introduction to the ways in which structural engineers approach problems and the history by J. P. M. Pannell (1964) gives a good overview of the development of civil engineering.

The development of the SABRE reservation system and other early software engineering successes are discussed in *Software Engineering* by Martin Shooman (1983). The experiences of the American Space Shuttle project in producing highly reliable software are covered in one of the chapters in the *The Capability Maturity Model* jointly authored by the staff of the Software Engineering Institute (Carnegie Mellon University) (1995). *Why Buildings Fall Down* by Matthys Levy and Mario Salvadori (1992) gives a good overview of some of the problems that have been encountered in structural engineering (it also covers the problems with the Comet aircraft).

A general introduction to the modern approach to quality management is best obtained by reading the works of some of its leading proponents such as *Out of the Crisis* by W. Edwards Deming (1986), and *Quality is Free* by Philip B. Crosby (1979). Introductions which also cover current quality standards include *TQM in Action* by Pike and Barnes (1996) and *ISO9000 BS5750 Made Easy* by Kit Sadgrove (1994). A good source of material on the development of quality concerns and the underlying statistical principles is *Quality: from Customer Needs to Customer Satisfaction* by Bo Bergman and Bengt Klefsjö (1994). The issues of quality assurance in software development are discussed in *Software Quality* by Sanders and Curran (1994).

Points to consider

1 In this chapter we have concentrated on the technical problems of software development; we have said little about human factors such as the problems of designing a system which fits in with working practices or which is easily understood by users.
Do these issues undermine the argument that software development is potentially an engineering discipline like any other? If not, how can systematic approaches be adopted to overcome these problems?
2 Given that quality approaches can, apparently, produce enormous increases in productivity and software reliability, is there any need for a

profession of software engineering? Are the problems in developing software really managerial rather than technical?

3 What kinds of problems might an organization encounter when trying to implement a more quality-oriented approach to software development?

4 To what extent do computer science (or other engineering) courses cover issues of quality in software development? Is this coverage adequate? What problems are there in instilling such ideas in a university environment?

5 From the experiences of some organizations it appears that it is possible to develop highly reliable software using quality management techniques. On the other hand, organizations may only reach that stage after years of gradual improvement. What are the implications for liability for faulty software? Is it reasonable for developers to be liable for faults in software? What about developers who have not yet managed to improve their practices? Should they be allowed a period of adaptation in order to adopt best practice?

CHAPTER 11

Societies for computing professionals

The software for the Therac-25 machine supplied by AECL, discussed in Chapter 1, was written in assembly language and ran on a DEC PDP-11 computer. It was developed over a period of several years by one programmer who then left the company leaving little documentation on the system. When one of the victims of the Therac-25 sued AECL, the victim's lawyers were unable to obtain information about the programmer from the company. Nor were the programmer's former colleagues able to supply details of his educational background or experience. This, in spite of the fact that he was developing complex, real-time software for a safety-critical application in a low-level language in which it is relatively easy to make mistakes. The lawsuit was settled out of court before any details of the programmer's qualifications were ascertained (Leveson and Turner 1993).

Overview

Although nothing is known for certain about the qualifications of those involved in the Therac-25 development it seems highly desirable that people engaged in the development of complex or safety-critical software should have appropriate training and experience. Professional societies have an important role in setting standards for training and for certifying that individual practitioners have attained an appropriate level of competence.

In this chapter we are concerned with professional societies for software developers and their role in promoting appropriate standards and good practice. We first consider what professional societies are and the functions they perform which the law does not. We then review the development of professional societies in engineering before outlining the current structure of the engineering profession in the United Kingdom.

The rest of the chapter is concerned with the computing profession in particular. We review the professional qualifications which are available to software engineers and computing professionals and how they may obtain them. Finally we look at the role of professional institutions in promoting training and development.

Relation to other chapters This chapter, which deals with the social development of professions, complements the previous one which considered their technical development. The need for professional societies to promote standards of competence arises out of the frequent problems which occur in software development, discussed in Chapter 1, and the wide gap which exists between current best practice and standard practice. The importance of establishing and respecting norms of professional competence also derives from legal liability issues outlined in Chapter 7. The role of professional societies in promoting and ensuring ethical behaviour is discussed in the next chapter.

11.1 What are professional societies?

Professions, such as medicine or the law, are distinguished from other occupations by the long period of training and experience which are required in order to qualify as a practitioner. They are also different in that they are regulated by professional societies, independent bodies with a separate legal identity, which control entry into the profession. Such societies are run by the members of the profession and represent its interests.

A profession which is run by its own members through the mechanism of a society has a degree of autonomy and independence. It is not under the immediate control of government or employers and can make its own pronouncements on issue of public concern. It can also set and enforce its own standards of professional behaviour and competence.

Professional institutions can be created in two ways: by statute (that is, by passing a law) or by Royal Charter. The statute, or charter, will set out the rules by which the institution or society will regulate its affairs as well as any duties or responsibilities that it has. For instance, a professional society may have a duty to advise the government on issues relating to its field or to set standards of training.

One important aspect of professions is that, in certain areas, membership of the appropriate professional body is a prerequisite to practising. For example, only a chartered accountant can certify that a set of company accounts gives an accurate picture of the company's financial performance. Similarly, it is illegal to practise as a dentist or to write a prescription for drugs without the relevant professional qualification.

The engineering profession

This is currently represented by a wide range of professional institutions, each of which is concerned with a particular area of engineering. Professional bodies for engineers have all been created by Royal Charters and the various institutions (e.g. the Institution of Civil Engineers, the Institution of Mechanical

Engineers, the British Computer Society and so on) tend to have broadly similar rights and responsibilities. The latter typically comprise:

- to advance knowledge in their area
- to uphold and seek to improve standards of practice (this will usually involve setting out a Code of Conduct for members of the institution)
- to set educational and training standards in their field (this may include running professional exams and accrediting appropriate degree courses)
- to advise the government on issues within their area of expertise (the British Computer Society has been consulted on the Computer Misuse Act and on intellectual property rights, for instance).

Engineering institution members are obliged to adhere to any codes of practice which their institutions set out and have the right to use certain titles and initials (members of the British Computer Society can use the initials MBCS after their name, for instance).

The involvement of professional bodies in setting standards of competence and conduct gives them a role which is complementary to the law. The law is essentially reactive in nature, it gives individuals or companies the means to obtain compensation or redress for injury or loss which they may have suffered as a result of other people's negligence or recklessness. But it does little to prevent problems arising. Professional bodies, in contrast, have an essentially proactive role. They set and seek to improve standards of training and competence. They serve as a forum for exchange of ideas and knowledge by professionals and promote ethical behaviour through codes of practice or conduct. Professional bodies in consequence have a role in helping to prevent problems arising in their specialist areas.

While it is a criminal offence to impersonate a doctor, anyone can claim to be an engineer (though a particular institution could sue the individual to prevent him or her using titles awarded by the institution). Given the safety-critical nature of much engineering some people have argued that only properly qualified engineers should have a licence to practise. Their argument is that an incompetent or poorly trained software developer, for instance, can cause as much harm as incompetent professionals in other areas, such as medicine (Shore 1988).

11.2 The history of engineering professions

When engineering was at the stage of a craft practice (as defined in the previous chapter), there were few formal mechanisms for the training of new engineers or for disseminating knowledge. The emergence of professional bodies to improve standards and ensure adequate training is therefore an important aspect of the development of a modern engineering discipline.

In the United Kingdom the first engineering institutions were learned societies set up to facilitate the exchange of knowledge among practising engineers. The Institution of Civil Engineers (ICE) was founded in 1818 and obtained a Royal Charter in 1828. Membership was relatively small, no more than a few hundred members for much of the nineteenth century, and there were no formal criteria for membership. The Institution included most eminent engineers of the period and was soon publishing accounts of its proceedings. It was not until about 1890 that the Institution set entrance examinations and published a syllabus.

In the early nineteenth century the term 'civil engineering' covered all forms of engineering which were not carried out for military purposes. Initially the Institution of Civil Engineers represented the whole engineering profession and continued to do so until after the middle of the century. Engineering had by this time developed differing, quite distinct, specialisms and in 1847 the Institution of Mechanical Engineers (IME) was founded. The IME concentrated specifically on mechanical engineering (locomotives, manufacturing, etc.) and had 100 members by the end of its first year.

When the IME was formed it was seen as being complementary to the ICE, concentrating as it did on a specific kind of engineering. Nevertheless, its foundation set a precedent whereby each branch of engineering set up its own institution (there were about 15 national engineering institutions by the turn of the century and there are about 40 at present). These newer institutions had similar constitutions and activities to those of the civil engineers. In part the proliferation of professional institutions in the second half of the nineteenth century reflected the growth of the engineering profession as a whole, which grew from 1000 members of engineering institutions in 1850 to some 40 000 by 1914.

Throughout most of the nineteenth century British engineers were firmly convinced of the value of practical experience as the basis of training. Most professional engineers learned as apprentices and often had relatively little formal education. This was in contrast to the system in many Continental countries which laid considerable emphasis on engineers having a mathematical background. Towards the end of the century, however, there was a change in this approach and engineering institutions began to set formal exams for admission and to publish syllabuses. This change was brought about by a growing recognition that British engineering was falling behind in comparison to Continental and American practice. The Tay Bridge disaster of 1879, in which a recently constructed bridge over the Tay collapsed in a gale dropping a train into the sea and killing over 70 people, was a critical incident in bringing about a re-evaluation of training and leading to a greater emphasis on formal education.

The institutional proliferation of the nineteenth century resulted in a profession in the twentieth which was fragmented and had difficulty in promoting its interests. Moreover, British engineering was not as successful as the engineering professions in other countries in helping to maintain an internationally competitive economy. Growing concern at the decline of the

UK engineering industry led, in the 1970s, to the government setting up a committee of inquiry under Sir Montague Finniston. The committee was charged with looking into the state of the engineering profession and making recommendations for improvements. The committee reported in 1979, making over 80 recommendations including specific proposals for the training of Chartered Engineers (The Finniston Report 1980).

Many of the recommendations of The Finniston Report were not implemented but one idea, for the establishment of the Engineering Council to represent and promote the profession as a whole, was followed. Nevertheless, engineering has not become as well established or respected as a profession in the United Kingdom as it has in other modern industrial countries. There are a number of reasons for this. Engineers are usually employees of large concerns and, as mentioned above, do not have an exclusive right to practise. Consequently they do not enjoy the same degree of autonomy in their professional lives as do lawyers or doctors. Another factor is the relatively low status of technologists in the United Kingdom as compared to other European countries (a phenomenon what has been blamed as one of the causes of the United Kingdom's long economic decline compared to other nations (Wiener 1981)). Lastly the profession has continued to be weakened by a plethora of professional institutions which have undermined its ability to promote its interests.

11.3 Professional institutions for software engineers

The two professional institutions which have most relevance for computer professionals are the British Computer Society (BCS) and the Institution of Electrical Engineers (IEE). The BCS is one of the most recent engineering institutions, having been founded in 1957 and received its Charter in 1984. The IEE in contrast has a long history, having been founded in 1871 when the use and application of electricity and electrical power were first becoming widespread. The IEE received its Charter in 1921 and is now the largest professional engineering society in Europe with a total membership of over 130 000. The scope of the IEE is far broader than the BCS in that it encompasses electrical and electronic engineering as well as computing. It is probably the case that software developers belonging to the IEE tend to have come from a hardware or electronics background. The BCS on the other hand has a smaller membership, 35 000, but probably more software developers. Consequently we shall concentrate on the BCS when discussing membership criteria and codes of conduct, though largely similar rules apply for the IEE.

The BCS's Royal Charter charges it with various responsibilities such as setting standards of practice, advising the government on matters relating to computing, representing the computing profession, accrediting computing courses, setting its own examinations, and acting as the UK member in various international computing-related organizations. The BCS also has a role in the dissemination of information about computing. To this end the Society has a number of special interest groups which discuss and exchange information on matters ranging from computer conservation to robotics, and publishes books and journals such as the *Computer Bulletin* and the *Computer Journal*.

Engineering Council

The Engineering Council acts as an umbrella organization for the 40-odd individual engineering institutions in the United Kingdom. It was created by Royal Charter in 1981 following on the recommendations of The Finniston Report. The Council represents the profession as a whole, promoting public awareness of the importance of engineering, advancing education, and advising the government on engineering-related issues.

The Council also has a role in regulating the profession and maintains a register of some 290 000 qualified engineers including about 200 000 Chartered Engineers. Registered engineers undertake to abide by a code of conduct which the Council publishes. All registered engineers are also members of individual engineering institutions.

Finally, the Engineering Council acts as the UK member in various international bodies such as the World Federation of Engineering Organizations and the Fédération Européenne d'Associations Nationales d'Ingénieurs (FEANI).

FEANI

FEANI represents the engineering profession at a European level and is made up of engineering institutions from 27 European countries. It was formed in 1951 to promote the interests of European engineers, improve standards of education, and encourage links between the engineering institutions of different countries. One important initiative of FEANI has been to foster engineering qualifications which are recognised across Europe. FEANI also maintains a register of engineers – to qualify for inclusion an individual needs to belong to a national engineering institution; to have a minimum of 7 years of engineering-related experience made up of at least 3 years of higher education in an engineering-related discipline; and to have at least 2 years of professional experience. Such engineers can use the prefix title 'Eur Ing' (standing for 'European Engineer') and have chartered engineer status throughout Europe.

11.4 Professional membership

Members of professional societies gain the benefit of meeting other profession-als in their field as well as access to other resources, such as libraries, seminars and special interest groups. Membership can be particularly important for those who work on a freelance basis since it is evidence that they have attained a certain level of professional competence and that they have undertaken to adhere to a code of practice.

Many software developers and computer professionals consider that the BCS is the obvious institution in which to seek membership. There are two kinds of membership: professional and non-professional.

Professional membership confers the right to be involved in the running of the society either directly or indirectly (by electing other members to executive positions). There are three such grades – Fellow, Member and Associate Member. Fellow is for senior professionals who have at least 8 years of practical experience and have achieved a position of eminence. Member is the standard grade: members will normally have passed exams set by the BCS or have a relevant degree and between 4 to 10 years of practical experience. There are special provisions to allow senior computing professionals without formal qualifications to obtain membership. Associate Membership requires a similar degree of experience as for full membership but the academic requirements are less stringent.

Non-professional grades of membership include Student, Graduate, Companion, and Affiliate. The Student and Graduate grades are for those who are studying for or who have obtained an appropriate degree but do not yet have sufficient professional experience to qualify for full membership. The Companion grade is for people from other professions, such as the law or accountancy, who have a significant involvement with computing. The Affiliate grade is for anyone with an interest in computers or information systems.

Professional membership of the BCS is available to those with the appropriate combination of professional experience and formal education. Experience is assessed from testimonials and interview; formal knowledge by examination. The BCS examinations comprise a Part 1 (corresponding to HND level), a Part 2 (corresponding to first honours degree level), and a professional project where the candidate demonstrates the ability to produce a computer-based system.

Course accreditation

Many computer science degree courses cover similar material to the professional examinations of the BCS. Such degrees are accredited by the BCS, so exempting their holders from the need to take some or all of the BCS's own examinations to gain membership (though they still need to be able to demonstrate the appropriate level of practical experience). For a degree course to give full exemption it must:

- cover the underlying theory and mathematics appropriate to computing
- have an emphasis on design
- promote understanding of ideas of quality
- cover systems development approaches

- cover ethical, legal, social and professional issues and
- include a substantial student project which involves the implementation of an application or tool using an engineering-based approach.

Registration with the Engineering Council

The Engineering Council maintains a register of qualified engineers at three levels: Chartered Engineers, Incorporated Engineers, and Engineering Technicians. To be registered as a Chartered Engineer an individual must have gone through periods of both formal training and professional experience. The training of a Chartered Engineer has four essential components called Engineering Applications, first outlined in The Finniston Report (1980) as follows:

- **EA1** an introduction to the fabrication and use of materials. In the context of computing this has been interpreted as signifying a good understanding of the representation and automatic processing of data.
- **EA2** the application of engineering principles in the solution of problems based on engineering systems and processes.
- **EA3** a thorough and structured introduction under supervision to industry which involves a range of practical assignments.
- **EA4** preparation for a first post with responsibility and working in the post with decreasing supervision.

The requirements of EA1 and EA2 are normally satisfied by the completion of an accredited engineering degree and EA3 and EA4 by a period of appropriate work.

The Engineering Council also maintains registers of Incorporated Engineers and Engineering Technicians. These grades correspond to engineers who do not have as advanced a formal training as Chartered Engineers but who have considerable practical skills or experience.

Many, but not all, professional members of the BCS are also Chartered or Incorporated Engineers. Those who have gained membership of the BCS on the basis of considerable practical experience and advanced professional standing may not have the academic qualifications which are necessary to qualify for Chartered Engineer or Incorporated Engineer status.

11.5 Professional development

The Engineering Council and individual engineering institutions advise members to continually seek to improve their skills and knowledge. The codes of conduct which these institutions publish also make it a professional responsibility to maintain a level of knowledge and competence which reflects current practice in a discipline.

The BCS has developed the **Industry Structure Model** to classify and differentiate the different roles and responsibilities which computing professionals may have. It identifies some 200 professional functions ranging from programming or technical support to management and strategy planning. These various roles are organized in a ten-level frame-work, from trainee to director level, which identifies key skills required in the various roles. The purpose of the Industry Structure Model is to help individuals and organizations to plan training and career development by identifying current gaps in knowledge or experience relative to career plans.

Training and keeping abreast of innovations is particularly problematical in computing since it is a wide and diverse field and developments take place very rapidly. To help computing professionals to deal with these problems, the BCS also runs two development schemes: the **Professional Development Scheme** (PDS) and **Continuing Professional Development** (CPD).

The PDS is designed to ensure that computing professionals have properly planned and verified training and development. In this scheme participants are given a logbook in which to record their work experience and training. Logbook entries must be signed off by a manager or experienced colleague who would normally be a BCS member and who would also have a mentoring role. The PDS scheme helps new professionals to obtain membership of the BCS since it provides an audited log of professional experience and development.

CPD is aimed at those who have already achieved professional qualification but who need to keep abreast of developments and broaden their knowledge. It is an Engineering Council initiative to encourage members of individual institutions to maintain and enhance their level of professional competence. Those participating in CPD are expected to plan their development, keep a record of activities and achievements, provide their institution with a record of their development, and encourage others to support and promote the scheme.

Schemes such as PDS and CPD provide a framework for monitoring and recording training. If properly followed and acted upon they can help a computing professional to avoid getting out of date or becoming trapped in one particular specialism.

11.6 Summary

In this chapter we have briefly reviewed the professional status of the engineering profession and its associated institutions. The development of such institutions is relatively recent and engineering is highly fragmented compared to other well-established professions, such as medicine or the law. The relatively low status of engineering in the United Kingdom has often been a matter for public concern and ultimately led to the setting up of the Engineering

Council to try to give the profession a higher profile and to improve standards of training.

Where computing professionals are concerned, the relevant professional institutions include the Institution of Electrical Engineers and the British Computer Society. We considered the membership criteria of the BCS in particular, since it probably has more computing professionals as members than any other engineering institution. Professional membership of the BCS is normally contingent on appropriate formal training and work experience. Members enjoy the advantage of being able to present themselves as full professionals and can benefit from opportunities for contacts with other professionals and supporting facilities which the society provides. Members of the BCS may also be eligible for registration as Chartered Engineers with the Engineering Council. Lastly we considered the need for continuing professional development and looked at two schemes which are run by the BCS.

Further reading

The Engineers by R. A. Buchanan (1989) gives a thorough account of the early development of engineering institutions in the United Kingdom.

The best sources of information on the British Computer Society, the Institution of Electrical Engineers, and the Engineering Council are their respective Web pages at:

http://www.bcs.org.uk/
http://www.iee.org.uk/
http://www.engc.org.uk/

which contain details on their activities and membership requirements.

The appropriate training for a software engineer is discussed in the articles by Shore (1988), Denning *et al.* (1989), Dijkstra (1989) and Parnas (1990).

Points to consider

1 There are estimated to be some 400 000 people working in computing in the United Kingdom yet the membership of the BCS is only in the region of 10% of this figure. What influence can an institution with such a small membership have on the industry?
2 Much of the impetus for the formation of engineering institutions was originally the need to exchange ideas and professional experience. Have modern communications largely taken over this role? If so, are engineering institutions left with any other significant role to fill?
3 In both this and the previous chapter it has been implicitly assumed that software development and other computing-oriented jobs are essentially engineering jobs. But many university computer science departments are in science or even management faculties rather than in engineering

faculties. What implications might such diverse views have for the way the subject is taught?

4 Is there any value in titles such as Chartered Engineer if they do not carry with them an exclusive licence to practise, which is not open to everyone?

CHAPTER 12

Professionalism and ethics

It is against the law to try gain access to computers on which one does not have an account. Is it morally wrong though? What if a programmer tries to gain such access purely out of curiosity or as a challenge? Is this really wrong and, if so, on what basis?

Objectives

In this chapter we shall look at some of the moral issues and dilemmas which a computing professional may encounter in the course of work. To many people in the field such issues may seem largely irrelevant to their professional life, so we first look at the reasons for considering ethical issues at all. Next we review some of the criteria which may be used for resolving ethical dilemmas. First we consider professional codes of conduct, in particular that of the British Computer Society. Such codes proscribe many dishonest or dubious practices but are not free from criticism. Since they are written to protect more than one interest group they can appear contradictory when applied to dilemmas involving conflicts of interest between groups. The problems which arise in such cases lead us on to consider some of the main strands of thought in moral philosophy. We give a brief introduction to the two most important kinds of ethical theories: consequentialism (the idea that acts must be judged in terms of their effects) and duty theories (which maintain that acts are inherently right or wrong), and see how these ideas can, in some circumstances, help to clarify ethical dilemmas.

Relation to other chapters In earlier chapters we have discussed issues which have an ethical dimension, such as privacy and databases in Chapter 2, and software ownership and computer crime in Chapter 4. We have also seen the response of British law to such issues; in this chapter we shall consider what ethical principles are involved in deciding such issues. We shall also consider the role of professional societies, discussed in the previous chapter, in setting standards of conduct for professionals.

12.1 Ethics and computing

Ethics is concerned with questions of right and wrong, good and bad, and determining how people should behave in particular situations. Words such as 'right' and 'good' are used every day in a wide range of situations to signify that something is desirable, sought after, or approved of by the person making the statement. 'Good food' is delicious, or healthy food; 'a good move' in a game is one likely to bring victory; 'a good driver' is one who drives carefully and obeys the traffic regulations, and so forth. The precise significance of 'good' and similar words, in these cases depends on the context where the word appears.

There is a different way in which words such as 'right' and 'wrong' are used. When people say 'It is wrong to murder people' they do not mean 'wrong in my opinion' or 'wrong if you don't want to go to prison', they mean that it is unconditionally, absolutely wrong. Ethics is concerned with right and wrong in this second, absolute sense along with issues such as ultimate values and standards of behaviour.

One kind of ethical issue which might face a computer professional is whether to disclose a conflict of interest to a client (Figure 12.1). A consultant, Sue, is offered a chance to recommend her own software to a client without their being aware that she will receive a royalty payment. Most decisions which people face are straightforward to the extent that they are concerned with making the best choice where the criteria for what is best are obvious: whether to accept a job with Company A or Company B, whether to shop at Store C or Store D. Such choices may be tricky but they do not involve any fundamental dilemmas; the objectives are clear, how to ensure the best career prospects or the lowest shopping bill. In deciding whether to disclose her interest to a client, Sue is faced with a different kind of choice, a fundamental one. Should she ensure that her software is sold and collect the royalty, or should she disclose her interest and run the risk that other software may be chosen? It is a choice between being open and risking losing the chance of a sale or deceiving and ensuring that it is sold. Such a choice is fundamental since it is between two irreconcilable alternatives: self-interest or openness.

Some writers (see, for instance, Martin and Schinzinger 1996) draw a distinction between the relatively small-scale ethical dilemmas which confront individuals or particular groups and the large-scale issues which affect society as a whole. The former include dilemmas like the one presented in Figure 12.1; the latter encompasses issues such as software ownership and encryption policies.

In this chapter we shall concentrate primarily on smaller-scale dilemmas. Many of these are not specific to computing, they are similar to the issues which may face professionals in other areas, particularly in engineering. These everyday dilemmas, which pit the interests of an employer against those of other groups, or the prospect of financial gain against honesty and openness, are not new, but they are the kind which most computer professionals will at some stage face. It is worth while to consider them for two reasons:

- Thinking about such issues in advance may make it easier to avoid getting into situations where people may take a particular kind of behaviour for granted.
- When people are presented with dilemmas in real life they are often under stress, and may not have much time to consider how to act. Moreover, there may be no disinterested party with whom to discuss the issue. In practice therefore it is not always easy to consider dilemmas dispassionately and react in the same way as one would wish with hindsight to have acted. Considering common moral dilemmas in advance helps overcome these difficulties.

Having looked at the nature of ethical choices and the desirability of thinking about such issues before encountering them in one's own career, the question arises as to how one should decide or choose when faced with an ethical dilemma. One obvious way, which we consider next, is to rely on the codes of conduct which are published by various professional bodies.

Sue is an independent consultant who specializes in advising clients about quality assurance. She has been hired by an insurance company to help them reduce the number of errors in the software that they develop in-house. As part of the assignment she is asked by her manager to look at software aids to testing which are available on the market and make recommendations as to whether the company should purchase any.

It so happens that one of the tools which is available, CheckIt say, was written by Sue in a joint venture with a small software house. The software house markets CheckIt and pays Sue £1000 royalty for each licence which is sold. Furthermore, CheckIt has not been particularly successful and Sue suspects that the software house is considering dropping it from the suite of products which they market.

The insurance company is unaware of Sue's involvement with CheckIt so she is presented with an opportunity to make a sale of her own software. She is fairly certain that there is no competing product and that the insurance company would benefit from using the tool. In any case the licence fee of around £5000 is small by the standards of an organization with an IT budget of many millions of pounds.

Should she notify the insurance company before agreeing to carry out the market study?

Figure 12.1. Disclosure versus personal gain

12.2 Professional codes of conduct

One of the characteristics of a profession is that it sets and enforces standards of behaviour for its members. Normally this is done through some formal code of conduct or ethics. One of the earliest and best known of such codes was the Hippocratic Oath, named after (though probably not written by) the Greek physician Hippocrates. This oath, which was developed in the fourth century BC, stresses the need for honesty and respect for the patient. It has become the foundation of many modern medical codes of practice.

The professional bodies of engineers also publish codes of conduct or practice. These generally stress the need to respect people's rights and legitimate interests, to deal honestly and fairly with clients, to help fellow professionals, and to maintain a high level of competence. For instance, the Code of Conduct of the British Computer Society (reproduced in Appendix I) lays down guidelines to be observed by computer professionals, as do the Rules of Conduct of the Institution of Electrical Engineers (reproduced in Appendix II).

According to the BCS Code, professionals are under a clear obligation to declare any interests they have in a service or product which they advise a client to purchase (rule 12) and to avoid conflicts of interest with their clients (rule 22). The IEE Rules give similar guidance on informing about conflicts of interest (rule 11). Consequently consultants who are asked to evaluate software packages should make it known to their client if they stand to gain when particular products are purchased (Figure 12.1).

The BCS Code of Conduct

The BCS Code of Conduct (Appendix I) comprises 22 rules which cover four main areas as follows:

1 **Public Interest** Professionals should take account of the public interest, and the rights and interests of third parties. One particular aspect of this is that practitioners should be aware of legislation which is relevant to their area of work. This means, for example, that a database administrator should know about the main provisions of the Data Protection Act to ensure that it is not unwittingly infringed.
2 **Duty to Employers and Clients** Professionals should discharge their obligations to employers or clients. This means that work must be carried out to a proper standard and that practitioners must not exploit their position to gain personal advantage. One implication of these rules is that practitioners should always advise their employers or clients if a project is running late and may not be finished on time.
3 **Duty to the Profession** Professionals have a general duty to uphold the reputation of the profession as a whole and to support other members of the profession. One implication of this is that a practitioner has a duty to

help junior members of the profession to develop. Consequently a project manager who has responsibility for a number of junior staff should try, as far as is compatible with other professional responsibilities, to give those staff opportunities to develop their expertise – perhaps by assigning them to a range of tasks, for instance.

4 **Professional Competence and Integrity** Professionals have a responsibility to carry out work to a reasonable standard and to keep their knowledge and expertise up to date (by participating in the Continuous Professional Development scheme discussed in Chapter 11, for example). Keeping up to date is particularly important in an area such as computing where technological development is very fast. One consequence of these obligations is that professionals should not misrepresent their knowledge – for example, an independent contractor should not claim to have knowledge of particular languages or packages which he or she has not used.

Consequently, in the situation outlined in Figure 12.2, where an independent consultant is worried that his level of expertise is being misrepresented, the Code is clear that the consultant should refuse to undertake the work (rule 20).

The BCS Code of Conduct is also supplemented with various Codes of Practice which give guidance as to how it is to be interpreted in particular areas (such as in safety-critical software development or for freelance contractors, for example). At the time of writing these Codes of Practice are under review, and so have not been included.

The BCS Code is not the only professional code that may apply to computer professionals; many software engineers are members of the Institution of Electrical Engineers and so governed by their Rules of Conduct (Appendix II). The IEE code is shorter, mainly because the BCS Code contains more rules which explicitly emphasize the public interest. This difference makes the BCS Code explicitly applicable to situations which involve issues of third-party rights (for instance, privacy) or activities which are in breach of the law. Overall the two sets of rules reflect similar concerns. They are also similar in both containing a mixture of rules concerned with general principles such as public safety (BCS, rules 1 to 4; IEE, rules 1 and 2) with narrower rules proscribing certain specific activities or behaviour (e.g. BCS, rule 10; IEE, rule 16).

Members of the BCS or the IEE who are in breach of the rules of conduct of their institution are subject to disciplinary action. This can lead to a formal reprimand, suspension, or even exclusion from their society.

Members of either institution who are chartered or incorporated engineers will also be subject to a code of conduct published by the Engineering Council. All these codes are largely similar to the extent that they lay stress on similar themes such as a general obligation to observe the interests of society and third

Paul is a freelance programmer and technical author whose experience is primarily in the development of PC database systems for small companies. For the past 6 months he has been working, on a contract basis, for a small software house who have often sent him out to work for their clients.

Now the software house has been asked by one of its regular clients to set up their Web site. Unfortunately all the staff that normally do this kind of work are occupied with existing projects. Nevertheless, the software house agrees to do the work and Paul is asked by his manager to go on site and set something up. When Paul points out that he has never set up a Web site before the manager tells him not to worry, given his knowledge and experience of technical authoring he should be fine and, if any problems should arise, he can always get in touch with one of the software house's Web experts to ask for advice.

Paul is keen to do the work since it will broaden his experience. When he asks whether the client is aware that he has never carried out this kind of work before he is assured that he doesn't need to worry about that. He should just do his best but not let on that he has never done similar work.

What should Paul do? He is sure that the client has been misled about his level of expertise. On the other hand, the software house is quite adamant that there is no problem. He doesn't want to upset them since they give him a lot of work and, moreover, the assignment is a good opportunity to broaden his expertise.

Figure 12.2. Misrepresentation of level of knowledge

parties, to put the interests of clients above personal interests, to keep technical knowledge up to date and so on.

Issues around professional codes of conduct

Professions and professional codes of conduct in particular are not without critics. One critic, John Ladd (1995), has outlined several objections to codes of ethics or conduct. First, ethical issues are complex and have to be resolved by individuals. It is not possible to resolve such dilemmas simply by producing a set of rules to follow. The second criticism centres around the distinction between micro-ethics (relating to the behaviour of individuals or small groups) and macro-ethics (relating to major issues of interest to society as a whole). Where micro-ethics is concerned, Ladd argues that there is no justification for any code, since the kinds of ethical dilemmas or problems which professionals face are no different from those which people encounter in general, regardless of whether they belong to a profession or not. Such everyday behaviour or problems require no new rules or special consideration. Where macro-ethics is concerned, a professional group may have a role in contributing to a general debate, but specific codes of ethics serve little purpose in this context. Ladd also argues that there may be secondary motives behind the establishment of codes of conduct, such as the desire to enhance the status of the profession. Moreover, such codes can, he believes, be harmful in that they may give rise to complacency: practitioners may think that so long as they observe the code they need not concern themselves with any ethical issues. One of his most important criticisms is precisely that such codes help to draw attention away from significant issues, such as how technology should be introduced or controlled, to smaller more immediate issues, such as the conduct of individuals.

Other critics have commented that the concern of professionals often seems as much to avoid being held responsible for problems or disasters as to prevent them (Adams 1995). Indeed cases have occurred where professional codes have been used to protect corrupt or dishonest engineers, as when two civil engineers criticized the behaviour of colleagues involved in the construction of a dam in Los Angeles. The engineers were expelled from the American Society of Civil Engineers in 1932 even though their comments helped to expose a major bribery scandal (Martin and Schinzinger 1996).

Nevertheless there are some strong arguments in favour of having codes of conduct. These really come down to the advantage that codes of conduct lay down common standards of behaviour. This means that clients or companies who employ computer professionals know what kind of service or behaviour they can expect. For example, they can expect not to be misled about levels of experience or likely delays to projects. The importance of this should not be underestimated since people and companies prefer to deal with those whom they believe to be honest and reliable.

From the viewpoint of individual professionals a code is important in supporting any refusal to behave unethically. In our example (Figure 12.2), Paul who is asked to misrepresent his level of expertise, can point to the BCS Code of Conduct (or the IEE Rules of Conduct) as sanctioning his refusal to comply. So although many codes of conduct can be criticized for containing rules which most people would take for granted, explicit statements about the need to take public interest or human rights into account do serve a purpose.

One difficulty which does arise with codes of conduct is that conflicts of interest can easily occur where a code appears to give contradictory advice. The BCS Code contains rules to protect both the interests of the pubic at large and the interests of clients and employers. What happens when there is a conflict between such interests? For example, what should a professional do who is working for a company which is going to sell safety-critical software which she believes is not safe (Figure 12.3)? The Code states that professionals must safeguard public health (BCS, rule 1) but it also states that work should be carried out in accordance with a customer's or employer's requirements. It appears to be sufficient for a professional to make clear the possible consequences if their judgement is overruled (BCS, rule 5). A similar conflict arises in the IEE Rules between safety (IEE, rule 1) and respecting employer confidentiality (IEE, rule 12). The IEE Rules do imply that it would be sufficient for a member to make an unambiguous statement about safety concerns to his or her manager (IEE, rule 7); of course, some engineers might not feel this was doing enough.

A separate problem with interpreting professional codes is that they are often written in a way which assumes that some kind of ethical or value judgement has already been made. To take one example, rule 2 of the BCS Code of Conduct states that members should take into account the 'legitimate rights of third parties'. This begs the question 'What is a legitimate right?' If a professional were in doubt about whether a right was legitimate the code is not of any use since it does not address the issue.

Moreover, it may be possible for someone who, for ulterior motives, does not wish to follow a particular rule to look for conflicting rules. For instance, Paul, who has been put forward to do work for which he is not really qualified (Figure 12.2) might avoid his duty to refuse to do the work (according to BCS

Jane works as a project manager for a company which produces medical equipment. She has worked for several years on software which will run in a suite of intensive care equipment. The software monitors heartbeat, breathing rate and so on and records these in a log. More importantly it also triggers an alarm when the patient's condition becomes unstable or critical. The software has been developed over a long period but is particularly error-prone. It now appears to be functioning correctly but, from looking at the amount of testing which has been carried out and the number of errors which were uncovered, Jane estimates that the software still contains a significant number of faults.

When she reports this to her manager at the end of a testing cycle she is informed that no more testing is to be carried out and that the equipment will soon be on the market as an upgrade to the company's existing intensive care equipment.

When Jane protests about this and points out that errors could have fatal consequences she is informed that the decision has been taken and that it is no longer her responsibility. Nevertheless she is extremely worried about the possibility of errors occurring when the machines are in service and wonders whether she should do more to prevent this.

Figure 12.3. A dilemma concerning confidence and safety

rule 20) by choosing to give greater weight to BCS rule 5, which says that members should carry out work in accordance with the wishes of their client.

12.3 A philosophical perspective on ethics

Although codes of conducts or rules may specify a clear course of action in most situations, there are circumstances where they are insufficient. There may be inconsistencies, for instance; ironically the longer and more comprehensive a set of rules is, the more likely it is that two or more rules may conflict with each other. When this happens an individual may need to consider issues more deeply. In any event, as Ladd and many others have pointed out, for behaviour to be truly ethical it must be based upon an individual's informed choice rather than unquestioning adherence to a set of rules.

Ethics, or moral philosophy, is that area of philosophy which is concerned with issues of right and wrong, and norms of behaviour. The original impetus for the consideration of these issues came in the fifth century BC when Greek travellers returned home with accounts of often very different cultures. These observed differences in customs caused early philosophers to reflect on the nature of moral codes and to look for common standards.

The value of moral philosophy is not that it provides answers to such questions but that it helps understand the issues involved: philosophy is first and foremost a subject which is concerned with clarifying assumptions and evaluating arguments. For much of its history, ethics has been dominated by religious thought, but in modern times much moral philosophy has been concerned with justifying moral codes or values in the absence of particular religious beliefs. This in particular has led to a search for underlying justifications for modes of behaviour or rules.

It is possible to identify two main approaches to ethical issues. Consequential theories evaluate actions primarily in terms of their consequences; duty theories in contrast lead to acts being viewed as right or wrong regardless of their particular consequences. We shall look in more detail at utilitarianism, the main consequentialist theory, and the theory of Kant, which stresses the role of duty in ethical behaviour before considering again the issue of how ethical dilemmas may be resolved.

Utilitarianism

When one is faced with a choice, what is the right thing to do? Utilitarians have an answer: one should do that which promotes the greatest happiness of the greatest number; happiness is the sum of pleasure minus the sum of pain. This simple rule is all that is required, according to utilitarianism, to decide any ethical issue.

A utilitarian would resolve the dilemma which faces Jane (Figure 12.3) by determining the consequences, in terms of total happiness, of any action she might take. This means assessing the advantages to her colleagues and the distress caused by occasional injuries or even fatalities if, on the one hand, she does nothing, against the damage to colleagues, if she takes another course of action (alerting the press, for instance). Of course, in practice such calculations may be tricky but, in principle, this is what needs to be done to resolve an ethical dilemma.

Utilitarianism was first proposed by Jeremy Bentham in the late eighteenth century and developed by the Scottish philosopher J. S. Mill in the nineteenth. These early proponents were very much reformers and were concerned in using utilitarian principles as a basis for legislation and social reform. Mill in particular expounded a version of utilitarianism which is sometimes referred to as 'act-utilitarianism'. According to this view, common moral imperatives, such as 'don't lie' or 'don't steal', were rules of thumb which encoded the ethically correct course of action in most situations. In more complex situations, however, ethical decisions needed to be made with reference to the greatest-happiness, greatest-number principle which utilitarians believe underlies all ethical behaviour.

For many people, utilitarianism is an attractive doctrine. It rests on a simple rule, based on pleasure, which has an immediate appeal and is also democratic in that it considers everyone's interests. Moreover, the rule is essentially forward-looking since it stresses consequences and has often been used as a guiding principle for legislation.

There are problems with act-utilitarianism. For one thing it often appears to sanction behaviour which most people would regard as dubious or obviously wrong. For example, a programmer who is going to make unauthorized copies of some software in order to sell it later (Figure 12.4) could argue that he was doing nothing wrong since it would result in more overall 'happiness' than if he did not.[1] Using utilitarian arguments, one can also justify knowingly punishing someone for a crime that he or she did not commit. This is on the grounds that the benefits of deterring people (though possibly not the real perpetrator) from committing similar crimes outweigh the distress of the unjust punishment to the innocent scapegoat.

Another criticism is that utilitarianism actually promotes two separate principles: maximizing happiness, and justice (that is, distributing happiness to as many as possible). But it offers no way to reconcile these two differing concerns. A programmer who commits what is called a 'salami fraud' (removing small amounts of money from many bank accounts, see Chapter 4) can argue that it is not wrong since the greatly increased happiness to the

---

1 Such copying is implicitly forbidden by the BCS Code which requires members to comply with the law (rule 3), and it is clearly against the spirit of rule 10 of the IEE which forbids a member from attempting to damage the business of another.

Bill is a New Zealander who is working his way round the world. He has been working in London for a software house which specializes in developing software for estate agents. The company has just finished developing a PC package which it intends to market under the name HomeFinder.

Bill was one of the main programmers to work on this software and he is due to leave the company and return to New Zealand after a final trip across North America.

Without his employers realizing it, he has come into the office one weekend to make a complete copy of the HomeFinder package. He hopes to use some of this software when he gets home in order to set up his own software house. He justifies this on the grounds that: first, the company behaves badly towards its employees so he feels no particular obligation and, second, since he will be in New Zealand he will not be in direct competition with his old employer which has no plans to market the software abroad.

Figure 12.4. Unauthorized copying of software

perpetrator far outweighs the hurt caused to the many account holders, who do not even realize that they have lost any money. Another utilitarian could argue that the same fraud does not spread happiness to the greatest number and so is obviously wrong.

One way that some proponents have attempted to get round these criticisms is to adopt a version of utilitarianism known as 'rule-utilitarianism'. In this version the greatest-happiness, greatest-number principle is used to derive a set of rules for everyday behaviour. That is, rather than use the utilitarian principle to answer the question 'What should I do in this situation?' it is used to answer the question 'What should people do, in general, in this kind of situation?' The answer to the latter question then gives rise to rules which should always be obeyed. Using this approach the copying of software (Figure 12.4) would be regarded as wrong. The problem with rule-utilitarianism is that it reproduces one of the problems that utilitarianism sought to avoid: following a set of rules will lead people to do the wrong thing in some situations, telling the truth when it might have been better to stay silent, for instance.

Utilitarianism has been criticized for other reasons as well. It is far from obvious that everything can be measured in simple terms of pleasure or pain. How can, for instance, the freedom to do as one chooses be measured in the same terms as a high salary or the satisfaction of climbing a mountain? The things which people seek and value are surely so diverse as to make comparisons between them impossible. A separate criticism is that utilitarianism takes no account of personal relationships or friendship. Someone acting according to utilitarian precepts would give no special consideration to his or her own feelings above those of others. Consequently the good utilitarian, confronted with the choice of rescuing his own mother or two strangers from a burning building, saves the strangers. Critics have pointed out that this is not how most mothers' sons would behave, or even be expected to behave.

Duty theories

The main alternative approach to utilitarianism, or other forms of consequentialism, advocates doing what is right, regardless of particular consequences. The best-known proponent of this view was the German philosopher Immanuel Kant who developed his ideas in the late eighteenth century, predating much utilitarian thinking. Kant placed great importance on respect for individuals and believed that the intention behind acts was what made them good or bad, rather than their particular consequences. He also stressed the central importance of people's duty to do what is right.

This begs the question: how do we know what is right in any given instance? Kant's answer was that a particular form of behaviour was right if one could be happy that everyone would always behave in that way. He expressed this principle, the **categorical imperative**, as follows:

> Act only according to that maxim by which you can at the same time will that it should become a universal law.

To illustrate this Kant gives the example of a man who is in dire straits and needs some money. He will only be able to borrow the money if he promises to repay it, but he knows that he will not be able to keep the promise. If he goes ahead and makes the promise anyway he is, in effect, acting according to the maxim 'When I have to, I will make promises that I know I cannot keep'. What would happen if this became a universal law, if everyone adopted the same maxim? Clearly promises would no longer have any value because everyone would be prepared to break them if it suited them. Consequently, according to the principle of the categorical imperative, breaking of promises is not right since no one can wish that such behaviour becomes universal.

According to this approach, Bill (Figure 12.4) should not make an unauthorized copy since he cannot truly wish that other people would feel free to do likewise. Presumably if his prospective New Zealand software house was successful he would not be happy about his future staff making copies of the software to set up their own companies. Likewise, Monica (Figure 12.5) must ask herself whether she would be comfortable with the idea that other people might read her e-mail without telling her.[2] She undoubtedly would not and so

---

2 The BCS Code, rule 2 appears to rule out monitoring on these terms (assuming that there is a 'legitimate right' to not have one's e-mail or files read by other people); there is no IEE rule which obviously applies to this situation.

Monica has recently taken over the role of support manager in a medium-sized company. The previous manager left suddenly after a stay of just a few months and Monica has been promoted to take over.

Shortly after she begins her new job she is asked by the IT manager to check up on how people are using e-mail and what they keep in their files. This she can easily do by making use of her access privileges to look at private files and e-mail files. Her manager explains that this is standard practice in the company to ensure that computers and e-mail are not used for private purposes.

When Monica protests that this is an invasion of privacy she is told that her predecessor made no objection and that the practice was well established in the company. When Monica points out that she has never seen any company notice saying that e-mail and files might be read by the support manager, she is told that honest staff have nothing to hide and would not be bothered by the practice.

Figure 12.5. A system manager is asked to monitor e-mail

should not behave in that way herself. On a more general level the categorical imperative cannot, unlike utilitarian principles, be used to justify punishing the innocent on the grounds that it will deter wrongdoing and so people will, on aggregate, be happier. No one would wish to be the hapless innocent of whom an example is made and so no one could agree to a situation where the innocent could be unjustly punished.

The categorical imperative is so called to distinguish it from hypothetical imperatives. A hypothetical imperative is an order to do something if one wants to achieve a particular result. 'Don't eat too much if you don't want to get fat' is an example: the imperative 'Don't eat too much' is contingent on not wanting to be fat – it presumably does not apply to Sumo wrestlers, for instance. In contrast, a categorical imperative is absolute; there are no conditions attached. 'Don't lie' is (according to Kant) such a categorical imperative; there are no conditions attached, one should not lie and that is that. There is a link here with what was said earlier: ethics is concerned with absolute notions of right and wrong, good and bad, rather than context-dependent meanings of these words.

The categorical imperative of Kant is not dissimilar to the ethical principle which appears in Judaeo-Christian (and other) religions: 'Do unto others as they should do unto you' or 'what is hateful to you, do not do to your neighbour', though the formulation is somewhat more abstract.

The categorical imperative goes hand in hand with a strong notion of duty. If something is the right thing to do then people have a duty to do it regardless of the consequences. This leads to a degree of inflexibility. For instance, according to a strict adherence to the principle an employee who is asked to disclose compromising information on a former employer for the benefit of the new employer (Figure 12.6) should do so for otherwise he or she would be lying and ignoring the duty to tell the truth.[3]

Ethical dilemmas

The principles discussed above do give some insight into ethical problems. An individual faced with a dilemma can resolve the issue by seeking to adopt the course of action which brings the most overall happiness to all those affected: a consequentialist approach. Alternatively, a particular course of action can be analyzed in the light of universalization: what if everyone were to adopt this course of action in similar circumstances?

Do these ethical principles tie in with any of the issues that we discussed earlier, such as software ownership or privacy? As far as ownership of software is concerned it seems that the arguments which are advanced by those who favour copyright protection are based on an appeal to universalization, that is, to duty ethics. They claim that copying software is wrong because were everyone to do it this would, in the long run, undermine the production of software; developers would become discouraged and turn to other activities. No one, they say, could therefore wish the maxim 'copy software when it suits you' to be enacted as a universal law so unauthorized copying is wrong. The arguments of those who are opposed to protection tend to be consequentialist: copyright protection makes software more expensive and ultimately reduces its use, it reduces cooperation between programmers, and it makes it harder to modify or develop software. They concede that individual developers or entrepreneurs will be worse off if there is no protection but maintain that there will be greater benefit overall.

The issue of data protection is interesting in highlighting one of the weaknesses in utilitarian principles. Debate in this area centres around the importance of privacy, yet it is not clear how privacy can be translated to the happiness of an individual who may be unaware of the information which others hold on him or her. How can information about John's creditworthiness, stored on some computer whose existence he doesn't even know of, affect John's happiness?

Both data protection and encryption issues are better clarified by the universalization approach. Rather than worry whether anonymity or privacy of correspondence equates to happiness in some way, it is easier to argue that most people would prefer to control the information held on them and to be able to have entirely private communications when they wished.

---

3 The BCS Code does not provide absolutely clear guidance in this situation; IEE rule 12 explicitly rules out improperly disclosing any information about the business of a former or current employer.

The activities of hackers, even if they do no damage, appear to be clearly wrong on the basis of both utilitarian and duty ethics. From a utilitarian perspective the disruption which a hacker causes makes the activity clearly wrong. Even if a hacker does not alter any data or programs on a computer, there is no way that the computer's owner or users can be sure of this, so hacking will inevitably cause problems. A hacker could argue that if his or her intrusion went undetected and no alterations were made, then no harm was done. This would be true, but there is no way for a hacker to ensure that an intrusion will go undetected. Alternatively, on an appeal to universalization, it is hard to believe that any hacker would be pleased to have his or her computer accessed without authorization. Consequently a maxim like 'hacking is acceptable' cannot be successfully universalized.

Although ethical concepts can help in understanding what issues are at stake, they do not always provide an obvious solution. For instance, Shirley (Figure 12.6) is really caught between two actual or implicit obligations: to respect her

---

Shirley works for a large software house in a division which specializes in development work for building societies. In her former job she worked for a much smaller software house which did all its work in this area.

Shortly after starting with the new company Shirley is asked to help out in putting together a proposal to a large society for carrying out a major development. Several other companies are putting in proposals for the work, including her old company.

The proposal is submitted and Shirley hears nothing for several weeks until she receives a phone call from the salesman who is dealing with the potential client. He tells her that the building society has narrowed the field down to just two companies: themselves and Shirley's old company. It appears that Shirley's former company has put in the best proposal but the building society is hesitating before giving it the business because it is a small organization and has never undertaken such a big project.

The salesman then tells her that he thinks all that is required to win the business is to undermine the building society's confidence in the smaller company. He asks Shirley whether her old company had undertaken any projects that had gone badly wrong so that he could mention these when he next saw the client. Shirley knows that just before she left her last job one project, which she was not involved with, had gone very badly behind schedule. She recently heard from friends that the client had brought legal proceedings which had been settled out of court. But she is reluctant to mention this to the salesman: it feels like betraying her old colleagues.

Figure 12.6. Conflict of interest of current and former employers

Paul has recently started work in a medium-sized software house. Formerly he worked in the computing department of a local authority and in his new job he is working as a team leader on a project to develop a system to calculate the tax liability of residents and to send tax bills out. The project is badly behind schedule though the software house is committed to delivering a working system within six months.

Paul left his previous job because he had found it stressful and the department had been understaffed. This had led to his working long hours and often not getting home until quite late. Consequently he had not seen much of his three young children in the week and his continual long hours had led to arguments with his wife. Paul had worried that if he continued working long hours it could lead to the break-up of his marriage.

Shortly after Paul joins the software house the project manager has an argument with one of the directors and leaves at short notice. Paul is then asked if he will take over the management of the project: this, it is conceded, will involve his working long hours and probably weekends as well. On the other hand, if the project fails the consequences for the software house will be severe. The rest of the team have agreed to work long hours and the management have promised everyone employed on the project a substantial bonus if it is completed on time.

Paul is left in no doubt that this is a significant opportunity for him to make a mark in his new job and, possibly, to secure a quick promotion. On the other hand, he is worried about the implications for his private life and the strain that it will put on his marriage.

Figure 12.7. A conflict of interest between work and private life

former colleagues, or to tell the truth when asked. Similarly, an individual who is forced to choose between family and work commitments (Figure 12.7) is unlikely to find any simple solution to his dilemma, either in codes of conduct (neither the BCS or IEE rules address this kind of situation) or in more abstract ethical principles.

The French philosopher Jean-Paul Sartre argued that all ethical decisions are ultimately personal. Even if an individual follows a code of conduct or seeks advice they have to make a choice about following the code or from whom to seek advice. They cannot avoid making the decision either directly or indirectly. Moreover, he argued that it is not possible to decide objectively how moral dilemmas should be resolved: each individual has to make his or her own choice knowing that others might decide differently. Sartre gave the example of a man living in Paris under German occupation during the Second World War.

His father is a collaborator and his mother is ill but is estranged from her husband. There are no other children. The man has the opportunity to travel to London and join the French resistance but, if he does, must abandon his mother who will have no one else to look after her. What should he do? On the one hand, he can join a movement to free his country but must desert his sick mother. On the other, he can stay but will be helping only one person. Sartre argues that it is in the nature of such dilemmas that they are hard to resolve (they wouldn't be dilemmas if they were not) and that each individual has, in effect, no choice but to make his or her own choice.

12.4 Summary

In this chapter we have been concerned with the kinds of ethical issues that a computer professional may come across in the course of work and the ways in which they can be analyzed. The value of considering such issues is, we have argued, that having thought about them in advance makes it easier to resolve such issues when they do arise and, perhaps, to avoid being put into difficult situations in the first place.

One obvious way of resolving ethical problems is to refer to rules of conduct, such as those of the BCS or IEE, for guidance. The BCS Code itself seeks to reflect the interests of various groups: society at large, employers or clients, and the profession as a whole. It also places an obligation on practitioners to maintain a high level of competence and to stay within their areas of expertise.

Professional codes have been criticized on the grounds that they do not define obligations or duties which are different from those that any other member of society has and can, in some circumstances, even be pernicious. Nevertheless, such codes do set a common standard and help individual practitioners resist pressure to behave unethically.

The weakness of codes of conduct is that they cannot always help individuals to resolve complex ethical dilemmas. Given that such codes seek to protect the interests of more than one group, it is inevitable that such interests will sometimes conflict, and when they do codes of conduct can appear inconsistent.

To help clarify such dilemmas, we briefly considered the main strands of thought in moral philosophy. These fall into two main groups: consequentialist ethics where the outcomes of particular actions are taken into account, and duty-based ethics where courses of action are tested against a criterion of universalization, that is, asking the question 'Would it be acceptable if everyone were to behave as I am about to?' Such ideas do help to clarify many ethical dilemmas but, as we saw, such choices are ultimately personal and not always easy.

Further reading

There are a number of texts which discuss the particular ethical issues which arise in the applications and use of computer technology. Among these are: *The Information Game* by G. Brown (1990), *Computer Ethics* by Y. Bynum (1996), *Computers, Ethics and Society* by M. D. Ermann *et al* (1990), *Computer Ethics* by D. G. *Johnson* (1985), *Ethical Decision Making and Information Technology* by E. A. Kallman (1993), *Practical Computer Ethics* by D. Langford (1995), and *Case Studies in Information and Computer Ethics* by R. Spinello (1997). The American ACM also has a Code of Ethics which we have not discussed: the contents of this code along with how it would apply to a number of cases is presented in the paper by Ronald Anderson *et al.* (1993).

The collection *Computers, Ethics and Social Values* edited by Deborah Johnson and Helen Nissenbaum (1995) contains a number of relevant articles including a critique of codes of conduct by John Ladd. The book *Risk* by John Adams (1995) also contains some criticisms of engineering codes of conduct (though not specifically of those of computing related engineers).

There are many introductory texts on moral philosophy though they often reflect their authors' particular standpoints. A general introduction to ethical issues is *How Are We to Live?* by Peter Singer (1997); Singer has also edited a collection of writings on ethics (1994) which gives a good overview of the field. One very readable short introduction to moral philosophy is *Basic Moral Concepts* by Robert Spaemann (1989). Other short introductions include: *Moral Philosophy* by D. Raphael (1981), *Morality: An Introduction to Ethics* by Bernard Williams (1973) and *An Introduction to Ethics* by J. Mabbott (1966). Longer texts include *Ethics* by J. Mackie (1977) and *A Short History of Ethics* by Alasdair MacIntyre (1966) which describes the development of thinking in this area.

Points to consider

1 Why worry about professional ethics? Some people may take the view that if they can get away with something and it is to their advantage (either in financial or career terms) then they would be foolish not to do it. Is it possible to convince someone who takes this view that they should change? What arguments could be used?
2 Should software engineers concern themselves with ethical issues any more or less than any other individuals in society?
3 As mentioned above, the codes of both the BCS and the IEE contain a mix of rules which are quite general (e.g. protect health and safety) and much more specific ones (such as declaring conflicts of interest). Is it possible to discern an underlying set of principles which have been enshrined in these codes? What are they and are they consistent?

4 Do computers and computer-related technology really raise new ethical problems or do they just present old issues in a new form?
5 Given some of the arguments advanced in support of codes of conduct (they ensure that clients know what they can expect from professionals, they support individuals when they refuse to carry out unethical work, and so on) could one argue that professional drivers should have a code of conduct ('Members shall not endanger other road users or pedestrians', 'Members shall refuse inducements to drive recklessly in order to speed up delivery of goods or to ensure that clients arrive on time' and so on)? Indeed is there an argument for every occupational group having a code of conduct which reflects their particular area of work (caterers, postal workers, airline pilots and so on)? What characteristics, if any, are there for a professional or occupational group which make a code of conduct appropriate?

Afterword

Modern information technology is really a combination of three related technologies: digital computers or processors, data storage, and digital telecommunications. We considered some of the problems and impacts of each of these in turn:

- Computer hardware is stable and largely reliable but software generally is not. It has proved to be very difficult to produce reliable software yet this has not stemmed a growing reliance on computer technology; there are now few areas of modern life which do not depend on software, yet most of that in use is of low quality.
- Advances in data storage now make it easy for private organizations and governments to store and analyze information on large numbers of individuals and, if they wish, to pigeon-hole people according to a set of predetermined profiles. This makes many aspects of life simpler, it is easier to get credit (for many people) than it otherwise would be yet such technology can also be used by unscrupulous governments to help monitor and stifle dissent.
- It is in the area of telecommunications that technological advances have perhaps been most dramatic. The ease of transferring data has facilitated globalization and reduced the power of individual governments to control the media or the exchange of information. We also saw how the availability of strong encryption technologies makes it more difficult for governments to monitor private communications.

As we saw, each of these areas has its own particular impact, but their combination into an integrated digital technology raises further questions and issues. We considered just a few of these: software ownership, computer crime, the apparent low pay-off of computer technology, and the impact on working conditions.

In the middle part of this book we looked at the way the law has adapted to computer technology. It was the case until recently that most lawyers were unfamiliar with computer technology, but this has changed since the advent of the PC has made computer technology generally available. Some early areas of uncertainty have also been resolved: software is protected by copyright, the storage and use of personal data is now constrained by data protection legislation, and the Computer Misuse Act has made activities such as hacking or virus writing illegal.

Nevertheless, there are many areas of the law relating to computer technology which are still uncertain. The liability of developers for errors in the software they produce still appears to be quite limited. However, recent decisions give reason to believe that the situation may change, at least where software developed under contract is concerned. Similarly, the trend with consumer protection legislation has been to progressively strengthen the rights of consumers and this may, in time, lead to package vendors having greater responsibility for the reliability of the software they market.

The poor quality of much software led us to consider, in the third part of the book, whether software development could properly be considered to be an engineering discipline in the same way as more established areas of engineering. The conclusion was that software development is not as different from other forms of engineering as it has often been claimed. Although many current practices are *ad hoc*, there is no reason why software development should not become as reliable an area of engineering as any other. In this context the use of quality management was seen as particularly significant, since it prepares the way for new techniques based on computer science research to be successfully taken up.

Another aspect of the development of software engineering is the emergence of a profession with standards of training and practice. We looked in particular at the British Computer Society and its role in promoting good practice. In the final chapter we considered some of the ethical issues and dilemmas which computer professionals may encounter and looked at how explicit professional standards can help to resolve many (but not all) such dilemmas.

The second and third parts of the book were largely concerned with legal and professional responses to the issues and problems raised by the technology discussed in the first part. These responses mean that computing professionals now need to have a wider awareness of the social context and legal implications of what they do than was formerly the case.

The process of reaction by the law and the computing profession to developments will continue. There is no reason to suppose that the impact of computing is going to diminish. Among the areas which, at the time of writing, look likely to become important are:

- The year 2000 problem: the precise effects and repercussions are unclear, but there are bound to be many problems at the turn of the century. Although this will have a negative effect on the way that computing is perceived, in the longer term it may help bring about some beneficial changes. It will increase understanding of the reliance which is now placed on computers and software and will help promote an awareness of the need for software engineers to be suitably qualified and trained. This could lead to a move away from the current situation where knowledge of the latest release of a language or system seems to be given more importance by many employers than understanding of design or verification techniques.

- Database technology will undoubtedly be used by some repressive regimes to help monitor and stifle political dissent. Even in more democratic societies there is likely to be a greater emphasis on the use of personal data for everything from marketing to crime detection. Whether the growing use of such data is met by increased concern about its possible misuse remains to be seen.

- The impact of the Internet is bound to become greater, but it is very hard to predict how much greater, or what significance this will have for the majority of people. It will certainly become much more difficult to censor and control information than it was in the past. It also seems unlikely that governments will be able to prevent private individuals from making use of advanced encryption technology.

- Perhaps one of the most significant issues considered in the book was the apparent poor payback obtained from computer technology. This issue is likely to assume greater importance as more users upgrade their machines and struggle with new versions of packages without getting an obvious return for the time and money invested. In the future, users may become reluctant to invest in new computers or software on the assumption that newer automatically means better.

- If electronic commerce does get off the ground then it is likely to be a fertile area for legal disputes. However, at present it seems unlikely that people will adapt to such technology in any numbers.

- Greater awareness that it is possible to produce high-quality software may also be important in improving current development practice. The more so if courts were to favour software users in disputes over software errors and quality. Such changes would also result in professional bodies having far greater influence and importance than they do at present.

Whether the impact of computers comes to equal that of the railways in the last century remains to be seen. The development of the railway not only transformed life in the countryside, but in the course of time it shifted the balance of power between nations. Railways shifted power away from maritime nations to the large, hitherto landlocked continents. Ironically the development of the railway, invented in Britain, was to be one of the factors which contributed to the end of British hegemony as the new technology undermined the importance of sea power.

Many people have predicted that computers and communications technology will in the future bring about just such dramatic changes. They predict a shift of power away from central governments and nation states to a highly educated and mobile elite. It is too early to tell whether there is any truth in such predictions but it is worth bearing in mind that few of those who participated in and witnessed the development of railway technology accurately foresaw its eventual impact.

BCS Code of Conduct

This Code of Conduct has been reproduced with the permission of the British Computer Society.

These rules are grouped according to the main areas to which they relate.

The Public Interest

1 Members shall in their professional practice safeguard public health and safety and have regard to protection of the environment.
2 Members shall have due regard to the legitimate rights of third parties.
3 Members shall ensure that within their chosen fields they have knowledge and understanding of relevant legislation, regulations and standards and that they comply with such requirements.
4 Members shall in their professional practice have regard to basic human rights and shall avoid any actions that adversely affect such rights.

Duty to Employers and Clients

5 Members shall carry out work with due care and diligence in accordance with the requirements of the employer or client and shall, if their professional judgment is overruled, indicate the likely consequences.
6 Members shall endeavour to complete work undertaken on time and to budget and shall advise their employer or client as soon as practicable if any overrun is foreseen.
7 Members shall not offer or provide, or receive in return, inducement for the introduction of business from a client unless there is full prior disclosure of the facts to the client.
8 Members shall not disclose or authorize to be disclosed, or use for personal gain or to benefit a third party, confidential information acquired in the course of professional practice, except with prior written permission of the employer or client, or at the direction of a court of law.

9 Members should seek to avoid being put in a position where they may become privy to or party to activities or information concerning activities which would conflict with their responsibilities in 1–4 above.

10 Members shall not misrepresent or withhold information on the capabilities of products, systems or services with which they are concerned or take advantage of the lack of knowledge or inexperience of others.

11 Members shall not, except where specifically so instructed, handle client's monies or place contracts or orders in connection with work on which they are engaged where acting as an independent consultant.

12 Members shall not purport to exercise independent judgment on behalf of a client on any product or service in which they knowingly have any interest, financial or otherwise.

Duty to the Profession

13 Members shall uphold the reputation of the Profession and shall seek to improve professional standard through participation in their development, use and enforcement, and shall avoid any action which will adversely affect the good standing of the Profession.

14 Members shall in their professional practice seek to advance public knowledge and understanding of computing and information systems and technology and to counter false or misleading statements which are detrimental to the Profession.

15 Members shall encourage and support fellow members in their professional development and, where possible, provide opportunities for the professional development of new entrants to the Profession.

16 Members shall act with integrity towards fellow members and to members of other professions with whom they are concerned in a professional capacity and shall avoid engaging in any activity which is incompatible with professional status.

17 Members shall not make any public statements in their professional capacity unless properly qualified and, where appropriate, authorised to do so, and shall have due regard to the likely consequences of any statement on others.

Professional Competence and Integrity

18 Members shall seek to upgrade their professional knowledge and skill and shall maintain awareness of technological developments, procedures and standards which are relevant to their field, and shall encourage their subordinates to do likewise.

19 Members shall seek to conform to recognised good practice including quality standards which are in their judgment relevant, and shall encourage their subordinates to do likewise.
20 Members shall only offer to do work or provide a service which is within their professional competence and shall not claim to any level of competence which they do not possess, and any professional opinion which they are asked to give shall be objective and reliable.
21 Members shall accept professional responsibility for their work and for the work of their subordinates and associates under their direction, and shall not terminate any assignment except for good reason and on reasonable notice.
22 Members shall avoid any situation that may give rise to a conflict of interest between themselves and their client and shall make full and immediate disclosure to the client if any conflict should occur.

APPENDIX II
IEE Rules of conduct

These Rules of Conduct have been reproduced with the permission of the Institution of Electrical Engineers. Note that they are published by the IEE along with guidance on their interpretation in common circumstances (not included here) and with the general instruction that members should put fair and honest dealing with other members of the community before their personal interest.

In the following rules, the term 'employer' should be taken as including 'client'.

1 Members shall at all times take all reasonable care to ensure that their work and the products of their work constitute no avoidable danger of death or injury or ill health to any person.
2 Members shall take all reasonable steps to avoid waste of natural resources, damage of the environment, and wasteful damage or destruction of the products of human skill and industry.
3 Members shall take all reasonable steps to maintain and develop their professional competence by attention to new developments in science and engineering relevant to their field of professional activity and shall encourage persons working under their supervision to do so.
4 Members shall not undertake responsibility as an electrical engineer which they do not believe themselves competent to discharge.
5 Members shall accept personal responsibility for all work done by themselves or under their supervision or direction, and shall take all reasonable steps to ensure that persons working under their authority are competent to carry out the tasks assigned to them and that they accept personal responsibility for work done under the authority delegated to them.
6 Members called upon to give an opinion in their professional capacity shall, to the best of their ability, give an opinion that is objective and reliable.
7 Members whose professional advice is not accepted shall take all reasonable steps to ensure that the person overruling or neglecting their advice is aware of any danger which they believe may result from such overruling or neglect.

8 Members shall not make any public statement in their engineering capacity without ensuring that their qualification to make such a statement and any association they may have with any party which may benefit from their statement are made known to the person or persons to whom it is directed.

9 Members shall not, in self-laudatory language or in any manner derogatory to the dignity of the profession of electrical engineers, advertise or write articles for publication, nor shall they authorise any such advertisement or article to be written or published by any other person.

10 Members shall not recklessly or maliciously injure or attempt to injure, whether directly or indirectly, the professional reputation, prospects or business of another.

11 Members shall inform their employer in writing of any conflict between their personal interest and faithful service to their employer.

12 Members shall not improperly disclose any information concerning the business of their employer or of any past employer.

13 Members shall not accept remuneration in connection with professional services rendered to their employer other than from their employer or with their employer's consent; nor shall they receive directly or indirectly any royalty, gratuity or commission on any article or process used in or for the purpose of the work in respect of which they are employed unless or until such royalty, gratuity or commission has been authorized in writing by their employer.

14 Members shall not improperly solicit work as independent advisers or consultants, either directly or by an agent nor shall they improperly pay any person, by commission or otherwise, for the introduction of such work; provided that, members working in a country where there are recognised standards of professional conduct, laid down in that country by a competent authority recognized by the Council, which are in conflict with the previous provisions of this rule, may order their conduct according to such standards.

15 Members acting as independent advisers or consultants shall not be the medium of payment made on their employer's behalf unless so requested by their employer; nor shall they place contracts or orders in connection with work on which they are employed, except with the authority of and on behalf of their employer.

16 Members standing as candidates for election to the Council of the Institution shall not undertake, or permit to be undertaken on their behalf, organised canvassing by means of circulars or otherwise.

References

Adams E N, 'Optimizing preventing service of software products', *IBM Journal of Research and Development*, **28**(1), 8, 1984.

Adams J, *Risk*. UCL Press, London, 1995.

Anderson R E, Johnson D G, Gotterbarn D, and Perrolle J, 'Using the ACM code of ethics in decision making', *Communications of the ACM*, **36**(2), 98–107, February 1993.

Arthur C, 'Ambulance system was "too complicated"', *New Scientist*, page 7, 14 November 1992.

Arthur C, *The Independent*, 25 May 1995.

Arthur C, *The Independent*, 23 August 1996.

Atiyah P S, *Law and Modern Society*, 2nd edition, OPUS, Oxford University Press, Oxford, 1995.

Attewell P, 'Information technology and the productivity challenge', in Kling R (ed.), *Computerization and Controversy*, 2nd edition, Academic Press, New York, 1996.

Baily M N, 'Great expectations: PCs and productivity', *PC Computing*, **2**(4), 1989.

Bainbridge D, *Intellectual Property*, 2nd edition, Pitman Publishing, London, 1994.

Bainbridge D, *Introduction to Computer Law*, 3rd edition, Pitman Publishing, London, 1996.

Barrett N, *The State of the Cybernation*, Kogan Page, London, 1996.

Beauchamp K G and Poo G S, *Computer Communications*, 3rd edition, International Thomson Computer Press, London, 1995.

Bennetto J, *The Independent*, 20 September 1996.

Bergman B and Klefsjö B, *Quality: from Customer Needs to Customer Satisfaction*, McGraw-Hill, New York, 1994.

Black L, *The Independent*, 1 November 1993.

Bott F, Coleman A, Eaton J and Rowland D, *Professional Issues in Software Engineering*, 2nd edition, UCL Press, London, 1995.

Boyle W, 'Handcuffed by IBM', *Computer Weekly*, 6 April 1995.

Branscomb A W, *Who Owns Information*, Basic Books, New York, 1994.

British Computer Society (BCS), *The Year 2000: A Practical Guide for Professionals and Business Managers*. Swindon, Wiltshire, 1997.

Brooks F P Jr, *The Mythical Man-Month*, Addison-Wesley, Reading, MA, 1982.

Brown G, *The Information Game: Ethical Issues in a Microchip World*, Humanities Press, New York, 1990.

Buchanan R A, *The Engineers: A History of the Engineering Profession in Britain 1750–1914*, Jessica Kingsley Publishers, London, 1989.

Burke N, *The Independent*, 9 January 1995.

Bynum Y, *Computer Ethics*, Blackwell, Oxford, 1996.

Campbell D and Connor S, *On the Record: Surveillance, Computers and Privacy*, Michael Joseph, London, 1986.

Card S K, Robert J M and Keenen L N, 'On-line composition of text', in *Proceedings of Interact '84*, pages 231–236, Elsevier, London, 1984.

Classe A, 'Emergency room', *Computing*, 12 June 1997.

Clement A, 'Computing at work: Empowering action by low-level users', *Commmunications of the ACM*, **37**(1), 52–65, January 1994.

Clough B and Mungo P, *Approaching Zero: Data Crime and the Computer Underworld*, Faber, London, 1993.

Coleman J W, *The Criminal Elite: The Sociology of White-Collar Crime*, 3rd edition, St Martin's Press, New York, 1994.

Connor S, *The Independent*, 26 March 1995.

Cook E, *The Independent on Sunday*, 11 June 1995.

Cooley M, *Architect or Bee: The Human Price of Technology*, Hogarth Press, London, 1987.

Cooper G, *The Independent*, 8 November 1995.

Cooper G, *The Independent*, 24 October 1996.

Cope N, *The Independent*, 15 November 1996.

Cornish W R, *Intellectual Property*, 3rd edition, Sweet and Maxwell, London, 1996.

Crosby P B, *Quality is Free: the Art of Making Quality Certain*, McGraw-Hill, New York, 1979.

Cusumano M A and Selby R W, 'How microsoft builds software', *Communications of the ACM*, **40**(6), 53–61, June 1997.

Dadak R, *Computing*, 31 July 1997.

Data Protection Registrar, *The Thirteenth Annual Report of the Data Protection Registrar* Wilmslow, England, June 1997.

Davies S, *Big Brother*, Pan Books, London, 1996.

Davies P W, *The Independent*, 20 June 1997.

Deming W E, *Out of the Crisis*, MIT Press, Cambridge, MA, 1986.

Denning P *et al.*, 'Computing as a discipline', *Communications of the ACM*, **32**(1), 9–23, January 1989.

Department of Trade and Industry (DTI), *Licensing of Trusted Third Parties for the Provision of Encryption Services*, London, 1997.

Dijkstra E, 'On the cruelty of really teaching computer science', *Communications of the ACM*, **32**(12), 1398–1404, 1989.

Doyle L, *The Independent*, 2 May 1994.

Edwards-Jones I, *The Independent,* 16 August 1991.

Elbra R A, *A Practical Guide to the Computer Misuse Act 1990*, NCC Blackwell, Oxford, 1990.

Ermann, M D, Williams, M B, and Gutierrez, C (eds), *Computers, Ethics and Society*, Oxford University Press, 1990.

Fincham R and Rhodes P S, *The Individual, Work and Organization*, 2nd edition, Oxford University Press, Oxford, 1992.

The Finniston Report, *Engineering Our Future, Report of the Committee of Enquiry into the Engineering Profession*, HMSO, London, 1980. Cmnd 7794.

Fisher P, *The Daily Telegraph*, 20 March 1997.

Forester T and Morrison P, *Computer Ethics: Cautionary Tales and Ethical Dilemmas in Computing*. MIT Press, Cambridge, MA, 1990.

Fox C and Fakes W, 'The quality approach: Is it delivering?' *Communications of the ACM*, **40**(6), 25–29, June 1997.

Freedman D, *The Independent*, 17 Febuary 1996.

Garfinkel S, *PGP: Pretty Good Privacy*, O'Reilly and Associates, New York, 1995.

Gibbs W W, 'Software's chronic crisis', *Scientific American*, **271**(3), 86–95, September 1994.

Givens J, *The Independent on Sunday*, 9 April 1995.

Gladden G R, 'Stop the lifecycle, I want to get off', *Software Engineering Notes*, **7**(2), 35–39, 1982.

Gosling P, *The Independent*, 28 April 1996.

Gould J D, 'Composing letters with computer-based text editors', *Human Factors*, **23**, 593–606, 1981.

Grant R and Higgins C, 'The impact of computerized performance monitoring on service work', *Information Systems Research*, **2**(2), 116–141, 1991.

Grayson I, *The Independent*, 29 July 1996.

Green H, *The Independent on Sunday*, 20 August 1995.

Gringras C, *The Laws of the Internet*, Butterworths, London, 1997.

Hafner K and Markoff J, *Cyberpunk: Outlaws and Hackers on the Computer Frontier*, Fourth Estate, London, 1991.

Halstead R, *The Independent*, 15 December 1996.

Handy C B, *Understanding Organizations*, 3rd edition, Penguin, Harmondsworth, 1985.

Harris P, *An Introduction to Law*, 4th edition, Weidenfeld and Nicholson, London, 1993.

Heap N, Thomas R, Einor G, Mason R and Mackay H, (eds), *Information Technology and Society*, Sage Publications, Newbury Park, CA, 1995.

Herbsleb J, Zubrow D, Goldenson D, Hayes W, and Paulk M, 'Software quality and the capability maturity model', *Communications of the ACM*, **40**(6), 30–40, June 1997.

Ilinchey M G and Bowen J P (eds), *Applications of Formal Methods*, Prentice Hall, Englewood Cliffs, NJ, 1995.

HMSO, *Britain's Legal Systems*, Aspects of Britain, London, 1996.

Hoare C A R, 'Programming is an engineering profession', in Hoare C A R and Jones C (eds), *Essays in Computing Science*, Prentice Hall, Englewood Cliffs, NJ, 1989.

Hoffman L J (ed.), *Rogue Programs: Viruses, Worms, and Trojan Horses*. Van Nostrand Reinhold, New York, 1990.

Horowitz P S, 'Mr Edens profits from watching his workers' every move', in Kling R (ed.), *Computerization and Controversy*. 2nd edition, Academic Press, New York, 1996.

Howlett D, *Computing*, 11 September 1997.

Hunt E, *The Independent*, 27 June 1996.

Icove D, Seger K and VonStorch W, *Computer Crime: A Crime-fighter's Handbook*, O'Reilly and Associates, 1995.

Jackson T, *The Independent*, 24 October 1994.

Johnson D G, *Computer Ethics*, 2nd edition, Prentice Hall, Englewood Cliffs, NJ, 1985.

Johnson D G and Nissenbaum H (eds), *Computers, Ethics and Social Values*, Prentice Hall, Englewood Cliffs, NJ, 1995.

Kallman E A, *Ethical Decision Making and Information Technology*, McGraw–Hill, New York, 1993.

Keenan D, *English Law*, 11th edition, Pitman Publishing, London, 1995.

Kemper J D, *The Engineer and his Profession*, 2nd edition, Holt, Rinehart and Winston, New York, 1975.

Khoshafian S and Baker A B, *Multimedia and Imaging Databases*, Morgan Kaufmann, Palo Acto, CA, 1996.

Kimball P, *The File*, Harcourt Brace Jovanovich, New York, 1983.

King J L, 'Where are the payoffs from computerisation? Technology, learning, and organizational change', in Kling R (ed.), *Computerization and Controversy*, 2nd edition, Academic Press, New York, 1996.

Kling R (ed.), *Computerization and Controversy: Value Conflicts and Social Choices*, 2nd edition, Academic Press, New York, 1996.

Kusserow R P, 'The government needs computer matching to root out waste and fraud', In Johnson D G and Nissenbaum H (eds), *Computers, Ethics and Social Values*, Prentice Hall, Englewood Cliffs, NJ, 1995.

Ladd J, 'The quest for a code of professional ethics: An intellectual and moral confusion', in Johnson D G and Nissenbaum H (ed.), *Computers, Ethics and Social Values*, Prentice Hall, Englewood Cliffs, NJ, 1995.

Landauer J K, *The Trouble with Computers: Usefulness, Usability, and Productivity*, MIT Press, Cambridge, MA, 1995.

Langford D, *Practical Computer Ethics*, McGraw-Hill, New York, 1995.

Laudon K, 'Information systems in a democracy', in Johnson D G and Nissenbaum H (eds), *Computers, Ethics and Social Values*, Prentice Hall, Englewood Cliffs, NJ, 1995.

Leveson N G and Turner C, 'An investigation of the Therac-25 accidents', *IEEE Computer*, 18–41, July 1993.

Levy M and Salvadori M, *Why Buildings Fall Down*, W W Norton, New York, 1992.

Mabbott J D, *An Introduction to Ethics*, Hutchinson University Library, London, 1966.

Macdonald M, *The Independent*, 29 June 1996.

MacIntyre A, *A Short History of Ethics*. Routledge and Kegan Paul, London, 1966.

Mackie J L, *Ethics*, Penguin, Harmondsworth, 1977.

Marshall S, *Computing*, 28 August 1997.

Martin M W and Schinzinger R, *Ethics in Engineering*, 3rd edition, McGraw-Hill, New York, 1996.

McCorkell G, *Direct and Database Marketing*, Kogan Page, London, 1997.

Morgan R and Stedman G, *Computer Contracts*, FT Law & Tax, 5th edition, 1995.

Neumann P G, *Computer Related Risks*, Addison-Wesley, Reading, MA, 1995.

Page D, Williams P and Boyd D, *Report of the Public Inquiry into the London Ambulance Service*, South West Thames Regional Health Authority, February 1993.

Pannell J P M, *An Illustrated History of Civil Engineering*, Thames and Hudson, London, 1964.

Parnas D, 'Education for computing professionals', *Computer*, **23**(1), 17–22, 1990.

Petroski H, *To Engineer is Human*, St Martin's Press, New York, 1985.

Pike J and Barnes R, *TQM in Action*, 2nd edition, Chapman and Hall, London, 1996.

Raphael D D, *Moral Philosophy*, Oxford University Press, Oxford, 1981.

Reed C (ed.), *Computer Law*, 2nd edition, Blackstone Press, London, 1996.

Roszak T, *The Cult of Information*, 2nd edition, University of California Press, 1994.

Sabbagh D, *Computing*, 15 May 1997.

Sadgrove K, *ISO9000 BS5750 Made Easy*, Kogan Page, London, 1994.

Sanders J and Curran E, *Software Quality*, Addison-Wesley, Reading, MA, 1994.

Schneier B, *Applied Cryptography*, 2nd edition, Wiley, New York, 1996.

Sharpe R, *The Independent*, 11 April 1996.

Shattuck J, 'Computer matching is a serious threat to individual rights', in Johnson D G and Nissenbaum H (eds), *Computers, Ethics and Social Values*, Prentice Hall, Englewood Cliffs, NJ, 1995.

Shaw M, 'Prospects for an engineering discipline of software', *IEEE Software,* 15–24, November 1990.

Shields R (ed.), *Cultures of Internet*, Sage Publications, Newbury Park, CA, 1996.

Shimomura J, *Takedown: the pursuit and capture of Kevin Mitnick.* Secker and Warburg, London, 1996.

Shooman M L, *Software Engineering*, McGraw-Hill, New York, 1983.

Shore T, 'Why I never met a programmer I could trust', *Commmunications of the ACM*, **31**(4); 372–375, April 1988.

Singer P (ed.), *Ethics*, Oxford University Press, Oxford, 1994.

Singer P, *How Are We to Live? Ethics in an age of self-interest,* Oxford University Press, Oxford 1997.

Software Engineering Institute, Carnegie Mellon University, *The Capability Maturity Model: Guidelines for Improving the Software Process*, Addison-Wesley, Reading, MA, 1995.

Software Engineering Notes, 12(4), October 1987.

Software Engineering Notes, 16(3), July 1991.

Software Engineering Notes, 18(1), June 1993.

Spaemann R, *Basic Moral Concepts*, Routledge, London, 1989.

Spinello R A, *Case Studies in Information and Computer Ethics*, Prentice Hall, Englewood Cliffs, NJ, 1997.

Stammers T, *Computing*, 7 August 1997.

Sterling B, *The Hacker Crackdown*, Penguin, Harmondsworth, 1994.

Stoll C, *The Cuckoo's Egg*, Doubleday, New York, 1989.

Stoll C, *Silicon Snake Oil*, Doubleday, New York, 1995.

Tanenbaum A S, *Computer Networks*, 3rd edition, Prentice Hall, Englewood Cliffs, NJ, 1996.

Taylor P, *The Financial Times*, 6 November 1996.

Turpin A, *The Independent*, 2 September 1995.

Victor P, *The Independent*, 16 November 1995.

Walker P, *Computing*, 5 June 1997.

Watts S and Pithers M, *The Independent*, 18 March 1993.
White R C A, *The Administration of Justice*, 2nd edition, Blackwell, Oxford, 1991.
Wiener M J, *English Culture and the Decline of the Industrial Spirit 1850–1980*, Cambridge University Press, Cambridge, 1981.
Williams B, *Morality: an Introduction to Ethics*, Penguin, Harmondsworth, 1973.

Index

active badge systems 64
act-utilitarianism 178
Adams, J. 8, 175, 186
Airline Reservation System (SABRE) 146,
  149
Anderson, R. 186
Anti-Crime Bill S.266 (USA, 1991) 42
appellant in criminal law 76
Apple v. Microsoft 97
arbitration 78
ARPANET 34, 35
Arthur, C. 14, 21
assignment of copyright 91, 105
Atiyah, P.S. 81, 84
AT&T, software failure 7
Attewell, P. 58, 61

Baily, M.N. 58, 59, 61
Bainbridge, D. 99, 115, 127, 138
Baker, A.B. 21
Bank of New York, overdrawn 7
Barnes, R. 156
Barrett, N. 48
Beauchamp, K.G. 48
Bell, A.G. 34
Bennetto, J. 28
Bentham, J. 178
Bergman, B. 156
Black, L. 67
Bott, F. 82
Bowen, J.P. 10
Boyle, W. 13
Brain computer virus 56
Branscomb, A.W. 48
British Computer Society 5, 15–16, 17,
  160, 162
 code of conduct 172–4, 192–4

British legal systems 72–3
British Nuclear Fuels, Sellafield software
  failure 7
Brooks, F.P.,Jr 17
Brown, G. 186
Buchanan, R.A. 167
Burke, N. 22
Bynum, Y. 186

calling line identification 35–8
  introduction of 37
  telephone numbers, ownership of 37–8
Campbell, D. 28, 31, 118, 125, 127
Capability Evaluation of software 153
Capability Maturity Model 15, 153–4
Card, S.K. 59
Carnegie Mellon University 156
case law 72
categorial imperative (Kant) 180
CCN Credit Systems 22
Chancery Division of High Court 77
Chappe, C. 34
chartered bodies 81
civil law 75–6
  procedure 78–9
clarification of case in civil law 79
Classe, A. 12
Clement, A. 65
Clough, B. 68
codes of conduct
  British Computer Society 172–4, 192–4
  IEE 195–6
  in software engineering 172–7
    criticisms of 174–5
    issues 174–7
commercial exploitation in engineering 142
common law 72, 73

203